Prince of Thieves

Also by Brian David Boyer

CITIES DESTROYED FOR CASH:
THE FHA SCANDAL AT HUD

Prince of Thieves

The Memoirs of
the World's Greatest Forger

By
Brian David Boyer

THE DIAL PRESS 1975

Designed by Jack Ribik
Manufactured in the United States of America
First printing 1975

Library of Congress Cataloging in Publication Data

Boyer, Brian D
  Prince of thieves.

  *1. Forgery—United States—Biography. 2. Crime
and criminals—United States—Biography. I. Title.*
HV6679.B68   364.1'63 [B]   75-15569
ISBN 0-8037-5387-X

For James Clair Boyer

This project began early in
1974 when I flew to Miami, Florida, for an initial interview
with the man I have called Peter "Tony" Milano. A week or so
earlier, I had been told some of the details of the career this
man claimed, and certainly it was interesting and worth a
writer's while to investigate. But the story seemed so much
larger than life that I suspected I was traveling to meet a mad
man, a crank whose fantasy life had outstripped his grip on reality. I had implied as much to Tony on the telephone before I
came and he was incensed that I, a nobody, dared to doubt
him, a master forger who had made millions and knew what he
did of the world.

We met at the Sheraton Four Ambassadors Hotel, where I
had taken a room. It was 9:30 AM on a Saturday; the day was
overcast, unusual for Miami, but to my winter-jaded Chicago
eyes the waters of Biscayne Bay sparkled through the hotel
windows. Still in a barely suppressed rage, Tony began our
meeting by having me call FBI Headquarters in Miami, where
he had me speak to the agent in charge of his case. No, there
was no doubt that he was a forger well known to the FBI, a
free-hand artist who had served time for several counts of the
crime in Lewisburg Federal Penitentiary. It wasn't bad for a
start, but then Tony has always had style.

From there we began the long process of interviewing, hours
and days and weeks of making tapes of Tony's recollections, of
my probing, trying to ferret out how much of what he was
telling me had actually occurred in just the way he was de-
scribing it, and how much was the truth as he wished it to be.

The hours I spent with Tony rolled by, first in Miami and then in Chicago, where we conducted additional interviews; by this time it was mid-summer and Chicago was hot and sticky. Tony had left Miami to join his wife and her daughters in California, having once again created a "clean" past for himself, on which to try to build a future. As I sat listening over and over again to his voice on tape, a certain eerie realization began to dawn on me. Sometimes Tony sounded like the man he should have been, given his boyhood: his speech was ungrammatical and overlaid with a heavy Brooklyn accent, although his remarkable intelligence always showed through. Sometimes, however, especially when relating an incident in which he presented the identity of a chemical engineer, say, to a bank official, his speech and demeanor would change measurably. Suddenly an educated man was speaking, one with a different voice, deeper and more assured, one with a different vocabulary, a vocabulary comprised of multi-syllabic technical terms and words of whose meaning I myself was not always sure. Reflecting back on our meetings, I remembered that at such times even Tony's posture changed: before my eyes, like a superb actor playing a role, he was that other identity.

What unnerved me was that Tony was not aware of any change in himself; he was not deliberately acting for me. In fact, when we met that summer, I often saw that he was not the skinny, balding man wandering unnoticed in worn jeans and an old shirt through the crowds in Lincoln Park that he seemed to be. Instead he was shivering with the imagined chill of the winter damp in Zurich as he hopped out of a limousine into the welcoming warmth of a bank. Or he was in London. Or Lisbon. But he was not with me. It was a strange revelation.

Later, as Tony and I corresponded about the various details that had to be confirmed as I wrote up the story, I saw another phenomenon develop. In the mail one day was an envelope I had apparently addressed to myself. Puzzled, I tore it open and then I felt a jolt of alarm—by now, when he wrote me, whether deliberately or accidentally, Tony had picked up the nuances of my handwriting. It was close enough to send chills down my spine. I suppose I am afraid, sometimes, that if he desired,

Tony could by taking over my handwriting, through that process, take over my whole personality as well.

There is something of a shock of recognition here, for an author constantly takes the threads of real stories and makes of them his own creation, part fiction, part fact. And in this instance I have stolen Tony, stolen his personality and his life, and used it to create a man now known as "The Forger," a being larger than life, and infinitely more appealing.

In short, from hundreds of pages of transcription of Tony's recollections, now both subject and author have Peter "Tony" Milano where they want him, safely in the pages of a book, where he remains as dangerous as a poem and as safe as the memory of a bull after the faena *has been completed and the carcass has been drawn away.*

Tony, as he is generally called in this hall of mirrors, vouchsafes that it's all true, an impossibility if only because some of the conversations recreated here were never witnessed by him. However, without question, Tony believes the story contained in these pages is real. The author does, too. The facts that can be checked out do hold together. But the reader may still have to make a judgment for himself every once in a while.

BDB
Chicago, Illinois

Prologue

A man who called himself Curtis Dall showered and shaved and put a blond wig over his bald head. Leaving the Lisbon Hilton, he hired a taxi to take him to the Baccarat Casino on the coast at the foot of a steep hill. He went directly to the manager's offices on the mezzanine and asked for Senhor Campos. He recognized the manager at once as one of Carlo Gambino's boys, known in New York as Fat Neck Nucci.

Fat Neck was a tall, thin man with a proportionately tall, thin neck and a high, reedy voice. His narrow lips appeared not to move as he talked.

"I don't know if I know any kinda Senhor Campos," Fat Neck said. "You're American, huh?"

"Brooklyn," said Curtis Dall. The narrow man who sat before him had grown up near his boyhood home in Canarsie, along with the Bonannos and the Colombos and the Gallos. Dall recalled that the dandified gangster, now dressed in a powder-blue linen suit, white patent-leather loafers, and diamond rings on both hands, used to complain about having to share a room with a younger brother and two fat older sisters who teased him and made his life miserable. The nickname was earned when Nucci gave a fat neck to a member of the original Anastasia gang: he put a meat hook through his Adam's apple and left the body hanging in the cooler of a butcher shop.

"There are lots of Americans here for you to play with," Fat Neck said to him. "Why not leave the Portuguese alone? Just my advice. I don't know no Campos. But the games are going on down in the casino. You wanna buy some chips and have

1

some fun, doncha? Here's a couple hundred to get you started."

The American smiled, but pushed aside the ten $20 chips Fat Neck piled negligently on the desk.

"I'm a friend of Jack Mace," Dall said. "Jack told me a couple of days ago Campos was going to meet me here this morning. I brought something for him from the states. It doesn't make any difference to me if he meets me or not. I think you should tell him that, Fat Neck."

Nucci swung the high heels of his patent-leather shoes off the desk with a clump. "Who the fuck are you that you call me a punk thing like that?" he asked.

"My other friend is Patriarca," Dall said calmly. "And I'm on business. Don't fuck with me in any way. Got it? Thank you. I'll be in the bar downstairs in about an hour, out back by the pool."

Deliberately turning his back on the tall gangster, Dall strode down the winding marble steps and went back to his hotel room. Prying back the window molding, he removed a tight roll of new US Treasury bonds worth $150,000 and placed them between the pages of an *Esquire* magazine.

Ignoring the light morning gambling action at the Baccarat, he headed, magazine in hand, towards the cabana chairs set under green umbrellas by the swimming pool. He saw the slim back of a suntanned woman sitting beside the water, and removed his aviator glasses. His eyes, dark brown in the gray light of New York City, now appeared to be bright, almost glass-green.

"A bottle of Dom Perignon for the lady," he told the waiter who hovered at his right shoulder. "I want a gin and tonic in a tall glass."

The waiter returned in a few moments with the bottle of chilled champagne in a silver wine cooler, and a single glass which he filled for the pretty girl in the pink bikini. Dall watched the waiter and the now-laughing girl trying to communicate in different languages.

Finally, the waiter simply pointed in his direction, and the young blonde lifted her glass to him and called out in English, "Thank you." The ocean breeze blew the words away, but Dall raised his own glass in return. Shortly, the girl caught the attention of the poolboy and wrote a message, which he brought over to the man under the umbrella.

"Angelica Antonia. Room 1014. Lisbon Hilton," the note read.

Dall waved his thanks, ordered a second drink, and put his sunglasses back on.

A large, swarthy man in a white linen suit, white shirt and tie, and a white George Raft wide-brimmed hat walked out to the poolside and directed the poolboy to pull a second cabana chair next to Dall's table. "How are you?" the man said, taking Dall's tanned hand into his fat one, covered on the back with thick black hair.

"I'm really fine," Dall answered, memorizing the thick face from behind his silvered sunglasses. The man obviously was not American, and not Italian—someone to be cautious in dealing with. "I'm Curtis Dall."

"They call me Campos," the big man said, having some difficulty with the English. "I am told you have package for me from Mr. Jack Mace."

"That's right," said Dall. "Where do you want to go?"

"I go nowhere," Campos said. "This is all my territory. Is OK."

Dall flipped open the pages of the *Esquire* magazine and handed the thin sheaf of Treasury bonds to the Portuguese gangster. The man counted them, grunting with satisfaction. He counted the bonds three times and then added and double-checked the total in a slim notebook until he was absolutely certain they totaled $150,000.

"Mr. Jack Mace is fast," he stated. "Thank you for coming."

"My pleasure," Dall told him, watching the blonde girl dive into the pool. "Mr. Mace will appreciate the compliment."

"Good," the gangster said, pushing away from the table. "I will go now."

"There may be some misunderstanding," Dall told him, sitting up in the lounge chair. "Mace told me you would deliver the money, and that I would deliver the money to the Spaniard this afternoon."

"Who said that?" the black-haired man asked suspiciously, raising his right hand toward a bulge in his suit jacket.

"Jack Mace said that," Dall told him, watching the hand with narrowed eyes. The fat man was sweating profusely, and the first beads of sweat appeared on Dall's forehead. He felt a drop slide down his body underneath his right arm.

"Do I care who is Jack Mace?" Campos asked.

"No, *I* care who is Jack Mace," Dall said in a lazy, taunting voice. "But you care who is Carlo Gambino, because Mr. Gambino cares who is Raymond Patriarca, who is my good friend and who is the very good friend of Jack Mace."

"This Patriarca is what you call . . . New England?" the sweating man demanded. Dall nodded and reached out his right hand.

"The bonds or the money," he said.

His attention was wholly on the bulge in the Portuguese man's jacket and the throbbing vein in his neck that might indicate whether or not the pudgy hand would reach for the gun in the shoulder holster. The blonde girl in the pink bikini got out of the water, then dove in again. Hopping out of the water a second time, she poured herself another glass of champagne, and for a second time raised the glass in Dall's direction. The sunlight was refracted through the yellow bubbles in the crystal, sending a flash of gold through Dall's sunglasses. The light brought a painful pleasure to the back of his eyes.

"It is nothing for me to kill you," the Portuguese said unexpectedly.

"Nothing," Dall agreed. "And nothing for you to be killed and chopped to pieces and the pieces fed to the fish in the ocean."

"Nothing," the man said, thinking. He plunged his hand into the pocket of his baggy white pants and found a roll of American currency bound by many strands of tan and red rubber bands. He threw the roll at Dall, who set it down on the table.

"Count it," the Portuguese ordered.

"I don't have to count it," Dall told him. "You're the one who has to add right."

The dark-haired man coughed and swaggered away into the shadows of the casino.

Dall stood up and waved good-bye to the girl, who waved

back. The only exit from the pool area to the street was through
the casino. Dall took several slow, even breaths and shifted his
shoulders to relax the muscles. He put the roll of bills into the
jacket pocket of his suit and put his hand into the pocket, holding the money. Leaving a fifty-dollar bill behind to pay for the
drinks, he walked across the white concrete away from the pool,
and entered the air-conditioned casino. The cold air gave him a
pain across his chest. Of the two dozen players in the casino at
this hour, about half were clustered at the chemin-de-fer table
on the far side of the room.

On the mezzanine above Dall, the casino manager was coming to the marble staircase. Two thin men dressed in clothing of
1930s gangster movies materialized, preventing Dall's return to
the pool.

Dall walked faster toward the casino entrance. The high-
heeled footsteps of the assassins stabbed into the carpet behind
him. Hitting the front door at a half-run, he sprinted across the
street, through an open courtyard doorway, across the plot of
grass and over a six-foot-high yellow stone fence.

At six thirty the following morn-
ing, four Portuguese fishermen carried a heavy, wet burlap
bag on board their boat and chugged away from the Lisbon
docks. They motored out for two hours into the Atlantic, past
the garbage that floats in the water near the shoreline, out to the
deeper water, past where the other fishing boats were working.
Finally they threw the drag anchor overboard.

Pulling the gunnysack out of the hold where it lay with the
putrefying remains of an earlier catch, they scanned the horizon
for other ships and airplanes, and then emptied the contents of
the bag out onto the deck.

What spilled over the filthy deck with a loose-limbed thunk
was the body of a man who had been shot five times in the back
with a Spanish-made .38-caliber automatic. A sixth shot had
been delivered as the *coup de grace* at the base of the skull.

The older of the fishermen picked up a large knife made to
cut fish, and with it severed the head. The other men picked up
similar knives and in a few minutes the body had been hacked

into half a dozen parts. The sections of the body were wrapped in fishing line weighted with heavy pieces of iron, and one by one the remains were dropped into the ocean.

The four men carefully washed the deck, removing all signs of blood, and then in a general spirit of housecleaning, removed the remains of the dead fish from the hold. A finger was found with the pieces of fish, but it was not wrapped with twine and weighted to sink forever beneath the surface of the Atlantic. It was simply shoveled overboard with the rest of the jetsam and fed on by the hungry gulls.

Chapter 1

Another Italian Kid in Canarsie

The time on the big round clock above the doorway to the seventh-grade classroom at PS 136 was 10:05. In less than two hours, school would be out for the summer. Ten minutes until recess. Peter Milano stretched his long, loose bones, and gazed through the rectangular windowpanes at the green trees set against Brooklyn's clear blue sky. He was bored out of his mind.

The thirteen-year-old boy watched a small, green fly buzz against the window pane and wobble in a looping path through the hot classroom air to the other side of the room. It danced above the blond head of Joey Gallo, who slumped behind the desk at the end of the second row. Humming, the fly spun past Frank Gambino, who chewed a piece of Wrigley's Spearmint with his powerful jaws. Frank's eyes were fixed on the rear end of Kathy Caruso. Pete watched Frank reach his hand under the desk and pinch the pretty girl's ass.

Kathy screamed and blushed. The thirty-five other students laughed.

But Miss Meyers slammed *Penrod and Sam* down on her desk, not a bit amused. "What is the reason for that outburst, Kathleen?"

Kathy wouldn't say, because she was terrified of the Gambino boy. Miss Meyers was too. She shook an arthritic finger at the whole class, warning them to behave while she went to get their final report cards.

When the teacher hobbled out of the room, Joey and Frank jumped out of their seats and ran to her desk, holding conspiratorial fingers to their lips. Their classmates watched intently.

7

Joey pulled open the desk drawers until he found Miss Meyers'
worn leather purse. He smiled broadly as he pulled a crumpled
five-dollar bill from the change purse and slapped it into Frankie's thick hand.

"Anybody says anything, I'll give him a knuckle sandwich,"
Joey announced.

Pete was proud of his friends. He winged the remaining half
of his art gum eraser at Joey's head. Tribute. Joey snatched up
the bouncing rubber from the dirty floor and threw it back.
Pete, pretending it was a grenade thrown by a Nazi soldier,
made the sound of an explosion. Joey and Frank slid into their
seats and folded their hands in front of them just as Miss
Meyers returned from the office.

At recess, Frank showed Pete the wrinkled money.

"You don't get none of it cause you didn't help us," Joey lectured. "Why dincha help us, Pete?"

"I dunno," Pete said, thinking about the wallop of his father's
razor strop. "I didn't want any of it anyhow. I got plenty from
the fish market."

"You're chickenshit," Frank spat.

Frank outweighed him by thirty pounds, but Pete was faster.
Slapping a left hand against Frank's cheek, he bounced a quick
right fist against the side of his head. Frank swung a haymaker
that went wild. Pete hit him again on the end of the nose with a
left jab. Frank dropped to his knees with a dazed look in his
eyes. But he wouldn't cry.

"I'll get you," he threatened.

Pete danced in the playground dust. "Come on, Frankie," he
taunted. "You want a couple too, Joey?"

"You shouldn't of hit him," Joey complained, helping Frank
to his feet. "He didn't do nothin' to you."

"He called me chicken. He can't go around saying that."

"But what if he had a baseball bat?" Joey pointed out.

"He ain't got no baseball bat," said Pete with perfect logic.

"You caught me by surprise," Frank said. "We'll go to the
gym, and see who beats who."

"I'll be the referee," Joey offered.

"Not if you got a bat," Pete said.

The three friends laughed.

School let out at noon. Pete tore his report card into little pieces because of the thirty-seven absent days marked at the bottom. Cutting school didn't make any difference to his mother, because she was old-country Italian who couldn't even speak good English. But his father knew what was going on. He wanted Pete and his older brother, Tony, to succeed in school and get rich in America.

Joey and Frank dumped their report cards in the trash basket, too. They failed everything anyway. In high spirits, the three rode the subway to the Fulton Market at the bottom of Manhattan.

"I ain't going back to PS 136 next year," Joey announced as they strolled toward the wholesale warehouses. "We're moving over to Bedford-Stuyvesant. We got a better place there to live."

"That Italian over there?" Frank asked.

"Sure, it's Italian. Sicilian," Joey said proudly. "It ain't no different than Canarsie, except there's more going on, you know?"

"There's plenty going on right where we live," Frank said.

"Italians own all the bars and restaurants in Bedford-Stuyvesant," Joey said. "My brother Larry's already got a job in one of them. They're letting him into the outfit."

Frank was jealous. "How old is he?"

"Fifteen," Joey said.

"I can get into the Black Hand anytime I want right now, and I'm only thirteen," Frank boasted. "I don't have to wait until I'm that old."

"You can't," Joey protested. "Nobody wants a shitty kid like you in their organization."

"I know everybody," Frank said in superior tones. "All them guys are at my house every day. My family's got real good connections."

"Why don't you guys talk about something else?" Pete complained.

"You don't know nothing," Joey said to him, lighting a Pall Mall and taking a puff. "That's cause you're not Sicilian. All your people gotta work for a living."

"You're crazy," Pete said. "My brother's already running numbers. My mother's from Calabria. They're tougher in Calabria than they are in Sicily."

9

"You really don't know nothing," Joey said. "You gotta be Sicilian or Abladon to be tough."

"Don't you worry about it, Pete," Frank said. "When I'm the Capo Don, I'll cut you in for some of the action."

"Come on, I'm hungry," Pete said as they neared the market, where boxes of produce flanked the sidewalk. "Anybody want some oranges?"

"Wait a minute," Frank called. "Come back here a second. Why oranges? Why don't we try to get some bananas, huh?"

"Yeah," Joey said. "A whole stalk."

"How the hell we gonna get a whole stalk?" Pete wanted to know. "There are about a million people on the street and Sergeant O'Shea's there, too. He lives right down the block from me."

"We'll go to the dock behind Russo's," Joey said. "That iron door just slides right open."

"That's a hell of a lot of bananas, a stalk," Frank said, considering the plan. "I can't eat all them bananas."

"We'll sell 'em down by the pier," Joey said. "Or are *you* chicken?"

"Well, I ain't chicken," Pete said.

Joey gave him one of the Pall Malls. "You in it, Frankie?"

"Gimme one of them," Frank said. "What the hell."

The three boys turned off Fulton Street, walking over the uneven brick behind the loading docks. Dropped and discarded melons, lemons, ears of corn, oranges, smashed bananas, crushed grapes, broken turnips, moldy potatoes, and broken heads of lettuce and cabbage lay everywhere. The air was thick with the smell of moldering and fermenting vegetables. Behind Rossetti's poultry store they came upon several wooden crates filled with chicken feet and heads, surrounded by a moving blanket of green flies. The smell of blood and death was overpowering. Joey took a splintered plank and spiked a chicken head with the sharp end, whipping it at his companions.

"Jesus, mother of God," Frank shouted. "You get diseases from them."

"You get lice from them," Pete added.

"Screw lice," Joey said, kicking over one of the boxes. Feet and bloody heads spilled over the bricks. The flies buzzed angrily, and rose in formation before landing again to continue their feast.

From 4:00 A.M. until noon, the loading docks thronged with draymen, teamsters, Italian shopkeepers in white aprons, and produce buyers from New York's myriad grocery stores and shops. Now at three in the afternoon, the area was as deserted as it would ever be.

Joey hopped onto the concrete loading dock that stretched past the doors of the wholesale houses, trying handles along the way, whistling "My Blue Heaven."

RUSSO'S TROPICAL FRUITS—BANANAS, PAPAYAS, AND PLANTAINS" was painted in red on the weathered sign ahead. Joey pushed at the iron back entrance beside the two big rusted garage doors that in the mornings swung open for the trucks. It didn't move. Reaching up above the iron ledge at the top of the door, he removed a short piece of steel rod which he inserted into a narrow opening at the door's left edge. Using the bar as a lever, he lifted the inside latch. The heavy door snapped open.

Still whistling, Joey replaced the lever and hopped down from the concrete dock.

"Them bunches weigh a hunnert pounds. Frankie and me been in there, so we'll snatch one. You keep watch," he said to Pete.

"This is pretty dumb," Pete said. "What are we going to do, take the subway all the way down to Canarsie Pier with a ton of bananas on our backs?"

"We gotta stick 'em in something," Joey decided. "Find a box."

Scouting the area, they found two discarded orange crates.

"We'll shove them in here and put the tops on," Joey said, satisfied. "You watch."

Joey and Frank scrambled inside the warehouse. When the door thumped shut, Pete began patrolling up and down the block, wondering how he would warn them if the cops appeared.

Inside the warehouse, Joey and Frank switched on an unshaded light bulb, and gazed with wonder at the immense crop of green bananas hanging like so many carcasses from iron hooks. The air was cool, with the faint odor of a conservatory.

"We can get a ton outta here," Frank said.

"Let's not mess around," Joey instructed.

Muscles straining, he lifted a huge bunch of bananas from its hook. "Find a knife to cut the stem, so we can get them into the boxes."

Frank found a long banana knife, and gingerly approached the stalk Joey laid on the floor. "Shake it, to scare away the spiders," he said.

Joey kicked the top of the stalk with his foot, and unexpectedly giggled.

"Tarantula," he exclaimed, springing at Frank with a grimace and his fingers curled like claws. "Arrrrrgh!"

Frank wasn't amused. "Don't mess around," he ordered, cutting the stem midway down its three-foot length. But the bananas were too bulky to fit into the orange crates.

"Cut 'em off," Frank said, slicing the bunches from the stem and putting them into the crates. "Hurry up."

When the crates were full, Joey slid open the back door and poked his head out.

"Is it clear?" he called to Pete.

"Yeah. Come on."

Joey and Frank carried out the heavy crates, slamming the door behind them.

"Take an end," Frank told Pete.

In each hand, Frank held the end of a crate, leaving the other ends to be carried by Joey and Pete. Sweating and gasping for breath, they trotted the fruit over the bricks and through a dirt alley, heading away from the market.

"We'll never make it out of the market," Joey said, setting down his end and leaning against a brick apartment wall.

"I know a grocer," Pete remembered. "He's by here. Let me ask him if he wants any fruit."

Little Mr. Bertini was sitting on a wooden chair in the back of his store looking at the headlines in the *Daily News*, drinking a Coke.

"*Buon giorno. Come sta?*" Mr. Bertini greeted the boy.

"*Buon giorno*, Mr. Bertini," Pete said to him politely. "You ever sell any bananas in this place?"

Mr. Bertini shrugged elaborately, and drank more Coke. "So you are in the banana business, my young friend?"

"This guy, we was helping him load over at the market," Pete said, improvising freely. "When we was done, he tol' us he didn't have any money, so we could take some bananas. Now we got two orange crates of them, and nothing to do with them. I only thought I'd ask."

"Bananas," said Mr. Bertini scornfully. "What can I do with two crates of them things?"

"They're real cheap."

"How much?"

"Ten cents a pound," Pete offered. "Ten dollars for the bunch."

Mr. Bertini picked up his *Daily News*. "And how do I tell the police, ten cents a pound?"

"I told you, I earned these bananas," Pete insisted. "Listen, I can sell them someplace else, you know."

"Five cents a pound, if they're not all bruised," Mr. Bertini said to him. "I'll buy a hundred pounds."

"That's great," Pete told him. "We'll bring them right here."

Mr. Bertini stood in the back of his little grocery store and the three boys carried in the two crates of fruit.

"Back here by the scale," he said. "Who are these boys?"

"This is Joey Cullo," Pete told him. "And this is Frankie Gambino."

"Your padre is named Carlo?" he asked Frank, after a momentary pause.

"My uncle," Frank said cockily. "Something the matter with that?"

"No, no," said Mr. Bertini, extracting five crumpled dollar bills from the pocket of his baggy pants. "When you speak to him, tell him please Mr. Bertini wishes him good health and pays his respects."

"Sure," Frank said, counting the bills. "I think there's more than a hunnert pounds of bananas in them crates."

"Don't worry," said Mr. Bertini, showing stained teeth. "Each of you boys have a candy bar."

"You got any Pall Malls?" Joey demanded.

Mr. Bertini gave him two packages. "No charge. Don't you worry about a thing."

"That's what respect can do for you," Frank told Pete as they neared Canarsie Pier back in Brooklyn. "We got ten dollars now. Someday we're gonna be rich."

"My father's not part of the organization," Pete pointed out. "What do I do about that?"

"Don't you worry about it," Joey said to him, throwing an arm over his friend's bony shoulders. "If you ever need anything, I'll let you in. You too, huh, Frankie?"

But Frank didn't say anything. He had caught sight of four older, black youths standing on the pier, throwing pieces of wood down into the polluted water. He bunched his shoulders, and swinging his arms, assumed a slightly pigeon-toed walk.

"Look at that," Joey said indignantly, "Spades messing around on our pier."

Pete felt adrenalin jolt through his system and his bowels tighten. He and Joey joined Frank, and shoulder to shoulder they marched onto the worn wooden planks of the pier.

"Say, you," Joey addressed the four black youths. "What the hell you doing, fucking around here at Canarsie? You got a license or something?"

The interlopers looked up from the water.

"There's a big dead fish down there," commented a tall, thin, black youth. He wore a mustache, and his head was wrapped in a do-rag. Baggy blue work pants hung from his hips and his construction shoes were tied with string.

"I don't care if it's a whale," Joey told him. "Anything around this pier is ours."

"Don't see no sign sayin' it belong to you," said the largest of the blacks. Frankie estimated that he weighed about 180.

"You musta missed the sign," Pete said. "It's back at the end. It says 'No coons.' "

Four pairs of black eyes tightened.

"You think you got an army someplace, you?" the big boy asked.

"You think you can come around here without askin' anybody?" Joey asked. "Get your asses off our pier."

14

"Sheet," drawled a third member of the quartet, picking up a length of tarred two-by-four. "Don't mess with us."

Pete moved slightly in front of Joey and Frank. "I can take the big spade if you can handle the others," he muttered to his friends, barely moving his lips.

Joey smoothed back his blond hair. "I'll kill the bastards," he said, loud enough for them to hear.

"You ain't gonna kill shit," said the youth in the do-rag, " 'less you can handle this." He extracted a straight razor from the front pocket of his worn trousers. With a shaking motion, he flicked open the blade and held it bent with an index finger across the back edge. Pete hesitated.

"I don't care what the bastard's got," Joey said, his voice rising in rage and indignation.

He picked up a long length of weathered board and thrust it like a lance into the shoulder of the youth with the razor. Stung, the young man swung the razor in an upward arc. Joey dodged aside and slammed the sharp end of the board into the middle of his face, cutting him across the cheek and nose.

"I'm gonna kill you, spade bastard," Joey screamed.

The biggest of the four threw a right at Pete, his knuckles slamming into the left ear. Pete jabbed three fast punches. He felt a moment's dizziness from the blow on the side of his head and danced away, his vision going and coming back again. He noticed that Frank was running at the two slighter black youths with a box held in front of him like a shield. The black with the two-by-four swung it like a bat, splintering the box. Frank clubbed back, and the broken boards tore through the shirt of the boy with the club.

"Watch out for that fucking razor," shouted Joey.

Pete barely got out of the way as the razor slashed the air near his neck. He kicked with his left leg, jamming the heel of his boot on the knee of the boy with the razor. With a yell, the boy fell sideways, dropping the razor onto the pier. Joey stabbed the board again into his face.

"I'll kill every damn one of you," Joey was shouting.

Facing the biggest boy, Pete bobbed his head, waiting for an opening, watching with intent hazel eyes. He saw that his oppo-

15

nent telegraphed his jabs with a drop of his right shoulder. Pete dropped his guard, presenting him an opening.

Seeing the right shoulder dip, Pete brought his right up and punched his opponent in the throat, just under his chin. The boy staggered back a step, both of his hands dropping. Pete danced forward, dropped down off his toes for solid footing, and executed a series of rights and lefts against the big youth's face. In his mind he could hear the crowd at the Garden thundering its encouragement.

The boy sank to his knees, his eyes glassy. Behind him, the other two black youths tackled Frank and knocked him down. One of them held Frank, while the other kicked him about the shoulders and chest.

"You bastards," Frank was yelling.

Pete went to his aid, throwing his shoulder against the back of the boy who was stomping Frank's head. The boy sprawled away, lost his balance, and fell over the side of the pier. The boy who held Frank pinned to the deck scrambled to his feet, dove off the side of the pier, and swam for shore. The boy in the do-rag snatched up his razor and stood back in a crouch, blood dripping down his face. The largest black joined his friend with the razor, their backs pressed against a rotted piling. Joey jabbed ineffectually at them with the board.

"I'll get my brothers and their pieces and we'll blow you away," he shouted.

Pete felt he had won his battle, and his taste for the fight ebbed.

"You guys had enough?" he asked. It didn't look like they had. In fact, the two remaining black youths looked much more dangerous now that they had been bloodied.

"Come and get us," they challenged. "You gonna have to kill us first."

Frankie, still lying on the deck, groaned loudly.

"You hurt bad?" Pete inquired.

Frankie lifted his head. "They stomped my brains out," he said.

"See what you bastards did?" Joey screamed. "You hurt him! I'll cut your nuts off!"

"Wait a minute, Joey," Pete said, helping Frank up. The side of Frank's face was scored with cuts and a huge bruise on his cheek looked like a damaged plum. "Holy Mary," he said, touching the bruise.

Pete straightened up. "Listen, you guys," he said to the two black youths who crouched menacingly at the piling. "Get out of here before somebody does get killed."

"I'm gonna kill them," Joey said, at a lower volume, regarding Frankie.

"What you gonna do with that crazy fucker?" said the black youth with the razor, motioning at Joey.

"We'll step aside, and let you get offa the pier," Pete offered. "OK, Joey?"

Joey sneered, but now he only blustered. "I'll give you to three to get offa here." He joined Frankie and Pete at the other side of the wide pier; the two black youths put their heads down and ran past them toward safety.

"Bastards," Joey shouted, throwing his plank after them.

Returning to shore, they found warm water at a tin shack used by the longshoremen in winter. Tearing up a pillowcase, they washed the cuts on Frankie's face.

"I coulda taken either one of them," Frank complained, wincing from the touch of the wet rags against the cuts. "Two of them was too many."

"I coulda cut that coon's head off with my spear," Joey boasted, lighting a Pall Mall. "He never touched me once with that razor."

Pete took one of the Pall Malls for himself, feeling very pleased with himself. He examined the torn skin on his knuckles and thought about the rights and lefts he had thrown against the larger youth.

"You're something else," Frank said to him. "That guy outweighed you by forty, maybe fifty pounds."

"He caught me a good one," Pete said, with suitable modesty.

"You oughta go pro," Joey told him. "You do some amateur bouts now, and in four, maybe five years, go pro. My brother knows some guys at the Garden." Then, shifting to business, he said, "I'll tell you what, Pete. We'll split everything we got today with you 'cause you done such a good job on that spade, right, Frankie?"

"Sure," Frank agreed. "Only there will be an extra buck left over."

"I'll take that, 'cause I lifted the money personal from the purse," Joey said. "Otherwise, we'll split even."

After Joey left to join his older brother at home, Frank and Pete walked down to the end of the long pier and watched the garbage float towards the Atlantic out of Jamaica Bay, snagging an occasional ocean-bound condom with long sticks.

"You ever had a broad?" Frank asked.

Pete looked at him with those unblinking hazel eyes and looked away without speaking. You didn't mess around with Italian girls. Their fathers and brothers beat and killed you if you did. The best solution to his virginal state appeared to be the Jewish girls who lived in the nearby neighborhoods of Sheepshead Bay and Bensonhurst.

"We'll go to the dance tomorrow night at the synagogue in Bensonhurst," Frank said, reading his thoughts. "Them broads are hot for us."

"Maybe I'll buy some new shoes," Pete said. "A pair of them sharp, black wing tips."

They entered the back door of the Gambinos' frame house on East 93rd Street, interrupting a heated conversation in the kitchen between Frank's father and a half dozen other rather threatening Italians drinking dago red out of jelly glasses.

Mr. Gambino was a heavy-set man with black, wavy hair starting to whiten at the temples. Although he was very polite and soft-spoken to him, Pete always gave him a wide berth.

"Hello, Mr. Gambino," Pete said, offering him his hand.

"You have a good way about you," Mr. Gambino said warmly, shaking hands. "See, Frankie, the good manners your friend has?"

"Sure," Frank muttered, holding the lacerated side of his head away from the summer sunlight, hoping his father wouldn't notice.

Carlo gestured at one of the dark-haired men who sat at the

kitchen table, and the man seized Frank by the shoulder, turning his face with the other hand. The others looked at the wounds and made sympathetic noises, looking to Mr. Gambino for approval.

"That doesn't look like victory," Mr. Gambino said. The sympathetic noises stopped. He lifted one of his thick paws and took Pete's hands in them. "These look like a winner," he pronounced.

Pete flushed with pleasure. "I only had one," he said. "Frankie had two." He shrugged, and spread his hands to minimize his achievement.

"Two," said Mr. Gambino, "and they were both standing on his head."

"And they both had to swim for shore," Frankie protested.

"That's right," Pete said.

"That's good," Mr. Gambino decided. He motioned for the boys to leave the room. "Tell your mother you were run over by a truck," he suggested, with a trace of a smile.

The men laughed and turned back to the conversation.

Fat Mrs. Gambino was setting the dining-room table with the help of Frankie's Aunt Carmela, who lived with them. When Mrs. Gambino saw Pete, she put down the plates and welcomed him with a cry of pleasure. She wrapped the boy in her arms, pulled his cheek against hers, and kissed him squarely in the center of his forehead.

"Where have you been so long?" she asked in Italian.

"I been workin' after school," Pete told her, beaming at the welcome. Mrs. Gambino was one of his favorite people in the entire world. She was as open as her husband was reserved, and as intimate as he was distant. The pleasant, fat woman always smelled wonderfully of sage and garlic and perspiration and lavender. She went to church every morning for six-o'clock Mass. Pete's mother said that Mrs. Gambino lit candles for the soul of her husband, one of the men who ran the Black Hand. Regardless of the reason, Mrs. Gambino had a crucifix over her bed, and a color print of Jesus Christ with a broken red heart hung in every room in the house.

Mrs. Gambino, like Pete's mother, made her own spaghetti from hard wheat flour, and dried it on racks on the back porch.

She cooked most of the day. Mr. Gambino, who made red wine every fall, sat in the kitchen all day holding quiet conversations with a steady stream of menacing men who spoke Italian.

Pete supposed that Mrs. Gambino never cried and carried on the way his mother did about his brother's work for the mob as a runner; she seemed oblivious to the world of Mr. Gambino, or inured to it. She was always so happy.

Aunt Carmela, Mrs. Gambino's widowed sister, wore black widow's weeds, and moved with an attitude of disapproval. When she went among the men in the kitchen to stir the bubbling spaghetti sauce, she indicated with her thin, colorless lips a general air of scorn and censure.

At the dinner table besides Mr. and Mrs. Gambino and Frank were his two brothers, Tony and Sam, his sister Rosie, and Aunt Carmela; Pete sat at Mr. Gambino's left. Aunt Carmela prayed.

"Such a terrible mark on the side of your face, Frank," said Mrs. Gambino, reaching for her son's face. "Have you been fighting?"

Mr. Gambino helped himself to a large serving of home-made vermicelli, covering it with the spicy tomato sauce and freshly grated cheese.

"I ran into the side of a truck down at the Market," Frank said.

"A truck with fists on it. Fighting! For shame," snapped Aunt Carmela. Frank looked to his father for support, but Mr. Gambino was wrapping the pasta around his fork.

"You haven't been to confession for ages," said Mrs. Gambino.

"Sure I have," Frank said, helping himself to the food. "Just the other day."

"It was Easter," said Aunt Carmela. "Unless you've been going to the church by yourself in the mornings."

"I want you to come with me to Mass tomorrow morning," said Mrs. Gambino.

"It's Saturday," Frank grumbled. "What's the sense in it? We have to go again on Sunday, anyway."

Frank's brothers laughed, but covered their grins.

"Get me a jug of wine Frank," instructed Mr. Gambino, letting him off the hook.

"You bet," Frank said, winking at Pete.

He carried in a fresh gallon of the homemade wine and then disappeared. After dinner, Pete found Frank in the back yard, standing under a spreading maple tree, the lighted end of a Pall Mall glowing in the dark.

"I swiped us a bottle of wine from the basement," said Frank.

"Give me a taste," Pete asked, already slightly woozy from the glass he had at dinner. The wine flushed his face as it warmed his stomach.

"I gotta go," he said. "My folks want me home by ten."

"I'll come by the fish market in Sheepshead Bay tomorrow, and go with you when you buy the shoes," Frank said.

Pete sang all the way home.

At six the next morning, Pete ate breakfast with his brother, Tony, who was decked out in new gray linen slacks with a high waist and pegged cuffs. His mother fried eggs over lightly and thick rashers of bacon. Mr. Milano slept late on Saturday before leaving at noon for the ammunition factory, where he made machines to support war production.

"Sharp pants," Pete said.

"Ten bucks," Tony said. When his mother's back was turned, he mouthed, "hot merchandise" to Pete.

"Your father won't like those pants," said Mrs. Milano in Italian as she set down breakfast. "They're nigger pants."

"Aw, Ma, this is the style," Tony protested in English. "All the sharp guys wear pants like this."

"Well, I don't know the styles," said Mrs. Milano, resigned to the fact that her children had adopted the ways of America. "But how can you work at the warehouse in fancy pants like them?"

"I'm taking my work pants," Tony said. "After work, I'm gonna play pool with some of the guys. OK?"

The truth was, Tony had quit the warehouse job months before and was now driving the yellow 1939 Chevrolet coupe owned by Vito De Bono, who ran the bookie joints. Sometimes Tony gave Pete a ride, and the girls about passed out when they saw the two handsome brothers tooling past in the bright yellow car.

Pete arrived for work at the Sheepshead Bay fish market at 7 A.M. The freshly caught flounder, mullet, mackerel, and other saltwater fish had already been purchased on the short trawlers and delivered to the market. Regular customers began to arrive at six thirty, to make sure that their fish was as fresh as it could possibly be. Pete wrapped himself in a wide white apron and began picking down the hundred-pound blocks of ice. He picked down a thousand pounds, carrying it in galvanized wash tubs to the green wooden display cases with glass tops and sides. Finished, he retired to the chopping blocks behind the cases, where he gutted and scaled the fish as they were purchased. He wrapped them in pages of newspaper that told about the war going on in Europe and the South Seas. The scales covered his hands and arms; he had to be careful not to cut himself with the sharp knives. A person could get blood poisoning from dead fish, or so Pete believed. If he drew his own blood, he carefully washed the wound and sucked at it until he couldn't taste fish anymore.

It was a good job. Pete was paid forty cents an hour for the ten-hour Saturday, plus a buck bonus if business was good, plus as much of the unsold fish as he could carry, because the store was closed on Sundays and the fish would go bad.

Frank sauntered into the back of the store at noon with a hat on his head, and told Pete that the police had raided one of the betting parlors, Rudy's Barber Shop on Rockaway Parkway.

"That's one of Tony's stops," Pete said.

He washed the fish scales from his arms, and the two boys walked through the mobs of Saturday shoppers to Goldsmith's shoe store on Flatlands Ave. Mr. Goldsmith was a short, fat Jew with a bald head and a German accent. The black winged-tipped oxfords looked wonderful on Pete's feet—lean and swift and dangerous. Wait until those Jewish girls see me in these, he thought. But the price, $6.95, was more than he could pay.

"I can put them away for you, layaway," Mr. Goldsmith offered. "Such terrific shoes as them, anybody come in here and buy them right up, and then where are you, eh?"

Pete handed him the three dollars in his pocket, and promised to be back with the rest of the money by five o'clock. He wouldn't have any money left for a soda after the dance, but maybe he could borrow fifty cents from Frank.

Only a block away from the shoe store, he saw the yellow Chevrolet speeding toward them down the street, with his brother at the wheel. Tony hit the brakes and beeped impatiently on the horn. He wore a maroon necktie and a white straw hat tilted back on his head; a Lucky Strike dangled from the corner of his mouth.

"Listen, kid, I was hoping I'd see you," Tony said. "I was making a pickup in a betting parlor when the cops raided it. I scrammed out the back, but one of the guys ratted on me. The cops are looking for me and reform school ain't where I want to end up. So I just enlisted in the Army."

"The Army?" Pete asked his brother, standing on the running board. "You can get killed in the Army."

"Them's the breaks," Tony said to him. "Actually, it should be fun. The pay ain't too bad, and if I fight the Germans, I'll probably get all kinds of medals. I'll learn how to handle a piece real good, too. I'm going home now to tell Mama. I left a message at the ammunition plant for Pops. Well, so long."

He held out his hand.

"Then I guess I won't see you anymore," Pete said.

"That's how it is," Tony said. "I ain't going to no reform school, no matter what anybody thinks. If the cops come around, you tell them I'm in Germany and they can kiss my ass. Here's for good luck."

Tony handed his younger brother a five-dollar bill, waved, and sped off down the street.

"That's somethin'," Frank said, "almost getting busted like that."

"I'm gonna go back and pick up those shoes, now I got the money," Pete said slowly. "God*dam*. I ain't gonna have a brother anymore."

Pete's mother was crying. She put her head down on the kitchen table and pulled at her hair. His father rocked her gently by the shoulders and reminded her that he had joined the Army himself at sixteen. Pete's own head was caressed and cried over as if it was going to be blown off, too. The hysteria ruined his appetite. That made his mother cry some more, so he had to force down the meatballs to prove to Mama that he loved her and wasn't ill.

Mr. Milano took his wife into the living room with a bottle of homemade wine and turned on the radio. Shortly thereafter, Mama went to bed with a sick headache. From the back of his closet, Pete removed a pair of high-waisted black gabardine trousers with sharply pegged cuffs, which he put on with a white shirt, black silk socks, and the new black wing-tipped shoes. He admired his wavy, long blond hair in the dresser mirror. His large hazel eyes looked tawny brown in the bedroom light. He rolled up the sleeves of the shirt twice, and made the muscles in his arms stand out.

Pete hurried past the living room where Pops sat drinking wine and listening to the war news on the radio. "I'm going to a dance with Frank and the guys," he called.

"I don't want you to be late," his father called back. "Church tomorrow, Pete."

"Yeah, yeah, yeah," he said, closing the apartment door behind him. Frank and Joey were waiting for him on the front step. Their clothes were identical to his own.

"You look extra sharp, man," Joey said, puffing on his cigarette. "I heard the guys saying that your brother is gonna get a good position with the organization when he comes back from the Army, good job he did today."

"What's that?" Pete asked.

"Got out, delivered the money, and disappeared," Joey said. "I'd do it just like that myself."

They boarded a bus for the trip from Canarsie to Sheepshead Bay for the regular Saturday night dance at Temple Beth Shalom. Paying their quarter to the chaperons and holding out the backs of their hands to be stamped with indelible red ink, they were models of deportment, hanging their heads down and addressing the adults as "Yes, Sir," and No, Sir."

But once inside the large basement meeting room where the lights were turned down low and Frank Sinatra crooned on the Victrola, they unbuttoned the top three buttons of their white shirts so the golden crosses around their necks showed, and threw their heads back in insolent contrast to the meek Jewish boys.

The pretty Jewish girls with their black hair, black eyes, full bosoms, and red lips caught their glances and tossed their curls with excitement, knowing that shortly those lean, mean Italian boys from Canarsie would pull them against their hard, muscular bones and jam their knees between their thighs and whisper in their ears about sudden, overwhelming passion and love. Of course the Italian boys were no good—poor students, Roman Catholic, the sons of fishmongers and vegetable peddlers with no culture and no future. But they were so wonderfully bad. The Italian boys stuck the tips of their hot tongues into your mouth and they got hard between their legs and pushed it against your stomach, making a girl tremble and blush. None of the Jewish boys, even the bravest, would ever cut in when one of the Italian boys was mauling one of the Jewish girls.

Myron Feinstein didn't understand what was happening when Joey Gallo tapped him on the shoulder and said, "Move it buddy, this is my dance."

"Rebecca's *my* girlfriend," Myron said, foolishly.

"I'm gonna leave here and come back with a .22 and shoot you in the head," Joey said to Myron, throwing a short arm over the tall boy's nervous shoulders. "Punk."

Someday, Myron Feinstein would make a quarter of a million dollars a year as a Wall Street attorney; he would collect art and go to the opera and tell his friends that he used to go to dances with Joey Gallo when they were kids together in Brooklyn.

But now, Myron bit his lips to keep from crying as the crummy Italian kid put his right hand possessively on the back of Rebecca's neck. Rebecca closed her eyes in the embrace. Myron told Samuel Singer, the chaperon, that the wiseacre Italian kids were saying swear words and threatening the girls.

Pete Milano was doing the fox-trot with a girl named Sheila who was only about five feet tall but had the biggest, softest chest he had ever embraced. Part of his dancing equipment stuck straight up in the folds of his pleated pants. Pete told Sheila that she had the nicest smell of any girl he'd ever danced with.

Mr. Singer, backed up by Mr. Cohen and Mr. Weisman, came

into the dimly lit room, Myron trailing along behind. "Excuse me," Mr. Singer said to Pete, snapping his reverie. "Are you Jewish?"

His dancing partner faded into the background.

"Sure, I'm Jewish," Pete said, wondering what was up. "I've been coming to these dances for a year now."

"Then what's your name?" asked the chaperon.

"Tony Milano."

"I see. I think you'd better come with me."

The three Italian boys were lined up in the hallway.

"Then why do you wear a gold cross?" Mr. Singer asked Pete.

"There ain't no damn sign up that only Jews can come to the dance," Joey protested. "You show me the sign. I know what's up. That rat bastard's trying to get me 'cause I danced with his girl."

Mr. Singer's face was frozen. "That kind of language," he said sternly.

"I'll tell you some language," Joey said, lifting his upper lip. "Eat this, fuckhead." Joey held the middle finger of his right hand up in front of Mr. Singer's nose.

"Christ, let's get outta here," Frankie said.

Laughing so hard that their bodies shook, the three ran up the steps out of the basement into the darkness of the street.

Telling each other lies about how they had scored with the Jewish girls, the trio walked all the way to Canarsie, feeling like wolves that had successfully slaughtered the sheep.

"Hey," Pete said as they walked along. "I got something to tell you guys. Call me Tony from now on."

Frankie and Joey glanced at each other questioningly, then at Pete, and shrugged.

"Sure, why the hell not," said Joey.

"Why's that?" Frank asked.

"Because it's a better name."

Chapter 2

When the man who called himself Tony Milano got out of bed on the morning of December 31, 1965, the temperature was eighteen degrees. Small, hard pellets of snow rattled against the windowpanes of his Manhattan apartment.

He made up the bed with military corners, then sat on the edge smoking a Marlboro. He had the body of a twenty-two-year-old athlete, a thick, muscular neck, long, sloping shoulders, and powerful arms. At 34, his stomach was flat. Not an ounce of fat had collected on his hips. But except for a short fringe of gray hair wrapped around his bony skull like a monk's tonsure, he was bald.

Sitting in the darkness, gazing passively at the snow outside, Milano questioned whether it was worth putting on his gray gabardine business suit and riding the subway to Wren's Appliance headquarters. He was a sales manager who felt he couldn't sell himself a cup of coffee. It was a nowhere job. He hated the owner's son, Barney, and didn't much like old man Wren himself.

Wrapping a gray-plaid robe around him, Milano plodded over the cold bedroom floor to the bathroom in his bare feet, flicking the light switch inside the door.

I still have my looks.

His face in the distorted mirror badly needed a shave but he still approved of it. A little gray in the beard and fringe, but he still looked like Paul Newman with his aquiline nose and high, arched eyebrows. The nose had been broken once, but it didn't show. The wide hazel eyes were set in a strong face with high cheekbones.

Like a motion-picture actor. Like Yul Brynner. Like Bill.

Glancing back into the bedroom, his eyes sought out the photograph of a man in a cracked leather frame at the edge of the dresser, his older brother, whose real name had been Tony but who called himself Bill. Both brothers had taken assumed names. Everyplace but work, his last name was Bartolini. Tony Bartolini. The first name of a dead brother and the surname of the mother.

Tony knew that his life had made more sense than Bill's, at least by a hairline. Back from the Army without any medals, Bill picked up his old job as a collections man for the mob and never did anything else again. Not that he had done badly in it. From 1947 until 1963 was a long time to go in the rackets without picking up a jail number. During those seventeen years, while Tony sold encyclopedias, used cars, real estate, and finally home appliances, Bill commanded the streets in sharp clothes, with a fat roll of ten-dollar bills in his pocket.

Even Bill's bust wasn't so bad, Tony thought as he went into the kitchen of his second floor walk up.

When the cops finally came for him they showed a form of deference and respect, a kind of familiar courtesy toward a man who had paid them off for nearly two decades. They explained that they had a quota to meet.

The judge, utterly bored with the charges, hammered down six months. Nothing. Six months for seventeen years on the other side of the law. Bill was back on the street, in a brand new 1964 Buick, in 120 days.

Milano felt his stomach churning as he ground dark Italian coffee beans and measured them into the aluminum percolator. The Buick didn't even have 5,000 miles on it when Bill dropped in the street with a brain hemorrhage. Dead.

Tony had gone to lots of funerals. But his own brother's had been different. Tony could have acknowledged it more easily if Bill had been shot down in the street. It would have seemed more in character. Bill would have liked it. A wiseguy shouldn't just fall sprawling on the dirty pavement like some square John

28

plodding home from the factory with a black lunchbucket swinging by his side.

But it made Momma happy. He died of natural causes.

She was so humiliated by Bill's career that she was almost glad when he died without any holes in his skin. Bill was just a little guy. There were no obituaries in *The New York Times* when he went. There were no FBI agents standing around in their black shoes at the funeral. There weren't many people at all. Plenty of flossy wreaths from the big guys who didn't send their names, for a lifetime spent in their service. A couple of official mourners who drove black Cadillacs. That was all. Another soldier off to the cemetery.

Milano poured heavy cream and stirred three spoonfuls of sugar into the thick coffee. He felt the year's end rushing in on him, blowing cold up his ankles, sweeping a draft over the damp linoleum floor.

I wonder why they call this a life? I should have stayed in the Army, after all. I'd be retiring next year.

Milano had enlisted in 1947, when he was fifteen years old. It hadn't been hard. He bought a blank birth certificate for a dollar and filled it out so that it made him eighteen years old. The bored recruiting sergeant knew the skinny kid wasn't old enough, but he would have to fill out one of these days. Milano wrote his mother a note and rode off to basic on the train.

The Army discovered that the tall kid who could barely read and write had a flair for mechanics and electronics. At seventeen Tony was sent to Germany as an electronics specialist for Army Security.

After more training at the Army Security Agency school at Arlington, and top-secret clearance, he ended up at the Pentagon in 1952 as a crypto-maintenance chief for the Army Security Agency. After six years in the Army he looked like a weightlifter; he moved back to civilian life in 1953, barely 21.

The Colombos, the Gambinos, the Gallos, his brother Bill, all wanted him to come into the outfit. The money's good, the work's easy. *You know.* You're good with your fists. But Tony never wanted to get caught. He didn't want to hurt people. He was naturally straight. He liked the guys; they were his friends. But he didn't like the business they were in.

Anyway, sales is a con. Ain't it?

Milano rented an apartment in Sheepshead Bay and found a job in Manhattan, selling *Encyclopaedia Britannica* door to door. His good looks and dazzling smile beguiled bored housewives into buying the expensive books they would never read. Dust-catchers. Home improvements were the next step—up or down, depending upon how you looked at it. New siding, new roofs, aluminum gutters that sometimes worked and sometimes didn't. The cat-and-mouse game between seller and buyer felt good. He could sell like hell. Even straight, the money poured in.

Milano drank the coffee, and thought about how much of the money had gone for broads. *Broads, booze, and big bands.* It cost a lot of money to run with Joey Gallo and his brothers. Frank Gambino could drop two hundred dollars a night and not feel it. You had to have something in your pockets to keep up. It was all a question of style. *Let me buy this round, Frankie.* A hundred here, another hundred there. Five hundred a week didn't go very far. Then he got married and there was less.

Sally was a waitress in the cocktail bar of the Golden Gate Motel and Restaurant. Pretty, with a slim, quick body and a hunger for enough spending money to erase her childhood in a Pennsylvania coal-mining town, she was positive that Milano was a gangster like his friends. There were three passionate weekends and an autumn trip to upstate New York to gawk at the leaves and wrestle endlessly on motel sheets.

"God, I love you, Tony, so much."

Maybe he loved her too. They were married in the New York City courthouse by a municipal judge, and they took up house-keeping in the Sheepshead Bay apartment.

And Sally found out I wasn't a gangster, after all.

Before long, Milano realized he had a lady he couldn't control. Sally wouldn't cook. She couldn't iron or clean house. But she could lie like hell. At the end of their first month of marriage, Tony arrived to pick her up from her job at the cocktail lounge. Only she wasn't there. He went home to wait.

At 5:00 A.M., Sally staggered in the door with her makeup smeared and whiskey on her breath. Tony got up from his uneasy sleep on the couch.

"Baby," Sally sighed, pressing her cheek against his chest, rubbing her leg against him. "I waited for you at the bar until after two. But you didn't come. So I had to take a cab all the way home."

"You're lying," he accused. "I was there lookin' for you at midnight. You weren't there. Where the hell did you go?"

Sally sank down on the sofa, all innocence. "I was probably in the john. I don't feel so good. I had to lay down."

"With who?"

"Screw you. What do you know?"

"You lying bitch. The owner said you left before ten with some of the guys."

"He probably said that because I married you and wouldn't shack up with him."

"Who the hell *were* you shacking up with?" he shouted, shaking her shoulders and whipping her head back and forth.

Sally clawed at his face, all pretense at gentleness gone. "You're a goddam square punk. You don't have any money. You don't have any respect. You don't have any guts, Tony."

Milano slapped her, and Sally dove for a knife, shouting more insults. He jerked the knife out of her hand, barely stopping himself from beating her senseless.

Sally snatched up her purse and ran out of the apartment. He didn't follow. When the sun was up and the bottom of a fifth of gin was dry, he cried. A wife was supposed to be at home.

The next day her father, a burly Polish coalminer with heavy calloused hands and a face permanently dirty from embedded coal, came with a .22 pistol.

"You asshole," Milano told him. "Don't you know who I am? I'm a goddam hardnose. I make my living breaking the heads of squares like you. You point that gun at me, and I promise that you'll be dead before you get outa the front door."

The old man believed it. Tony poured him a drink. The two of them discussed how lousy women were until Sally contritely came home at dinnertime. Her face was clean, her light brown hair set in a soft, new style. She burned the chicken Vesuvio and forgot to add the garlic, apologized, and placed a bottle of chianti on the table in front of him. Her father left. They made love for hours that night.

The next weekend, she was gone again.

Milano opened a tin box from the top shelf of the closet, and rummaged through it until he found an old photograph of Sally and himself, arms over each other's shoulders, smiling.

Smiling, always smiling. Even the day she packed her bags and split.

Still it made him sad. At loose ends with no woman, he resumed his travels through the mob-owned bars of Brooklyn with Frank Gambino and the Angulo brothers, working hard all day selling and partying hard all night, keeping up a front. He never mentioned to his friends who wore revolvers strapped under their suitcoats that Sally had disappeared.

Milano knew he should have married an Italian girl. Italian girls recognized instinctively what a family was supposed to be about. The man went out and enjoyed himself and spent money. The woman stayed home, cleaned the house, bore children, didn't complain or ask questions, and went to church on Sunday. And Milano wanted kids. A lot of them.

Should I have been such a gentle man?

The people he ran around with would kill a woman who ran around; kill her, or scar her, or beat her like a whimpering animal.

Almost tenderly, Milano put the picture back in the box, and put it away. If he had ever caught her with somebody, he might not have been so gentle. But he never did. She moved quickly. She was good at covering her tracks. He followed her trail, but could never catch up with the girl. Or her boyfriends, either. He had enough of faithless wife and witless father-in-law. He filed for divorce on grounds of adultery. It was official after only six months of marriage. Milano never saw her again. He moved to Manhattan and hoped she was far away.

The shame of marrying that kind of girl. A whore. A lousy whore.

It haunted him; he couldn't completely get over it. He

couldn't get close to another woman again. He seemed isolated in the bars, at the parties. He wore a quiet, solitary mien that made him seem like a sworn member of the brotherhood, without ever having participated. He behaved like somebody a wiseguy could respect.

Tony was an ear into which Joey Gallo could pour his plans and worries and ambitions. He never volunteered an opinion of any kind. He was a frequent traveling companion of Bill Bonanno, a jovial hanger-on. The rapidly rising mobster made him attractive job offers. To Frank Gambino he was the childhood friend who appreciated his growing newspaper legend. For the Angulo brothers, for many others, he was a regular guy to bullshit with and find broads with in the bars.

And his friends were getting rich. Adding up the money in his checkbook and savings account, Milano found that he was worth just over $2,000 after fifteen years as an honest man.

Nearly an hour went by on the kitchen clock. Still sitting at the metal kitchen table, the cup of cold coffee in front of him, a pile of half-smoked cigarettes in the ashtray, the opened checkbook to the other side, Milano realized the real feeling he had about his friends' lives in the mob was jealousy. Intertwined with his lifelong fear of jail was envy of their lives. Sure, the brotherhood was dangerous. He knew about the hits, the assassinations, and the near misses; he knew about being barricaded in bare apartments during gang wars, the constant surveillance by the federal officials and local police, bugged telephones, federal indictments, and grim grand juries.

There was that other side, though, that he couldn't stop thinking about: the three-hundred-dollar suits, a couple of grand in spending money in the pocket, the new Cadillac, the big house, the high-class, expensive broads that a lousy appliance salesman couldn't even think about. Now the year was ending. Next year he would be thirty-five. His life was that of a hanger-on, a do-nothing, a chickenshit bastard with a bald head, a crummy apartment, and $2,000 in the bank.

It was certain that he wouldn't be going in to work that day, so Milano needed some action to shake himself out of his strangely unsettled mood. If it hadn't been winter he would have taken his fishing poles and gone after some trout. But today his own company wasn't good enough; he needed companionship.

He took a steaming shower, shaved, and dressed in his best black mohair suit, a white button-down shirt, and a blue-and-red striped tie. Slipping a pair of rubbers over his shined black shoes and buttoning the gray wool overcoat, Milano left the apartment building for the bank, where he cashed a thousand-dollar check. It felt good to have cash warming his pocket.

Forty-second Street. Yellow taxicabs moving slowly through the slush. He held the gray Stetson down on his bald head and shouldered through the wind. Madison Avenue was as empty as Sunday. New York was vacant between Christmas and New Year's Eve. He walked uptown against the blowing snow, his mind blank. He remembered a telephone number. A broad on West 62nd. He turned into a restaurant for a drink.

The restaurant was named Leon's. An orange neon sign above the door glowed in the gray air. Inside, Milano's black-gloved hands brushed the snow, small irregular flakes, from his shoulders. He removed the hat and wiped his forehead with a white handkerchief. There was no checkroom. No headwaiter. No customers. He unbuttoned the topcoat and draped it over the back of a high green plastic bar stool. On the other side of the aisle, blue poles wrapped with tiny red-and-green Christmas lights formed an open divider. The bartender stood counting bottles at the bronze cash register.

"Quiet," Milano said.

"Quiet. Everybody's out of town," said the bartender.

"Black and White, double, on the rocks," Milano said.

He took a handful of dimes from his pocket and went to the stand-up telephone at the back of the restaurant, dialing the number of Frank Gambino.

"Happy New Year, Frankie," Tony said. "What's happening?"

"Tony?" Gambino asked. "Where the hell you been? I thought you would come over Christmas."

"I came by early," Milano said. "Didn't see nobody home but a plainclothes man in an unmarked car. So I didn't stop."

"That bastard," Frank said. "I think it was a fed. I don't know. They're around all the time."

"How was your Christmas?"

"No subpoenas," Frank said to him. "Listen. What's going on? Anybody around?"

"Everybody's with their kids. The holidays," Tony said. "You?"

"I wish I had gone to Miami," Frank told him. "It was a nice Christmas. The family. Everything's quiet, you understand."

"It's too quiet," Tony said.

"I can stand it," Frank replied. "What do you have in mind?"

"Not much," Tony said. "I'm taking some time off work. No business now. I thought I might go up to Lundy's in Sheepshead Bay tonight, have dinner, a couple of drinks."

"I wouldn't mind getting out of here," Frank said. "The kids are driving me nuts. You want to meet me there?"

"Sure," Tony said. "About seven?"

"Yeah," Frank said. "You going to bring somebody?"

"Maybe," Tony told him, thinking about that telephone number, and a girl with red hair named Kelly. "Maybe she's got a friend."

"You hear that?" Frank said to the federal agent he thought bugged his telephone. "Call the grand jury. I'll see you about seven."

Tony called Kelly.

"Are you up?"

"What do you mean, am I up?" she asked. "Who is this? Is this Tony?"

"Probably. What's going on?"

"I'm doing housecleaning," she said. "Some guy you are. You been in jail or someplace?"

"Just working," he said, visualizing her. "Why don't you get your hair done or something, and we'll go to Lundy's tonight for some fish?"

"How do you know I'm not already busy?" she asked.

"I'm asking."

"How can I get my hair done this late? What time is it? One or something?"

"Yeah," he said, consulting his Bulova watch. "You won't have anything to worry about today. If they're open."

"Lundy's," Kelly said. "Just me and you?"

35

"Frankie Gambino," he told her. "I thought maybe you had a girlfriend, that tall girl—Barbara somebody."

"She's married," Kelly said. "I could ask her, maybe."

"Do that," Milano told her. "Meet us there at seven."

"I'll find somebody. But the weather's real bad out, Tony."

"Take a cab. I'll pay for it."

There was another man sitting at the bar when he came from the telephone, a very drunk, sandy-haired man about Tony's age, in a blue suit with a blue vest. Milano sipped at the scotch, washing it down with a swallow of ice water.

"Christmas stinks," the man said, addressing Milano. "It's just a bunch of wrapping paper to stick in the fireplace and burn. This goddam city stinks, too."

"So where are you going?" Milano asked. "Philadelphia? Boston?"

"Just keep your ass out of Westchester," the man said. "Fucking women, drive you out of your mind. Are you married?"

"Nope," Milano said.

The man was drinking brandy. He called the bartender, and ordered one for himself and one for Milano. "Everybody's divorced in Westchester. Did you know that? Alimony. Child support. Christmas presents. I played halfback for Amherst, for Christ's sake. I didn't think it'd be like this."

Milano looked critically at the man's cheeks, criss-crossed with red veins, and his paunch under the blue vest. "You musta been fast," he said.

"Fast," the man said. "No cigarettes, no booze. Booze, maybe, but no wife. No fucking Westchester."

"Why not?" Milano asked him. "I hear it's nice there. Pretty. Comfortable."

"It's the women," the man said. "Wear you down. You look like you take care of yourself. Where did you play?"

"Football?"

"I don't care," the man said. He held out a hand with cigarette tar stains. "My name is Frank Gallagher. Amherst. Westchester. Divorce court. The whole thing. I'm in banking."

"Tony Bartolini," Milano said. "I'm a gangster."

Gallagher looked at him and swallowed down the shot of

brandy, opening his mouth and closing it again. Milano saw the bartender listening attentively.

"Now that's something," Gallagher said. "You don't look like one, you know what I mean?"

Milano shrugged, buying new drinks. "What should I look like?"

"It's just—I never met one before," Gallagher said. "You just look like an ordinary businessman."

"It *is* business," Milano said. "Like anything else, you got to make a buck."

"I'll tell you, being a banker isn't such hot shit," Gallagher confided. "You got somebody on your ass all the time. People think that bankers have it all taken care of. Wait until the lawyers get done with them. They're fucked up like everybody else." Gallagher peered at Milano, closing one eye and moving his face close to his. "Hey," he said in a low voice. "You ever *hit* anybody?"

"Hit?" Milano asked. "Boxing?"

Gallagher winked, raised a finger, and crooked the thumb. "Powie," he said.

Milano laughed. "Go on," he said. "Everybody doesn't do that stuff."

Gallagher looked very disappointed. "You know somebody wants a contract?" he asked. "I'd pay somebody five thousand to get rid of my wife."

"I don't do that kind of stuff," Milano said, injury in his voice. "I don't even carry a gun."

"What kind of gangster are you?" Gallagher asked, his voice rising louder.

Milano stood up and put on his overcoat. "Hey," he said as he left. "I'm lyin' to you. I'm really an electrical engineer."

"For Chrissake," exploded the exasperated drunk.

The bartender cleared Milano's empty glass from the bar, and picked up the tip left behind.

"I'll tell ya," the bartender said to Gallagher. "That guy ever comes in here again, I wouldn't mess with him, I was you."

"An electrical engineer," the banker snorted.

"Listen," said the bartender. "He left me a ten-dollar tip."

Buoyed by the scotch and his little joke, Milano found a taxi-cab and told the driver to take him to Wren's Appliance head-quarters. Except for one of his salesmen standing in the cashier's office, the main floor was deserted. Aluminum tinsel hung in ropes from the ceiling in Christmas colors, above the refrigerators, washers, and dryers. Bright red-and-yellow signs advertised a New Year's sales extravaganza. In the second-floor offices he greeted the ancient receptionist with a grin, asking for his messages.

"Nothing, Mr. Milano," Maura told him. "But Mr. Wren wanted to see you."

"Junior or senior?"

"The young one," she said. "He was looking for you this morning."

"I want to talk to him anyway," Milano said.

He hung his overcoat on a wooden hanger in his large corner office, and walked to Barney Wren's corner office at the other end of the room. At the gray steel desks, a dozen clerks and ste-nographers tried to look busy as they watched the hands of the clock moving towards 5:00 P.M. Barney, working in his shirt-sleeves, looked sourly at the sales manager as he sat down in the armchair across from his desk.

"You shoulda called in or something," Barney said. "I wanted to talk to you this morning about the newspaper sale ads."

"You see, I couldn't make it," Milano told him. "I was having a cup of coffee, and then I had to take a shower, and then I had to walk across town for a couple of drinks." He smiled at the angry expression that tightened Barney's face. "Why don't you talk to me now, bubbie?"

"What the hell is with you?" Barney exclaimed. "I don't think you realize I own this business."

"Your father owns the business. You work for him, the same as I do."

"You really got some attitude," Barney said, shoving his papers aside. "You're supposed to call in, you don't come to work in the morning. Who's going to take care of the cus-tomers?"

"I don't think you realize, I don't give a shit. I want to tell you something, Barney, about you being an asshole."

The owner's son turned red in the face. "Close the door," he commanded.

"Close it yourself," Milano said. "You're not only an asshole, you're stupid. An' I been wanting to tell you about how I fucked your wife."

Young Wren jerked his head so quickly Milano thought he might throw it out of joint. The plump, moon-faced executive left his desk and slammed the door of the office. "Are you drunk, coming in here like this?" he asked, totally ignoring the challenge.

"I screwed your wife at the office picnic in July," Milano said calmly, with a great deal of satisfaction. "You had the secretary in the boathouse, and I took Susanne into the house and I drilled her in the laundry room. She was horny as hell. She has," Milano said, remembering the details, "a little scar to the right of her belly button where she had her appendix taken out. She says you don't get it up anymore, Barney."

Wren's short fingers were trembling. "Tell me about it, Tony," he said in an oddly constricted voice. "Give me all the details. Why the hell are you coming in here like this?"

"Then she called me here all the time," Milano said, looking at the bright red color of the man's ears. 'Come on over here and bang me,' she said all the time. She would have fucked me to death, I'd of let her."

"You're sure as hell not going to go on working here after this," Barney said. "I mean, you're fired, Tony. You gotta understand that."

"How do you explain it to your old man? I mean, so you say, 'I fired Tony because he was sticking it to Susanne'? I don't think the old man gives a shit."

"Why the hell do you hate me so much?" the pudgy man blurted out. "I gave you a hard time sometimes, but what the hell, I'm president of this company. I gave you bonuses and everything."

"How you going to explain this to your old man?" Milano asked levelly. "What do you say?"

"Jesus, I can't have this," Barney said, rubbing his face and looking puzzled. "There's gotta be something I can do about all this."

39

"Money," Milano suggested.

"This is something else," Barney said. "You go and bang my wife, and I gotta pay for it."

"Three months severance pay," Milano suggested. "I'll take it now, with what's due me."

"Horseshit!" Barney said strongly. "I wouldn't give you more than a grand, no matter what the old man says."

"You owe me six hundred. I'll settle for two thousand total, but I want it in cash."

The president met his gaze for a second, nervously moving his eyes away. "I'll divorce the cunt," he said. "I knew you couldn't be trusted the first day you came in here, Tony."

"Come on, now," Milano said, pointing to the door. "Get me the money and stop dicking around. I got some people waiting for me."

When he left with the money wrapped in a wrinkled brown paper bag, the solitary salesman on the floor waved his right hand through the air, like a swimmer going down. No lifeguard.

Lundy's was crowded. The maitre d' held a chair for him at the bar, courteous, even deferential. Kelly came in the door, her short red curls bouncing, and just behind her came the blonde, Barbara. The maitre d' found the three of them a table in the bar, a vacant chair next to the wall waiting for Frank Gambino.

"It is some night out there, sweetie," Kelly said, drinking a Manhattan. "The cab *slid* all the way here, I'm telling you."

"I'm telling ya," Barbara said, a vacant expression on her pretty face. Milano thought it was pills. "If Kelly hadn't of called me up, I woulda stayed home and read a magazine. But I told my husband that Kelly had split up with this guy, and I had to go hold her hand." She giggled, gulping down gin over ice.

"I wouldn't say anything to Frankie about any husband," Milano said to her. "He's old-fashioned, you know?"

"Have to get out sometime," she said, over the noise in the restaurant. "Is this a nice guy?"

"The greatest," Milano said. "A gentleman."

"This is a nice place," Barbara said, looking around at the red-checkered tablecloths, the men in dark suits, the women in bouffant hairdos, diamonds on their fingers, pearls around their necks.

Tony grinned. Half the men were mobsters out with their girlfriends. A few, more quiet and sober, were with their wives. Kelly put her hand on Tony's arm.

"Frankie's here," she said.

Gambino entered, snow flecking his tan cashmere topcoat. The fat man who followed just behind took the topcoat and hat, giving them to the girl at the checkroom. Handsome, freshly shaved, Gambino greeted friends, bending down to listen for a moment to a small, gray-haired man who scurried up to him from one of the tables. He frowned and shook his head no. The maitre d' brought Frank to their table, and Frank stood smiling as Milano introduced the girls. Barbara appeared to be a little short of breath.

"The car wouldn't start," Frank said, sitting down beside the blonde girl. "Brand new Coupe de Ville, and the battery was dead. Had to come in Mickey's car, and the heater didn't work. I'm frozen through."

"Have some of this," Barbara offered, handing him her glass.

Gambino took a taste of the straight gin and stuck out his tongue. "Trying to poison me with that stuff?" he asked. "I want Chivas with a little soda and a twist," he told the waiter. Leaning over the table he addressed Milano.

"The asshole in the unmarked car didn't budge when we went past in Mickey's Buick," he said, delighted. "He's still sitting back there staring at the Cadillac."

"So what's happening?" Milano asked.

The girls, prepared to be ignored, were chatting about beauty parlors.

"Business is good," Frank said. "But the heat's on. Everything is complicated. But I got no complaints. You?"

"I quit Wren's today. I had enough of those people. This is the kind of work I like," Milano said, placing an arm around Kelly. She smelled of Christian Dior and face powder.

"Honey, tell me about you," Gambino said to the blonde.

"I'm just an ordinary housewife," she said stupidly, draining her second drink.

Gambino shot Milano a questioning glance. The bald man

raised his eyebrows imperceptibly and Gambino shrugged. He was in a good mood. He took the menu for all four of them, and ordered lobster for them all, plus four bottles of Dom Perignon 1957.

Three waiters scurried back and forth from the kitchen and the bar under the direction of the maitre d' and the watchful eye of the fat man who had followed Gambino and was now at the bar. He drank, to his great disgust, ginger ale. Men who wanted a word with Gambino first approached the bodyguard, who heard their request before permitting them to come to the table. No business would be conducted tonight. The lower-ranking soldiers paid Gambino their holiday respects and wishes for a prosperous New Year. Gambino laughed a great deal, shoveling down forkfuls of food and drinking waterglasses of the expensive champagne. Barbara was very drunk, leaning against Gambino and kissing his neck and face. Milano laughed at the passionate antics of the blonde girl. Kelly's right hand held the inside of his thigh, tickling. His leg jerked, the knee kicking the underside of the table and rattling the plates. They all jumped and laughed at the blush that colored Milano's hairless dome; Barbara got the hiccups and excused herself. Kelly gathered up her purse and went along.

Frank put one of his broad hands on Milano's arm.

"Listen to me, Tony," he said with warmth in his voice. "I've got a good job for you. You can manage one of my legitimate businesses. Maybe the liquor distribution. Maybe the construction company. You just tell me. You need any bucks?"

"I'm set," Milano said. "I'm in good shape."

"You can do lots of things. You're clean. You got no record. I can really use you."

"Thanks," Tony said to his friend. "If I need something, I'll let you know."

Gambino nodded. He turned to the fat man, Mickey, motioning him over.

"This is Tony," he said. "We went to school together. He ever asks for anything, I said give it to him."

"How do you do," Mickey said in a high voice, taking Milano's hand in loose grip.

"Make that call now," Gambino told his bodyguard. "There's

42

a pay phone in the back. Don't worry. This place is all right."

Mickey's broad back churned away on his fat legs.

"That's the best trigger I ever got," Frank said. "Nobody knows him. He's outa California."

"Why?" Milano asked.

"It's tight around here. I pay him a lot. I can trust him."

"You don't know him," Milano said.

"He's checked out. He's never lost a client."

"Don't be the first."

"I don't intend to be," Gambino said. He pointed to the other side of the room, where a mild-looking young man with long curly black hair sat alone, methodically chewing on a steak. "Remember Danny? That's his kid brother; he's from the neighborhood."

Smiling confidently, Gambino stood up as the women returned from the washroom.

"I drank so much I couldn't stop going," Barbara said inelegantly.

"Maybe you should fill up on something else," Gambino said.

"Oh, baby," Barbara said, kissing him on the lips. "Let's go. I don't care how cold it is outside."

Mickey had returned to his post at the bar. Gambino stood, snapping his fingers at him. Milano saw that as Frank rose, the young man with long hair put money on his table and disappeared outside.

"Gotta strike while the iron is hot," Gambino said.

"You go on, Frank, I'll take the bill," Milano told him.

"It's taken care of," Gambino said. From his pants pocket he removed a wad of hundred-dollar bills and slid one of them under his plate. "So's the tip."

"The next one is on me," Milano said, bothered that Frank wouldn't let him even pay the tip.

"Absolutely," Frank said. "Can I give you a lift someplace?"

"I thought we'd grab a cab and go on over to Sonny's Lounge, and listen to the singer."

"That is not the place to go tonight," Gambino said urgently, all traces of drunkenness gone. "You understand me, Tony?"

Milano felt uneasy, as though he had been narrowly missed by a car in the street. "I understand the singer's no good, anyway," he said, standing, as Mickey brought coats for Gambino and his date.

Gambino, his smile back and a twinkle in his eye, took Barbara possessively by the arm of her black-dyed rabbit coat. "Come around next week, we'll talk." He disappeared out the door.

The exit was grand enough to warrant applause. Tony watched with an ironic expression on his face.

"He is swell," Kelly said to him.

"Swell," Milano agreed. "Your friend doesn't seem to have much upstairs."

"She's got plenty downstairs, though," Kelly said. "Not as good as me, lover, but she's OK. Why did Frankie say that about Sonny's Lounge?"

"You don't really want to know," Milano answered.

They had a nightcap and retired to Kelly's one-bedroom high-rise apartment on Madison Avenue. Kelly was hot, but despite the fact that Tony hadn't been with a woman for more than a week, he was preoccupied and prefunctory in their lovemaking. When they lay quietly together under the gentle warmth of the electric blanket, Kelly asked him again about Gambino's warning.

"Nothing," he said, irritated by her inquisitiveness. "Forget it."

"Something bad was going to happen there," she said. "What was it, Tony?"

"Not a thing."

"Somebody was going to get killed," she guessed. "That's right, isn't it, Tony? Did Frank have anything to do with it?"

"You ask too many questions," Tony snapped, getting out of bed and putting on his trousers.

"Don't get mad," Kelly said, following him out of bed. "Let me get you a drink or something. It's just that something happened there and I read about it in the newspapers and I wondered what was going on."

"You don't understand," he said with a deep frown on his face. "I take you to a place, you see some people, have a couple of drinks and a laugh or two—you don't read the newspapers the next day. Why the hell are you always reading newspapers?"

"Everybody reads newspapers," she said, bewildered.

"I don't read any goddam newspapers," he stated. "I have a drink. I go to work. I mind my own business. Don't you see?"

Kelly didn't understand.

"I been dating you for months," she said. "I don't know anything about you, except that you know a lot of some people."

"What people?" he challenged.

"Like Frank Gambino," she said. "Like the Gallo people. Like Bill Bonanno."

"What the hell are you talking about?" he said. "I don't know no people."

"Who do you think we had dinner with tonight?" she replied.

"That depends on who I tell you we had dinner with tonight," he said. "If I tell you we had dinner with Frank Gambino, we had dinner with him. If I tell you we had dinner with Joe Schlepp, you say we had dinner with Joe Schlepp. Maybe I say we didn't even have dinner, but went to a movie. Maybe you haven't seen me for a month."

"And maybe we didn't just fuck right there in that bed," she shouted at him. "You crazy or something? Frank Gambino, Frank Gambino, Frank Gambino. I know who sat right across the table from me."

"Stop shouting," he ordered in a quiet rage. "You say that name again, I hit you in the mouth and you won't have any more pretty teeth. I'm telling you right now, we went to a movie and had a hamburger and a beer and came home and went to sleep. You tell that to your friend, too. Otherwise I'm not responsible for what happens."

Kelly started to cry. "What do you do, Tony, that you're so concerned? How are you mixed up in all of this?"

Milano put on his shirt and jacket, folding the tie in his pocket.

"I don't do anything," he said. "I'm unemployed. I'm a bum."

When Tony slammed the door of the apartment, Kelly was certain that she would never see him again.

It was much colder now outside in the street, but the wind

had died down and the snow had stopped. Tony began walking again, the snow on the sidewalks squeaking under his rubbers, past the closed bars and stores and great buildings.

December 31, 1965. All day he had been taking stock of his life, winnowing it, paring off pieces, people, even parts of himself that he didn't want or couldn't use. There wasn't much left: no job, no wife, no girlfriend, a distant elderly mother he hadn't seen for years, and the old friends whose lives he wasn't really involved with, whom he knew mostly in bars and restaurants.

I'm nothing, Tony thought, *I don't exist.* But instead of making him feel depressed, the thought excited him. He felt oddly joyous, lightened by having gotten rid of the last remnants of somebody called Peter Milano. In his place now, a man called Tony Bartolini walked quickly through the streets of New York, tall and anonymous, a gray figure simply passing by.

Even the occasional shivering hookers seemed to look through him or looked casually away as though he didn't exist. Tony thought that he might be invisible.

At home, he undressed and lay naked on top of the bed, his open eyes looking up through the darkness at the black ceiling. Whatever he had been approaching in the street was receding from him, and he felt fear start to close in on him. There was something wrong. Something that he couldn't shake was keeping him from beginning again, from starting new, something was preventing him from being absolved of his old self.

Then he remembered the money. In the blackness, he smiled. He realized that to shake free he had to get rid of the money.

But despite his determination, thirty-five years of cautious living had made him careful with a buck. It took nearly two months for him to squander the money, and then he had to give most of it away.

It wasn't until February, 1966, that Tony Bartolini reached into his pocket and couldn't come up with anything. He was broke. Now he was ready for the next step.

Chapter 3

In February, the weather got warmer and wetter, unpleasant all the time. The sky was always close, with clouds at the tops of New York's gray buildings. Everything turned gray—the sidewalks, the shop windows. White people and black turned gray.

When Tony asked the cab driver to take him to the *Times* building on 43rd Street, his money actually wasn't completely gone. He still had $150 in small bills in the right-hand pocket of his trousers, under the wet raincoat. He tipped the driver, and with the late-afternoon rain coming down and water seeping through the thin soles of his shoes, he went into the bar across the street from the *Times*. The man he was looking for, Philadelphia Charlie, sat on a stool at the bar, facing the door.

"Hi, Tony," Charlie said. "Come on, sit down. Have a drink. Lenny, give my friend a snort."

The bartender, a short, thin, gray-haired man from the Bronx, wore a gold jacket with a white shirt and a black tie. He looked like the field marshal of a South American dictatorship. "What do you want, sir?" he asked Tony.

"A beer. Rheingold draft."

Philadelphia Charlie smiled. He was an ordinary-looking man until he smiled. Then you could feel danger coming off him, as from a hungry animal in a cage. "What do you look so disgusted about?"

"Money," Tony said, sipping the beer. "I lost my job a couple of months ago, and I've been spending money like it ain't nothing. I've got to do something."

"That's too bad. What kind of a job are you looking for?"

"Don't know. I just don't have any idea."

"Well," Charlie said, looking less dangerous. "How would you like to make some fast cash?"

"That's just what I want to do. All the money I got is in my pocket. I don't even have a bank account any more."

That made Charlie laugh. "I work for John Bonnano," he said, in an ordinary tone that the bartender ignored. "We move checks. Business checks. We hit the banks. We got a system."

Tony looked at him. His hazel eyes were as gray as the rain outside. "OK," he said.

"There are usually four or five of us that go out."

"That's cool," Tony said.

"I want to know if you're interested," Charlie said.

"I'll go along with it," Tony said.

"Meet me here at six o'clock tonight, and we'll go see John in the Hotel Dixie, right next door."

When Tony came back at six, Charlie was still sitting on the same stool. They found John Bonnano drinking coffee in the Hotel Dixie restaurant.

"Welcome to my office," Bonnano said, extending a hand to Tony. "Charlie here says you're interested in coming into my business. I'm interested you're interested."

Tony sat down across from him. "Why's that?"

"I know about you from some of the guys. Frank Gambino. How come you don't want to do business with Frank?"

"Too rough," Tony said to him. "You can get killed, that kind of business."

"This is better. All you kill are the banks."

"How's the money?"

"Terrific," John said. "Here's how it works from my end. The guys you're going out with tomorrow are all working for me. I'm supplying everything—the checks, the check-writing machine, the typewriter. These are good checks. A full book. It's just been lifted."

"I don't know anything about this business," Tony explained. "Do banks cash stolen checks?"

Philadelphia Charlie made a calming motion with his hand.

48

"Don't worry, John," he said. "I'll explain how it works to him."

"You better," John said. "Listen Tony, don't worry about it."

"How much do I get?" Tony said.

"I was comin' to that," John said. "On this kind of a deal, when it's all my crew, you get twenty-five percent of what you take in."

"How much is that?" Tony asked him.

"A lot," said Philadelphia Charlie.

"You're going to enjoy this," John told Tony. "It's a good crew. Everybody but you has worked it before."

"There's nothing to it," Philadelphia Charlie said. "Give me the checks. I got some other things I got to attend to."

John lifted a large commercial checkbook from the seat of the booth. Philadelphia Charlie opened the checkbook on the pink formica table: four hundred checks, Metropolitan Tool and Die Company.

"They look good," Charlie said. "How hot are they?"

"I just got them today, for chrissake," John said. "They were acquired only a couple days ago. Burglary. The company probably doesn't even know they're gone."

"That's good," Tony said, relieved.

"I just want to tell you, Tony, there are other kinds of deals, too," John said. "For example, there is a ten-percent, twenty-five-percent, fifty-percent deal, if you're taking more responsibility."

"You said *this* was a twenty-five-percent arrangement," Tony said.

"But not on top of fifty percent of the take," John explained. "You get that if you're working your own crew. The best arrangement for making money is to go into business for yourself. Then I just sell you the checks and stuff, and you take it from there. But no guarantees."

"I better find out how this works," Tony said to him.

"I need some cards," Philadelphia Charlie told John. "I want a full set to get the account opened."

John put a small manila envelope on the table, and shook out credit cards for American Express, Diner's Club, and Mobil

Oil. They all bore the name of Roger Metcalf. "Good enough?"

Philadelphia Charlie riffled through them. "I need one to get a car," he said.

John grunted. "I forgot," he said. "This is how it gets so expensive." Reaching into a shirt pocket, he removed a Hertz credit card. "This is a brand new card. It cost me a hundred bucks. I woulda used it myself." Shrugging, he threw it onto the table with the others.

Tony felt self-conscious about John's openness.

"Don't you worry about people watching this?"

John laughed. "This is my office, honest to God," he said. "I got a regular place to live in, in the hotel. It's my place, Tony. Either I know everybody here or they don't make any difference, anyway."

Philadelphia Charlie placed the credit cards in an empty wallet, and wrapped the checkbook inside the fold of a newspaper. "I'll pick you up in the morning, about eight," he told Tony.

John smiled at Tony. "You look real good," he said. "You look square."

"I am square," Tony said.

He stayed home that night, nervously smoking and fretting about being caught. He awakened at 5:00 A.M., showered, and dressed in a gray gabardine suit, a blue oxford-cloth shirt, and a red-and-blue striped tie. The doorbell rang exactly at eight. Going outside in his tan raincoat, Tony found Philadelphia Charlie and two other men in a new rented Chevrolet.

Tony got into the front seat, next to a huge, fat man whose stomach rested on the steering wheel.

"This is Tony," Charlie told the others. "This is Fat Louie and this fella is Little Steve."

"Pleasure," said Little Steve, a small man about thirty years old.

Fat Louie thrust out a large, very fat hand. "I'm delighted to meet you," he said. "Charles has been telling us about your decision to join the rolls of dangerous felons. To the untrained eye, we may not look like very much, but any experienced eye could tell that we are a hearty band of desperados."

"What's with this guy?" Tony asked Charlie.

Fat Louie started the car with a trembling hand.

"That's what you get, going to college," Charlie said. "Louie went to private school and everything."

"The Valley Forge Military Academy," said Fat Louie. "And I graduated from Yale with honors. If my poor patrician father could see me now."

He was a very inept driver, and stalled the car twice before getting it to the corner. "Condensation in the carburetor," Fat Louie explained. "The Hertz people don't maintain their cars very well these days."

Pulling out into traffic, he cut off a sedately moving school-bus.

"Goddammit," cursed Little Steve. "You can't drive, Louie. Let me take it."

"I am a superb driver," Fat Louie said. "I never saw it, the way it shot up on me."

Rain pelted the windshield, but Fat Louie had apparently forgotten about the windshield wipers. With the hairy back of his thick hand he cleared a small circle of steam away from the inside of the windshield, peering out intently.

"The day is strangely somber," Louie said, slamming on the brakes at a traffic light. The others were thrown forward.

"I'm telling you I can't stand how the hell he drives," Little Steve shouted. "You make me too goddam nervous, Louie. Why the hell won't you let me drive?"

"Experience and talent can't be identified in the first instant," Fat Louie said, as he inched the Chevrolet through the intersection. "When we sail down the highway, the incredible skills I possess will be apparent even to nervous little ragamuffins like yourself."

Tony watched the fat man's hands and arms shaking on the steering wheel. Louie appeared to have been taken by an enormous chill. His huge, ashen face had the color of candlewax, and he sniffed frequently.

"You got some cold," Tony said to him.

Fat Louie smiled, showing small, separated, but perfect teeth. "It's my metabolism," he said. "I suffer from low blood sugar."

"Bullshit," Little Steve said in the back seat. "Tell him that you need a drink. Tell him to stop the car, Charlie, and get over the DT's, or I'm getting out of here and to hell with it."

"That's a good idea," Charlie decided. "There's a tavern open there. Let's stop and have a snort before we get going. How's that sound to you, Tony?"

"I don't usually drink in the morning," Tony said.

"Ah, but it's better drinking in the morning," Fat Louie said dreamily. "It awakens the spiritual forces."

He pulled the car in front of the tavern and led the way into the bar. The time on the Budweiser clock was 8:25. "What will you have, gentlemen?" the fat man asked. Philadelphia Charlie and Little Steve opted for beers. Tony requested a glass of soda water, and raising it said "*A noi.*" Fat Louie downed his glass of vodka and pushed it forward for a refill with utter concentration.

"What's the deal?" Tony asked Philadelphia Charlie.

"We're going to the Ben Franklin Banks in Long Island," Charlie told him. "Louie's gonna go in and open up an account in the name of that Metcalf— that Roger Metcalf. Then he's going to put two hundred into Roger Metcalf's account."

Charlie smiled, bringing a violent look to his eyes. Tony saw Fat Louie down the second glass of vodka, and push forward the glass for a third.

"How much does he drink?" Tony asked.

Little Steve chuckled. "Two fifths a day, maybe. Poor Fat Louie is one hell of an alcoholic."

"You can kill yourself like that," Tony commented.

"He gets too nervous otherwise," said Little Steve. "A guy can't work something like this if he's so nervous he shakes all the time."

"He's makin' me nervous," Tony said.

"Don't worry about Louie," Charlie told him. "He does his job all right. You watch. He'll walk out of here sober, no shakes."

Tony shrugged, and returned to business. "Why do you put the money in the bank?"

"That's so we can make more deposits," Charlie told him. "We make up the checks to Metcalf." Opening his briefcase, Charlie displayed a pile of the Metropolitan Tool and Die Company checks, now imprinted in red for $600 each, to Roger Metcalf. "Then we go to a window, and give them a deposit slip for *two* hundred. The teller checks the number, and it's OK. Metcalf is making a deposit, not making a withdrawal, so she hands over *four* hundred. We do that at every branch."

"Every branch!" Tony whistled.

"Easy," Philadelphia Charlie told him. "We hit four windows at the same time, and all branches. When those checks start going through the clearing house tomorrow morning, them bastards are going to die."

"Die," said Little Steve. "That's right."

Tony began wishing he had had some of Louie's vodka, but no expression of any kind showed on his handsome face.

"Gentlemen, we have a day's labor awaiting us," Louie said. "Shall we depart?"

Fat Louie's hands had stopped shaking, and he drove much better now that he had consumed a pint of vodka.

At the Ben Franklin Bank in Farmingdale, Long Island, Louie pulled the car into a parking space and peered moodily at the old facade.

"Once again, old horse, into the battle," he said mostly to himself.

Philadelphia Charlie leaned over the back of the seat, and handed him the three credit cards. "You got two hundred bucks?"

"Indeed, my friend," Fat Louie said. "What a dismal fate for a graduate of the great academic mother, Harvard."

With another sigh, and a wet honk of his nose, he pushed out of the Chevrolet and walked heavily through the front doors of the bank.

"I thought he said he went to Yale," Tony commented.

"He went someplace," answered Philadelphia Charlie tensely. "He'd better not blow it."

"He can panic," Little Steve said, lighting a cigarette. "He does that, sometimes."

"What happens then?" Tony wondered.

"We see him come like a bat out of hell through that front door," said Little Steve. "One fat bat."

53

"Shouldn't we be ready to make a getaway?" Tony asked.

"It's not our skin," Little Steve said. "He's not holding up the bank, for chrissake. He's just opening an account."

"Then why does he panic?"

"Why does he drink?" asked Philadelphia Charlie. "His nerves are shot. That happens in this business."

"What if somebody comes after him?" Tony asked.

"If he chickens out, nobody will come after him," said Little Steve. "They'll just think he's a nut."

"And John's out about fifteen hundred in front money, and my ass is on the line to come up with it," said Charlie. "That's plenty."

A tense half hour went by.

"Banks are busy," said Charlie. "It's a good sign, he's gone long. It means that he's being taken care of."

Tony watched the bank entrance. Finally, he saw a heavy, dark shape lean against the door, and Fat Louie came shambling out.

"Look at him," he said.

"Good," Charlie said. "He's limp. He didn't get caught. Tony, you drive. He won't be worth a shit now until he gets another drink."

Fat Louie sagged gratefully into the Chevrolet. His cheeks were fiery red and his nose was purple, but he was beaming with pleasure.

"A piece of cake," he said. "I even have the checks for my new account. Now, a drink."

"Good work," Charlie told him, taking the credit cards and the new checkbook.

At the tavern, Fat Louie, Philadelphia Charlie, and Little Steve all drank whiskey with beer chasers; Tony sipped another soda water. Despite his turbulent feelings, he noticed that his fingers were the only ones that were steady.

At the Ben Franklin on Farmington Boulevard, Tony pulled the car into the bank's parking lot.

"Just go to the window and make a two-hundred-dollar deposit," Charlie instructed the novice. "We'll be at other windows, doing the same. Don't say anything that you don't have to, and don't worry about anything. If there's any sign of a fuss, don't bolt. Don't run. If you feel like you have to leave, walk slowly out the door. But don't go back to the car, or you'll blow it for the rest of us. But nobody ever catches on that there's more than one person doing the same thing, anyway."

"Doesn't sound so safe to me," Tony said.

"Nothing in this world is truly safe," rumbled the fat man. "Only the grave, where we joust with the worms."

At fifteen-second intervals, the four men went into the side door of the bank. The Wednesday-morning customers stood in short lines at the teller's windows. Tony chose the line nearest the door, with three people ahead of him.

Just in front of him stood a burly man with a short, gray crew-cut. The woman who was making a deposit with the pretty girl at the teller's window removed a canvas bag from her purse, and emptied its contents—a thick stack of checks, and a large pile of loose coins. Then the woman began counting and examining the checks while the teller counted the change.

"It looks like we're in for a little wait," said the man in the crewcut.

Tony, intently watching his companions move up to their windows, started. "What?" he asked.

He saw that the burly man wore the collar of a Roman Catholic priest.

"I'm sorry, Father," Tony said. "I was wool-gathering."

The priest had a cheerful, avuncular way about him. "That woman. I should know better by now than to get into line behind her. She works for a little heating business, and every Wednesday she brings in the week's checks. She could just turn them in, and trust in the bank's adding machines. But she's afraid of having made a mistake."

"How long does she take?" Tony asked.

"Maybe ten minutes," the priest said. "You might be better off if you went to another window."

"I can wait."

"People are usually in such a hurry," the priest said. "I haven't seen you before. Do you live around here?"

"No, Father," Tony said respectfully, thinking of the irony of speaking with a priest before he commited his first real crime. "I live in Manhattan."

"I don't want to pry," the priest said. "I'm rector of a church near here, and I'm always looking for people to join my flock."

"How did you know I'm Catholic?" Tony asked him.

"You look like a fish-eater," the priest said to him. "Actually, I could tell by how quickly you said 'Father.' "

"Really?" Tony asked him. "Can you always tell a Catholic?"

"I think that I can, but I'm not always right. Usually I find I'm talking to fallen Catholics. It's unbelievable how many have strayed."

Unbelievable, Tony thought. "I'm one of them, I guess."

"It's never too late," the priest told him. "Not that many people believe in the church these days. It's usually the old women. Men *never* were good Catholics. The Irish always considered themselves the most devout, but that was hangover religion. Every Irishman's sin consists of overindulgence in alcohol." He smiled broadly. "I'm Irish; when I'm sent to hell, it's scotch that will send me there."

The woman with the pile of checks finally concluded her business and left the window. The man next in line cashed a check quickly.

"You go ahead of me," the priest offered. "You have less time than I do."

"Not at all." Tony desperately wished he had hours before he got to the window. "I've got plenty of time."

The priest greeted the teller, made a small deposit in his account, and smiled farewell at Tony as he left.

"Hi," the cute teller said to Tony. "Father McCarthy's a nice guy, isn't he?"

Tony nodded. "There aren't many like him." He smiled thinly, feeling sweat dripping from his armpits. His whole body felt on fire; perspiration soaked his palms. But except for the strained smile, his face showed no emotion as the teller accepted the deposit slip and check. Tony's thighs felt quavery as she turned over the check and pushed it back towards him.

"You forgot to endorse this, sir," she said.

"Yes, I did," Tony said with a panicky feeling. He had forgotten who the check was made out to. "Do you have a pen?" he asked with a frown.

The girl handed him a black ballpoint. Hesitating briefly, Tony turned over the check, reading the name Roger Metcalf. Tony wrote a fancy signature unlike anything he had ever written before. As he wrote the name he felt himself become Roger Metcalf—an engineer, he thought, for a small machinery company.

"Here it is," he said with relief.

The teller counted out $400 in $50 and $20 bills.

"Thank you, sir," she said handing him the deposit record with the money.

"Thank *you*," Tony said to her. "Tell Father McCarthy thanks, too."

The teller looked slightly puzzled as he left.

"What the hell took you so long?" Little Steve asked him as he got into the car.

"Some dame with a lot of checks," Tony said. "Who gets the money?"

"Hang on to it," Philadelphia Charlie told him. "We'll total up at the end of the day."

The exit went beside the drive-in teller's booth.

"Stop," Charlie instructed. "One more hit."

He inserted a deposit slip and a fifth $600 check into the metal box, and watched gleefully as the teller recorded the transaction and returned another $400 in cash. "Now go."

From Ben Franklin branch to branch they worked steadily without breaking for lunch until shortly after three, when Fat Louie's nerves snapped. Tony saw Louie approach the teller, fumble the paper in his hand, and drop the check onto the floor. He lunged onto a knee to capture it.

For a moment, it didn't look as though the obese man would be able to pull himself back to his feet. Grasping the edge of the counter with both hands, he swayed dizzily. Louie put the palm of a hand against his forehead, and grinning sickly, turned from the window and stumbled out of the bank.

Louie was trembling violently in the car. "God, I'm sick," he moaned. "I think I'm having a heart attack."

"He's having a heart attack?" Charlie asked Little Steve.

The small man took Louie's pulse. "Don't think so," he said. "I think it's low blood sugar."

"Mock a sick man, and you shall be mocked by the gods," Louie muttered.

He rolled down the window and vomited against the side of the car.

"Christ," said Little Steve. "Goddam rummy."

Philadelphia Charlie, Little Steve, and Tony hit five more banks before the last of them closed at five o'clock, raising the day's total to 12 Ben Franklin branches. Tony figured that they had taken $19,200, of which $1,200 was his.

Philadelphia Charlie counted the day's take as they drove back to Manhattan, handing Tony $1,225.

"What's the extra twenty-five for?" Tony asked.

"The one at the drive-in window," Charlie told him. "What do you think of this business, Tony?"

"Terrific," Tony said to him. "Do we do it again tomorrow?"

"Why not?" Charlie said. "Anybody want to go to New Jersey?"

They all wanted to go to New Jersey, except for Fat Louie, who wanted, with a firm, almost ferocious determination, a drink.

Tony touched the fat roll of money in his pocket and experienced an emotion very much like pride. *It's not so hard being a criminal*, he thought. *It's easy.* He stopped the car at the first decent looking cocktail lounge, ordered a double Chivas, and tossed it down without tasting it. The liquor couldn't cut through the euphoria: he felt already intoxicated, almost dizzy with success.

Goddammit, he thought through dinner with his confederates, *what a hell of a thing. I was born for this kind of life.*

Tony drank heavily that night, trying to take himself off the high edge of terror and success. But he was calm and sober when Charlie dropped him off at midnight. In the shabby bedroom, Tony laid the bills evenly over the entire top of the dresser, chuckling softly. Eventually he removed the sweat-stained suit, and threw it in a heap in the corner, taking a long shower that washed the salty residue of fear from his skin. He put on pajamas, turned off the light, and thinking of the priest, tried to present a prayer.

"Jesus Christ, now I'm a crook," he prayed. "I can get busted. Will I get busted? How good is this thing? Now there's no turning back. I broke the ice, and that's it. Make me rich, make me cold, make me fearless. Make me glad."

This is blasphemous, he thought, and slid into a dreamless sleep.

Philadelphia Charlie called Tony shortly after nine the next morning; a crushing hangover made it impossible to work. Tony felt very disappointed, as though a woman he wanted had just broken an important date.

To work off the energy building up in him he went to the handball courts and played until he could barely stand up. The hard needle shower reinvigorated a taste for excitement, and Tony decided that he ought to spend some of the money he had made.

Walking the streets, he found a one-bedroom apartment in Tudor City on the East Side which he rented on the spot, putting $250 down as security and paying the first month's $250 rent. He bought a pair of $35 Florsheim Imperial shoes, black, a gray-flannel suit made by Petrocelli, half a dozen white-and-blue broadcloth shirts, and four new ties. But the taste for excitement wouldn't go away. He telephoned Charlie at his home, asking what other kind of action was around.

"You're nuts," Charlie told him. "You actually like this stuff, eh?"

"It's a way to pass the time."

"I might have something," Charlie said. "Come on up."

What Charlie had was a bank guarantee card from the First National City Bank of New York, good for up to $100. He added to it a recently stolen personal checkbook from an upstate physician. Tony paid him $300 for the twenty-three unused checks, and set out on his own.

By closing time, riding taxis from branch to branch, Tony had hit the bank for $1,500 at $100 a crack. He bought several bottles of wine and two quarts of Chivas Regal, which he brought to Charlie as a way of saying thanks.

"But why the fuck do I have to give someone else seventy-

59

five percent?" he asked the other man, whose eyes still appeared to have been boiled in whiskey. "Where the hell did you get that card?"

"You like it?" Charlie asked. "You get them around. I bought it for a hundred bucks."

"I'll give you two hundred," Tony told him. "It's worth it."

"No, I don't want any money," Charlie said slyly. "I don't want the card, either. See, I already used it a couple of times."

Tony rose out of his seat with a yell. "You cocksucker, you already used that card in the same banks?" he shouted.

"Hey, cool it. You didn't get caught with it, did you?"

"The risk," Tony said. "Are you trying to set me up?"

"You're crazy," Charlie told him. "Don't be so fucking paranoid."

Tony calmed down when Charlie offered to take him to one of the hot-goods markets where he bought identification, credit cards, checks, and other hot merchandise. They rode a Yellow Cab to the Horn and Hardart across from Grand Central Station, the timeless cafeteria where shabbily dressed old men dropped their hoarded quarters hopelessly into the coin slots.

"This is really a classy place," Tony said to Philadelphia Charlie. "Looks like a bathroom, if you ask me."

"Don't be so critical, for chrissake. It all depends on what you're looking for."

Charlie pointed out a heavy black-haired man with a huge pot belly at a far table. The man wore a bright purple silk shirt with shiny brown pants, an expensive pair of black-and-white summer shoes, and fluorescent orange socks. His thick hair was pulled back away from his puffy face, plastered down with heavy pomade.

"That's Mike the Greek," Charlie said. "You wanna meet him. He's got credit cards. Anything you want. The guy sitting by him—see that little Jewish guy?—he's Cy. Diamonds. They sell more diamonds in this cafeteria than in Africa."

As Charlie led the way to Mike the Greek's table, Tony observed intent business conversations at several tables throughout the cafeteria, amid the solitary dinners of the lonely and the coffee of the cold.

"You, Charlie, wow, good to see ya," Mike the Greek said,

proffering a greasy hand with black fingernails. "Who's the frien' witcha?"

"Tony," Charlie said. "You mind if we sit down with you for a minute?"

"Always my pleasure. What can I do for youse guys today?"

"I just wanna get you to know this man," Charlie told him. "This guy is a fella who works with me. Anything he wants, it's OK. I vouch for him. All right with you?"

"Always glad to have new customers," said Mike the Greek. "What can I do for you today? Cards? No full decks today, but I could probably get them in twenty-four hours. Tell ya something good that's comin' in. American Express. One thousand unused cards are coming in. Interested?"

"Real interested," Charlie told him. "How clean?"

"Just as clean as can be. Right out of the vault. Should be good for seven days, no matter what. What the hell—maybe longer."

"How do you get cards like that?" Tony asked him.

"Some creepy clerk steals them. I should know? I got my sources. These will be two hundred each," Mike told him. "Normally, an American Express is only one hundred. But these are the best kind you can get."

"I want one," Tony said.

"So do I," said Charlie.

"Come by Monday night," said Mike, "but a little later. I keep the store open on Mondays until eight."

"You have a store for credit cards?" Tony asked.

Mike laughed loudly. "I got a clothing store in Brooklyn," he explained. "A legit place. Well, mostly. Say, if you're interested, I got a hell of a sale going on Thom McAn shoes."

Charlie lifted an inquisitive eyebrow.

"I got a whole truckload of Thom McAns," Mike boasted. "These guys lifted the trailer, and I bought the whole thing."

"Don't the Thom McAn people wonder how come you're suddenly selling their shoes?" Tony asked him.

Mike drank down his coffee. "Nobody counts, nobody notices nothin'," he said. "I useta wonder about that myself. But with so many thieves in New York . . . You know something? I got cops come into my store, buy all kinda suits and things, never ask any questions. Maybe they don't care, maybe they don't notice. I stopped worrying about them kinda things a long time ago."

"Is there anything else that I'd be interested in?" Tony inquired.

"Passports?" Mike said. "Ever need any passports?"

"I never went anyplace," Tony said. They all laughed.

Mike waved broadly at somebody behind them, and leaned over the table. "Little broad, nuts about me," he said.

A tough-looking but attractive bleached blonde who looked about sixteen years old walked insolently to the table wearing a new black leather jacket and very tight plaid slacks.

"Gracie," Mike thundered, "give me one a them big wet ones."

Obediently, the teenager took Mike's loose, fat face between her thin fingers and kissed him deeply on the mouth. Tony saw their tongues working back and forth, and felt embarrassed. The girl sat down next to the fence, who heaved a heavy arm over her shoulders.

"How about this merchandise?" Mike crowed, pinching Gracie's right nipple with his fingers. She started at the pain, but didn't move away. "Either of you guys interested in some hot stuff like this?"

"We ain't even been introduced," Charlie said.

"We're all friends anyway," Mike said. "Gracie, this is Charlie and Tony."

Gracie politely said, "Pleased to meetcha," and fell silent with her arms wrapped around Mike's ponderous stomach.

"This little girl here gives tremendous head," Mike said loudly. "Ain't that true, honey?"

Gracie nodded.

"Anyplace," Mike continued. "She'd even do it right here, wouldncha, sweetie?"

Gracie nodded again.

"Either of you guys interested?" Nick asked them.

Gracie's small blue eyes watched them unwaveringly. Tony didn't much like either Mike or his little girlfriend.

"How much?" Charlie asked, never able to resist a bargain.

"Twenty-five bucks," Mike said. "And she'll do it right here."

Charlie considered it for a moment. "Nah, I got too much to do," he said.

"Just a thought. Any time you want this little honey, just tell me."

"Thanks," Charlie said. "We're gonna push on now. I want Tony to meet some of the other guys here."

Charlie moved ahead of Tony, greeting Cy the diamond fence and passing him by for a small man in a gray suburban jacket who had a pair of crutches lying across the chair.

Tony and Charlie sat down with the crippled man, Little Eddie, another dealer in hot credit cards. They were joined shortly by an emaciated man in a blue shirt.

"Frankie the Cat Burglar," Charlie said. "Tony, this man is something special."

Tony was impressed by the strength of the thin man's fingers.

"Who you with?" Frankie asked.

"I'm with Charlie," Tony said.

"A new man on the route," Charlie explained. "Gonna be a real good one, I'm telling you. I'm bringing him around to people today so he gets to know what's going on."

"There's enough going on," said Little Eddie.

"*Plenty*," Frankie snickered.

"That's what he's finding out," Charlie said. "Now, like this guy," he said to Tony, indicating the burglar. "You could tell Frankie, you could say, 'Now, Frankie, I want a book of business checks.' And Frankie will go steal them on order. Greatest burglar you ever saw. Get in any office building. Right, Frankie?"

"Right," Frankie said. "Four hundred for a full book."

"Fresh," Charlie said. "When you get them from Frankie, you know the checks are fresh. He went and got them for you. Biggest worry a check-casher has is to buy some checks and maybe some sonofabitch has used some of them, and they're on the list. Or they're old and they're on the list. You have to watch who you buy from."

Little Eddie and Frankie the Cat Burglar nodded their approval.

Charlie, sitting at the end of the table, spied a man wearing a soft hat enter the cafeteria. The pupils of his eyes turned into pinpoints. "Polack Joe," he muttered. " 'Scuse me. Have to call a friend."

After a brief conversation at the pay phone, Charlie returned, stopping to greet the long-nosed man in the soft hat, who had taken a table nearby. Polack Joe wolfed down a sweet roll and a candy bar. He looked slyly at the check-passer.

"Haven't seen you for a while," he said. "Everything all right?"

"Terrific," Charlie said effusively. "Everything's been going *good.*"

Polack Joe relaxed a bit. "That's good," he said, picking up a piece of icing from the plate. "No problems?"

"No problems at all," Charlie said. "Everything's a piece of cake."

"I'm glad," Polack Joe said, really meaning it. He hesitated, and then decided to approach his concern. "Was everything cool with those checks?"

Charlie smiled. Even ten feet away, Tony could feel the rage in Charlie's bared teeth. "Great," Charlie said.

"I thought they'd be OK," Polack Joe said.

Charlie returned to his own table. Several minutes later, two hulking men wearing longshoremen's jackets entered the cafeteria, looking over to their table. Charlie unobtrusively pointed out Polack Joe. The men, one tall and gangling, the other short and compact, went to Polack Joe's table, and sat down on either side of him, smiling. Polack Joe shook his head, and covered his face with his hands. "Don't think so," Tony heard him say.

"But Charlie, Charlie—" Polack Joe called over.

Charlie acted as though nothing was going on.

The two men stood up on either side of Polack Joe, who reluctantly rose to his feet like a man in a trance, to be escorted out. Charlie grinned lupinely.

"That's it," he stated. "Let's go, Tony."

Whatever was going on, Tony knew that he didn't like it. "I think I'll get on home," he told Charlie as they left the building.

"Come with me, just a minute."

Reluctantly, Tony followed Charlie around the block, and

walked down a nearby alley. He heard the sound of quiet protests and blows. The two men had Polack Joe pressed up against a wall. They were mechanically punching him in the body.

"Don't break nothin'," Charlie said. "I don't want him killed, this time."

Polack Joe vomited, and the taller enforcer stepped back, waiting for him to finish.

"I didn't mean nothing," Polack Joe pleaded. He was crying.

"The message is, don't sell me used checkbooks," Charlie said. "I had to run out of that bank with the fucking security guard on my tail."

"It was an accident," Polack Joe said.

"Screw you," Charlie told him. "Maybe I don't care if they *do* kill you—accidentally."

He handed the tall enforcer five $100 bills. The man counted the money, then resumed punching Polack Joe like a man returning to work after his coffee break.

"Let's go," Charlie said.

Tony was disturbed. "I don't like this violent stuff."

"Sometimes you gotta protect yourself in this business. That guy's a burn artist."

"Then why did you do business with him?" Tony asked.

Charlie didn't really understand the question. "He said he had some checks. I said, are they OK, like I always do, and he said they were, and they weren't. Half the time his checks aren't any good, so he hasta be taught a lesson."

"Why do business with somebody you don't trust?"

"See, he vouched for them," Charlie tried to explain himself. "What are you gonna do?"

It was still raining Friday when Tony, Charlie, Fat Louie, and Little Steve drove to New Jersey, where they burned eighteen branches of Franklin National Bank for $28,000. After the last bank, Charlie rolled down the window and threw away the three credit cards Fat Louie had used to open the account, and the checkbook, which still contained more than two hundred checks.

"What if somebody finds them?" Tony asked.

"What difference does it make?" Charlie said. "They ain't our checks. Maybe somebody can use them."

Back in Manhattan, Tony put on the new suit, and joined the others for dinner at a Sutton Place restaurant. Tony learned Fat Louie once had been very rich, the son of a New Jersey manufacturer who died, leaving him the business and more than $1 million.

"First it was racehorses," Fat Louie explained. "I lost a lot on the bobtails, because I liked to play them. But I really lost when it came to having my own stable: five horses; every one a loser. Then it was gambling, and always booze. As I lost more of my father's fortune, I began to swell up to these immense proportions. I often reflected that I should be in a psychoanalyst's office rather than in a restaurant squandering my inheritance."

"So what happened?" Tony asked.

"I sold the business when the money was gone, and that got me several million more. When *that* money was gone, I turned to crime. Few Yale graduates have led as sordid an existence as I, my friend."

He spoke with great relish, as if amused by his own disintegration. Fat Louie pushed away from the table, and lurched heavily towards the men's room.

"Why did he do all that?" Tony asked.

"He's kinda nutsy," Little Steve said. "He's smart and all that, but he likes to ruin himself."

"I wouldn't work with him, except he can get those accounts open better than anybody else," Charlie said. "I think that's the hardest part, facing some bank vice-president with all that phony ID, and pulling off a story about having a business and all. I've tried it myself, and it doesn't feel right to me."

"I could do it," Tony said. "It sounds easy to me."

"So try it," Charlie said.

After dinner they followed Fat Louie to his girlfriend's apartment, about five blocks away on Sutton Place. Francine was a beautiful black-haired prostitute who could match Fat Louie drink for drink. She had long, brown-tipped breasts that Fat Louie removed from her dress and, dipping them in his drink, sucked on with loud slurping noises.

"Stop that," Charlie said. "That's making me too horny, goddam it."

"They're here for anybody who wants them," Francine offered. "Say Baldie, you want to suck on these?"

"I don't like to share," Tony said, laughing.

"Then we'll party," Francine said, going to the telephone.

In a few minutes, they were joined by three of Francine's girlfriends. Young, well-dressed, and reasonably stupid, they reminded Tony of the secretaries and clerks he knew from the appliance store. As the best-looking man, Tony got most of their attention, until Charlie began to get jealous.

"This is supposed to be a party for everybody," Charlie said, taking one of the girls by an arm and leading her away to a bedroom.

Francine and Fat Louie lay tangled drunkenly together on the couch, with no signs of passion despite their disarrayed clothing, while Tony and Little Steve danced with the other two girls. Tony was not really enjoying himself, although the girl he danced with clung passionately to his body.

When the doorbell rang, Tony was certain that they were being raided by the police.

Francine disengaged from Fat Louie's embrace and pulled herself together, peering through the sentry hole in the door. "What do you want?" she asked. "What time is it, anyway?"

"It's two o'clock," a young man's voice said. "We got a date now, Francine."

"Oh, God, I forgot," Francine said, opening the door for a nervous young man with his hands in his pockets. "What's your name again?"

"Tom Ballbach," the young man said, wondering why all these other people were in the apartment. "I talked to you this afternoon on the telephone."

Francine swayed drunkenly, placing a hand on Ballbach's shoulder for support. "I fuckin' forgot," she said. "I'm sorry. My friends came up, and we're having a party. I don't think I can do you now, since we're having a party."

"I can come back," the young man wished he had never come.

"Nah, meet my friends," Francine said, pulling him into the

room and locking the door behind him. "Tom—Bullock? Whatever your name is, everybody introduce yourself. I don't remember." She realized that the front of her dress was still unbuttoned, and pulled it closed.

"Hi," Ballbach said, trying to be sophisticated and friendly. "I'm in computers."

Fat Louie cleared his throat of phlegm, and stared at the young man. "Then you are a genie," he said. "I always wondered what made the fucking things work." He leaned back his head, and fell asleep.

Philadelphia Charlie and the girl came from the bedroom to find out who the visitor was.

"Hi, I'm Tom Ballbach. I'm in computers." He pulled back when he saw that the older man was wearing a shoulder holster with a gun in it.

"I steal," Charlie said to him. "What the fuck are you doing here, kid?"

"He had a date with me. I forgot," Francine said.

"This is a John," Little Steve said.

Charlie drank scotch from the mouth of the bottle, wiping his mouth with the palm of his hand. "Then fuck her," he told the computer man. "It ain't like we're going to be offended or anything."

The young man tittered.

"What the fuck are you laughing at?" Charlie asked belligerently. "Get it on, kid. Screw the broad, and get the hell out of here."

"Maybe I'd better go," Ballbach said to Francine. "I don't want to break up your party."

"I'm tired of you not listening to me," Charlie said to Ballbach. "You tryna do this lady out of her money?"

Ballbach was shocked. "Of course not," he said. "I just didn't know there would be so many people here, that's all."

"What's wrong with our company?" Charlie asked, menacing. "Crooks ain't good enough for you?"

"I *like* crooks," Ballbach protested. "You're fine by me."

"Then pay the lady her money," Charlie ordered. "Francine, how much this creep owe you?"

"He doesn't owe me nothing," Francine said. "I just forgot about my date, is all."

"You owe her a hundred bucks," Charlie decided.

"But—" the young man said.

Charlie tapped the gun on his shoulder. "Pay."

"Yessir," the young man said, hurriedly taking the money out of his wallet and handing it to him.

Charlie brushed his hand away. "Not me, stupid. Her."

"Here," Ballbach said, giving the money to Francine, who began to cry.

"Honest to God, I don't want it," she sniffled. "I don't do business like this."

"You're all crazy," Charlie said. "You wanna be screwed out of your money?"

The young man stood near the front door with the bills held out in his hand, grinning sickly. Tony felt he had enough.

"That's OK, kid," he said, taking the bills and placing them in Ballbach's jacket pocket. Tony took out his roll and peeled off a hundred-dollar bill, which he handed to Francine.

"See, Charlie, Francine has her money," he said. "Right?"

"Yeah?" Charlie said.

"Yeah," Tony told him. "Do you have your money, Francine?"

"I don't want any money," Francine cried. "I came from a good family and everything."

"Cool," Tony said, patting her shoulder. "Look, Charlie, I got a meeting with somebody, so I've got to get out of here. This kid's going to come with me, because I need somebody to give me directions. All right with you?"

"What if it's not?" Charlie said.

"Are we partners?" Tony asked him.

Charlie nodded.

"OK," Tony said, grabbing his coat. He pushed Ballbach out the door ahead of him. They rode down the elevator in silence.

"You really helped me out there," Ballbach said to Tony in the building lobby. "Take this money."

"I don't want your money," Tony said. "Don't be a jerk all your life. You want some advice, kid?"

Ballbach said he did.

"Stay away from hookers, thieves, politicians, and people who give you good advice."

"Are you a thief, too?" Ballbach asked him.

Tony looked at him through half-closed eyes, utterly exhausted.

"No, I'm not a thief," he said. "I'm an electrical engineer."

"I'm in computers," Ballbach said, smiling.

Chapter 4

There were stains of indelible blue ballpoint ink on Tony Milano's hands.

Carefully, patiently, very curiously, the bald man sat at the new kitchen table in his luxurious apartment on First Avenue, copying the signatures of other men and women.

First, he laid tracing paper over the signatures and drew over them. Hours later, he placed the signature to the left and a blank sheet of white paper to the right, and as swiftly as possible tried to repeat the other person's most personal hand.

What amazed the forger was how easy it was for him to capture the soul, the essence, the intrinsic personal meaning of somebody else's signature. To test this new-found talent further, he copied whole paragraphs from the letters women had written to him over the years, and was startled to discover that once his copy had been made, even he, unless he carefully looked, couldn't tell the original from the fake.

The talent—the trick, as he thought of it—must have lain dormant inside him. The discovery excited the forger.

After that first week with Philadelphia Charlie's crew, Tony began to branch out on his own, rather than sharing his earnings with anybody else. It made more sense to him to work alone, paying cash up front to one of the hot-check merchants for the paper and necessary identification.

He had discovered that hot American Express traveler's checks were as good as money anyplace, and could be purchased from thieves like the Goldman brothers for as little as ten cents on the dollar.

Tony's first week's take, about $7,000, was the smallest since

71

he became a forger two months past; his illegal take since then had been as high as $12,000 for three or four days' careful work a week.

He had decided to try his penmanship because many stolen credit cards and traveler's checks were already countersigned. Most check-passers refused to touch this kind of merchandise, because of the problems of copying the existing signature; consequently, countersigned materials cost much less than blanks.

Although it hardly seemed possible to him at the time, Tony had made more than $60,000 over the preceding eight weeks— and spent more than $50,000 of it. Some sign of it remained in the form of the two dozen expensive suits and sports jackets hanging in the bedroom closet, and the dozens of brand-new shirts and ties. All of the apartment furniture was new—expensive, custom-made pieces purchased for more than $5,000. His cufflinks were 18-karat gold, his watch a brand new Buccellati that had set him back nearly $2,000. But most of the money, nearly all of it when it came right down to facts, had been squandered in restaurants, on women, on jewelry and perfume and silk scarves and dresses to make them happy, and on a new-found luxury that he couldn't get enough of—chauffeur-driven limousines. For Tony Bartolini no longer went from bank to bank in taxis if he could help it. He hired limousines for the driving, to relieve himself of the bother of hailing a fresh cab each time.

When you don't have any change in your pocket, he thought, it's hard to imagine how you could spend $6,000 or $7,000 a week just playing around. Things such as rent and overhead amounted to so small a part of that money each month that they didn't even count. It was hard for a person to spend more than $500 a week on food, even if he ate fancy French food in expensive restaurants, which Tony didn't. He went to the best restaurants, because he had grown to appreciate the silent service, the step of the sommelier, the unfolding of the wine list and the gentle, knowing, friendly smiles of the maître d'. But his taste for foods had remained simple. Six days out of seven, he ordered only a good sirloin or porterhouse steak, sliced tomatoes, and perhaps olives and *peperoni*, the little green Italian peppers pickled in wine vinegar. On the seventh day, he preferred fish in an Italian or Greek restaurant—usually sea bass, with the eyes still intact, and a side dish of salad with cheese, olive oil, and vinegar. Wines, of course, were very expensive in good restaurants. With fine wine at every meal, and a woman along to drink it up, he could spend another $500 each week with no trouble. That brought the total up to $1,000 a week, plus maybe $200 for rent, and walking-around money. Say $1,200, say $1,400, and make it easy on himself.

Where in the hell did the rest of it go? Well, the broads weren't cheap. The previous weekend, Tony had encountered a young advertising art director at P. J. Clark's. The girl's name was Alice Carmichael. She had come from the Midwest, a small Illinois town called Pekin; but she was a Vassar graduate, a tall, black-haired, full-hipped young woman with gold hoops hanging from her ears, unpainted but manicured fingernails, tight slacks, a cashmere sweater over which was thrown a second cashmere sweater, and two gold bracelets on her wrists. He couldn't remember her shoes, but her brassière covered her breasts only to above the nipple, and was transparent anyway. Her panties were the bikini kind, silk, in a rose color, through which showed her shiny black pubic hair. She was, of course, married, but that didn't make any difference. Tony had come to know these young, perfumed, off-handedly casual Eastern college women who made $20,000 a year in New York and thought they had the world by the balls. They amused him, these same lovely and cruel women who had once frightened the church-going Catholic boy in him, and he was passionately in sex with every one of them.

And they him. It wasn't just his clothing, although the cut of the $400 suits made him appear very sophisticated and conservative at the same time, and it wasn't just the muscular body that moved so easily underneath the cloth, although that also played a large part in their fantasies about him. Rather, the charm had something more to do with the large, square, bald skull in which the luminescent hazel eyes shone so wisely and appraisingly under the half-closed lids. It may have had even more to do with the incredible confident calm that he exuded, the calm that said *I already know you naked and waiting for me in my bed, and I already know my hands on your body and*

your head pressed against my stomach. And there was something more than that, too.

That other feeling he exuded had to do with danger—invisible but tangible waves of danger, short, pulsing waves that you
could almost feel with the palm of your hand should you place
it just for a moment, in a friendly gesture, over the back of his
neck, or on the bicep of his arm. There was no sound of the
danger in his low, level, and pleasant voice, no sign of it in his
rock-steady hands, and no feeling of it in his easy and relaxed
movements.

The feeling of danger came from his eyes, if he let them
linger directly on you for too long. Because in the black centers
of those hazel eyes—which could turn from pale blue to the
deepest of browns—there was the rapt attention of a camera that
recorded your every movement, your every weakness and desire, and transmitted that information to the brain where you
knew you would never be forgotten. Even if you wanted to be.

But the girl, Alice. Alice had felt him approach, and her hips
turned slightly, and she pressed her thighs together for just a
moment before loosening them for his approach and turning
around with a cool smile on her frosted lips and the tip of her
pink tongue just touching the outside of them, like a resting cat.
In a place like this, everybody bought drinks. Everybody makes
offers, too. But only the electrical engineer suggested that when
they go someplace for breakfast, it was to Miami. At 3:00 A.M.,
after a limousine ride to Kennedy, Alice and Tony were rising
side by side together, heading for Miami.

"And this guy, honey, is something else. He takes me right to
breakfast. No fast tuck-and-woo in between leaving the airplane
and getting something in our stomachs. Right away he orders
eggs Benedict, and champagne, and caviar, and then a couple of
long rum drinks in fresh orange juice. By that time, I was exhausted. Beat out. Ready to fall in. He rents a suite in the Fon-
tainebleau, a three-room suite, and I crawl into bed hardly able
to move, but waiting for him to come to me and get it over with.
He's got to get something out of all this, right? In fact, I was
starting to feel like he wasn't interested in me, or something.
But I fell asleep quickly and don't remember really what was
going on.

"But I started to find out in the morning. Very gently, just pulling me out of sleep, he entered me from behind as that Florida sun was streaming in the window and I was starting to think, *I must be in the South, there's no sun like this in New York in March or any other time of the year.* He's a big man, very slow, very careful. He pulled a climax out of me twice, before he turned me over and lifted me up and put me down on him and started moving his hips up and down, stabbing that goddam dick of his up to my heart. I thought I was going to die at first, and then I started to get behind it, and I just went wild. And then there was another time in the shower, while we were laughing, and then in the living room of the suite, where the fruit was still packed in the wicker basket, and then another time, outside, beside the pool, lying on a large beach towel, where nobody could see. But I don't know if he cared who saw what. I don't know if I cared that much, either. At night we went dancing, and he bought everybody in the club a bottle of wine, and drinks later at another place, and bought the orchestra for an hour to play every goddam song I could remember, and he danced and seemed to have bought the whole world for me, and finally he put this fucking gold bracelet on my wrist, and took me back to the suite and screwed me all night. I don't know what in the world he really does, but he's richer than hell, and knows how to spend money like nobody I've ever met."

Tony had a black friend who had served three years in the federal penitentiary at Leavenworth, who called what he had a "pussy jones," *jones* being vernacular for habit. But since he didn't gamble, and he didn't take drugs, then why the hell shouldn't he do what he wanted to?

Then it cost $3,000 to find a decent apartment in Philadelphia for his aging mother and pay the rent on it for a year. It cost another $2,000 to send her down to Puerto Rico for the first real vacation of her life. And it costs plenty to pick up the tab when you're traveling in style with the boys. But it didn't make any difference. There was all the money in the world waiting for him, waiting in the banks, just begging for somebody to smile and sign for it and take it away.

Tony leaned over the table and with his miraculous hand wrote new and more interesting signatures, thinking, *This one* *is worth $1,500; this one is worth $2,000; this one is worth whatever I want.* But he never really thought he'd become a millionaire.

"See, it's like this," Moe Green told Tony as they sat together in the Carousel Restaurant eating ham and eggs for breakfast one Sunday morning.

"This guy, he's a dentist. Respectable. Owns a home. Nice wife. Kids. You know, the whole thing. But he has this one problem, Tony, which is why he comes to me. Guess what that problem is?"

"Broads?" Tony asked.

"Horses. See, he's a fucking freak for the horses. Every goddam day that he don't have his fingers in some poor sucker's mouth, he's out at the race track with the green sheet, trying to figure out how he's going to crack the mutuel for a million bucks. Always got a new plan—a new angle. If he's not at the track he's handing money over to the bookies. Same difference. Always going to make a killing, get even, and then stop playing them horses. You play horses, Tony?"

"Nope."

"That's good. I played them when I was younger, but I'm not so goddam young anymore. Anyway, this dentist. Not two-dollar bets, mind you. Fives and tens. Then it starts growing. A dentist makes a lot of money, right? But that don't help you when you throw it away on fucking horses. So the mortgage isn't paid, and the car payment ain't made. His wife gets on his ass, yellin' at him all the time for losing the money, and he's fucking miserable. So he decides he's got to get out of this hole that he's in, and do something, fast. So, like any normal horse-player, he decides that the horses are how to get out of the horseshit that the horses got him into in the first place.

"That always means one of two things. One—the perfecta, the daily double, the quintella, whatever it is that can complicate your life and lose you money faster than before. Or two, bigger bets. Or three, both. So the dentist does. And naturally he wins some and he loses some. But he ends up losing his ass, and he's into the bookmakers for ten thousand bucks."

"Uh-huh."

"So they give me a call, and naturally I talk to this guy, and he borrows the ten grand from me. The terms ain't bad for that kind of money on short notice. The interest is a thousand a week and the principal is a thousand a week, so it's all over within ten weeks. Nothing for a dentist. But this jerk, this schmuck, keeps playing the horses. First, he don't pay me back the principal; just the thousand interest. So I figure every week he doesn't want to pay the principal, he owes me another grand. I explain it to him like a gentleman. He says he doesn't understand. I explain it to him just like he's a baby. 'This is Patriarca's money,' I tell him. 'Raymond don't like to be fucked around.' He never heard of Raymond. I say, 'Where the hell you think ten grand comes from so you can pay off the bookies?' Nothing. It doesn't punch in. He's going to lecture me about usury. 'What the fuck is usury?' I say. 'You wanted ten thousand; you got ten thousand. Now you won't give the money back.' You understand what I'm telling you?"

"Yeah. He's not paying the money back."

"You got it. I thought he understood what I'm talking about. Now here's the crazy part. I go to his office last Friday when the money is due, and he's got nothing for me. Nothing. Not a red fucking cent. He says he's added it all up and figured out that he's paid me fifteen grand in interest. <i>He</i> thinks he's paid off the loan.

" 'That's an annual interest rate of two hundred percent,' he says to me. 'The law in New York says that you can't charge more than 18 percent on consumer loans,' and so on. The point is that he's a deadbeat.

"The funny thing of it is, I'm even nice to him. I think that it's the Jewish thing. It makes me feel kind. I tell him, he now owes me fifteen grand, and yet here I'm still only charging him a thousand a week interest, when everybody knows that it ought to be fifteen hundred a week, since the amount of the loan has gone up.

"So now it's a week later. And my question is, Tony, what am I going to do?"

"Yeah."

"That's what I mean. I'm in business like anybody else. But he won't understand. So now I can't sit here and enjoy my breakfast like a normal person. I got to go visit him at his house in the Bronx. Would you give me that package?"

"It's heavy, Moe. What's in it?"

"A fucking axe."

"Yeah?"

"Cost me twenty-five dollars. It's brand new. Now that fucker owes me fifteen thousand, twenty-five dollars."

The heavy man carried the long box out of the Carousel Restaurant and unlocked the door to a Buick Riviera at the curb. Driving to the Bronx, he turned on the radio, listened to the Sunday morning religious broadcasts for a while, and irritably turned the radio off.

He got to the Bronx shortly after noon. The rain had stopped at last. The goddam sun was even coming out. The puddles on the concrete were drying up, and the temperature had risen.

Spring was in the air.

Moe Green looked at the new green grass on the Bronx lawns and the leaves of the tulips pushing up in the flowerbeds, and he approved. He liked people who took care of their things. Moe was a little disappointed to find out that the dentist's house wasn't one of the imitation Tudor houses that he admired so much. It was a modern white stucco house, for chrissake, with one geometrically curved corner, and a big picture window with gold draperies pulled closed behind the glass.

Parked in the driveway was a shiny new Cadillac Sedan de Ville. Moe recognized it. It belonged to the dentist.

Tunelessly whistling one of the goddam Christian hymns, Moe Green parked the Buick Riviera in front of the dentist's house. Being careful not to step on the new, growing grass, he walked up the driveway apron to the sidewalk to the front door. For such a big man there was something fastidious about his movements, as though he were as worried about hurting the pavement as the blades of grass.

Shaking his head with regret, Moe pressed a square finger on the doorbell. Dr. Marvin Rose came to the door in an old pair of tweed slacks stained with white and tan paint. When he saw Moe Green standing at his front door in a black overcoat and a black hat, he got very nervous, and rubbed one of his long hands over his bald head.

"My God, Moe, what are you doing here?"

"I wanna come on in the house and talk to you," Moe said. "It's about money."

"My God, what would my wife think?"

"You going to keep me standing here outside, or are you going to let me in?"

"My God, this is my neighborhood. Can't you understand that?"

"You owe me fifteen thousand fucking dollars, Doc. I gotta talk to you about the money you owe me."

"I told you how I thought about that. It's usury. It's against the law."

"I want my money today, Doc," Moe said. "The money is past due. *Way* past due. I've been giving you a pass. The pass is up. I gotta get that money today."

"Who is it, Marvin?" called the dentist's wife in a shrill voice. "Who's at the door?"

"My God, Moe, get out of here!" the dentist hissed.

"I want the money by five o'clock today," Moe told him.

"I'll talk to you about it at the office."

"Look," Moe said. "You got a fancy house. You got a fancy car. That's your Caddy in the driveway, isn't it?"

"What's that got to do with anything?" the dentist asked.

"You dumb shit," Moe said. "I told you, if you don't get me the money, you'll be sorry. Right?"

Gladys Rose joined her husband at the door. "What is it, Marvin?" she asked him.

"Pleased to meet you," Moe said.

"It's nothing," said the dentist, trying to order Moe away from the doorway with the fury and terror in his eyes.

"What can we do for you?" asked Gladys Rose.

"I hate to have to do this," Moe said. "But I hope you understand."

The large, gray-haired man in the black overcoat nodded courteously at the dentist's wife and walked slowly down the walk, back down the driveway to his car. He unlocked the door, tore open the cardboard box, extracted a bright red fire axe, and carried the fearsome weapon back up the driveway to the front of Dr. Rose's Cadillac. Taking a deep breath, Moe lifted the axe above his head and smashed the blade down in the Cadillac's hood. With the pick end, he broke the headlights. With the blade he smashed in the windshield.

"Stop him! Stop him! Stop him!" screamed Gladys Rose. Her husband held her inside the house by an arm. "Help! Stop him! *Please.*"

Moe, breathing heavily, drove the axe through the side windows, and broke in the back window as well. He chopped two holes in the Cadillac's trunk, and methodically splintered the taillights. Opening the car door, he drove the pick end of the axe into the butterscotch leather upholstery, and tore up the car's seats.

Mrs. Rose wasn't trying to rescue the car anymore. She lay inside the entrance, crying and beating her head against the floor. The neighbors, alerted by the screams and crashes, stood at their windows with mouths open.

Moe was worn out. He had enough exertion. The car was destroyed. Tucking the axe under an arm, he puffed to the front door of the house and stood outside the screen door, staring at the dentist.

"See this fucking fire axe?" Moe asked him.

The dentist could only nod.

"You bring me the money by five o'clock this afternoon or I'm going to chop you up just like I chopped up this fucking Cadillac of yours," Moe said.

"My God," the dentist said.

"Five o'clock," Moe said.

"Yes sir."

Moe smiled. "I hope you and the missus have a nice day," he said. Tipping his hat, careful not to crush the soft grass of the lawn, he returned to the Buick and drove away.

The handsome bald man in the tan linen slacks sat in the barber shop of Chicago's Palmer House, talking about the New York Mets, in town to play the Cubs. He liked the Mets, and whenever he had a free afternoon, bought a box seat and went to the game to cheer their fortunes. The barber, a quiet-spoken elderly man, snipped the chromed scissors around the customer's ears, trimming the short, graying fringe of hair. This was the second time in eight days the meticulous, well-groomed gentleman had been to visit him. The manicurist finished buffing the customer's fingernails, and smiled at him. He was well liked in the Palmer House barber shop; he handed out $5 tips.

"So, you've been enjoying Chicago," the barber said, holding up the hand mirror behind the customer's head.

"Tremendous town," said the customer. "I'll be sorry to go."

"Here on business?" the barber asked him.

"Consultation," said the customer. "I have some clients here that I've been meeting with."

"What business are you in?" the barber inquired.

"I'm an electrical engineer," said the customer, handing out the tips as the black porter carefully brushed the last short piece of cut hair from the shoulders of his custom-made white shirt. The porter held the silk-lined suit jacket so the man could slip his muscular arms into it. The customer smiled at everyone as he left the barbershop.

"That's a *gentleman*," said the barber.

"Don't see many of them, anymore," said the second-chair barber.

"A ten-dollar tip this time," said the first barber, beaming proudly. "He likes my haircuts."

Smelling pleasantly of Habit Rouge cologne, the bald gentleman walked through the hotel's lobby and almost reluctantly forced himself out of its air-conditioned comfort into the baking August heat. Handing the hotel parking ticket and a dollar to the doorman, he walked down the block to Michigan Avenue to gaze for a moment at the sunbathers in Grant Park. For a moment, he was undecided about what he should do for the rest of the day. The Mets *were* playing the Cubs in Chicago. Yet, he had come to the windy city for work, not for baseball. Deciding, he returned to the hotel where his rented blue Ford was now parked at the curb, and drove the Outer Drive toward the city's northern suburbs.

In the slim leather attaché case on the seat beside him were several checkbooks from Chicago's major banks—Continental, First National, Exchange, American National, Lake Shore National, and the National Boulevard Bank. His first activities in the city had been to open accounts at each of them, depositing $100 in each account. Each checking account was in the name of a different man, and for each name the attaché case also contained a complete set of IDs—credit cards and social-security cards. There was no sense in burning banks in Illinois with the fake-deposit trick; laws in that state forbid branch banking. But retail businesses were another story.

When he hit Evanston, he searched for large supermarkets, and found a National Tea store. Going in, grateful to be out of the heat once again, he selected a shopping cart, and into it put half a dozen cans of cat food, a jumbo box of Tide detergent, apples, a small prime roast, a large tube of Gleem toothpaste, twelve jars of baby food, and a cellophane tube containing three bright red tomatoes. From the magazine rack, he selected a copy of the latest *Esquire*, which he leafed through as the short line ahead of him moved past the checker. The checkout girl rang up his order, which came to $15.38. Nodding, he removed one of the checkbooks and a fountain pen from the inside pocket of his suitcoat. Making out the check for $100, he handed it to the clerk.

"I'm sorry, sir," the checkout girl said. The name on the plastic identification badge she wore pinned to her blouse read "Marge." "Do you have your check-cashing number?"

"I don't have a number," he replied. "I'm new in Evanston."

The girl hesitated a moment, looking at him. "You'll have to get this OK'd by the manager."

"Sure. Where is he?"

"I'll page him."

She called for Mr. Luddington over a loudspeaker. A young blond man with a ruddy face appeared at the register.

"This man isn't registered with us," the counter girl told him, handing him the check.

The manager looked at it and asked the customer for identification. Opening his wallet, the forger took out credit cards, apologizing for not having a driver's license too. On the back of the check, the manager wrote down the number of the American Express card.

"You ought to fill out a form for your check-cashing number," the manager said.

"Do you have one?"

The manager brought one of the forms for the forger. "No problem, Marge," the manager told the checkout girl, who gave the customer $84.62 in change and packed the food in a large brown paper bag.

Smiling pleasantly and wishing the girl a good day, the bald man carried the bag outside, removing from it the *Esquire* magazine. He appeared to be looking for something; placing the bag on the hood of the car, he waited in the sunlight until he saw a trio of grade-school boys coming down the sidewalk.

"Hey, kids," he said. "You on your way home?"

"Maybe," said one of the boys suspiciously.

"Well, there." The bald man handed him the bag of groceries. "Take this home to your mother. But don't let it lie around. There's a roast in it that could go bad."

Getting into the car, he threw the magazine in the back seat, waved at the children clutching the bag of groceries, and drove away.

The man in the car permitted himself a feeling of satisfaction. There wasn't much sense in beating a grocery store out of eighty-five bucks. Punks did that. There wasn't much professional accomplishment in doing what hundreds of thousands of average citizens did every week, in one way or another. But he liked to begin the day's serious activities with a small burn like this one, just to test himself. Because they were hit with bad checks so often, supermarkets were always suspicious, and made a worthy test.

And there were the small details that defined his professional skills. Small-time operators in grocery stores always bought cigarettes, beer and liquor, and expensive gourmet foods like smoked oysters. The forger's purchase had been just what any suburbanite might need for his order on a Thursday morning. The amateur would have resisted the checkout girl calling the manager, or acted nervous or even bolted when he approached. But the forger knew from experience that store managers always OK'd checks if the situation looked right, because they didn't want to offend prosperous new customers. The risk was real. But nobody refused to cash a check for a man who bought baby food.

The original $100 deposit had been almost immediately withdrawn. The identification he used was stolen several months ago in Florida, useful only to provide a false identity and give the manager a sense of security. But if the manager had checked the signatures on the credit cards and on the check that he signed—carelessly, he hadn't—he would have seen that the forger's work and the real signature were indistinguishable from one another.

Pulling into a diagonal parking space in the suburb's downtown shopping district, the forger opened the attaché case and removed from it a cashier's check made out to Wallace Stevens for $840. Nine other cashier's checks for $840 to Wallace Stevens remained in a white envelope. The forger had prepared them himself the night before in the hotel room. He replaced the identification he had used in the grocery store with credit cards made out to Wallace Stevens, slid the attaché case under the front seat, and walked into an expensive furniture store, browsing among the room settings, feeling the fabrics on the easy chairs and sofas.

"Good afternoon," the salesman said, approaching him. "Can I help you today?"

"I don't know if you can," said the forger. "I'm looking for a French Provincial living-room chair in some kind of muted tapestry."

"Let's see what we have," the salesman said. "I think that we may have just the thing."

Leading the way, he showed the bald man a selection of chairs, many of which, the customer agreed, were very pretty, durable, and good bargains.

"But," said the customer with a worried frown, "do you have anything of a little bit better quality?"

It was obvious that he didn't want to offend, but he was seriously interested in good things. "This is for our eleventh anniversary. It's a surprise for my wife."

The salesman appreciated the thoroughness of the customer's inspection of the quality chairs, and thoroughly approved of his final selection of a tall-backed chair in brown and white, with just a touch of russet thread through the pattern. The price was $395.

"Well, there's one other problem," the customer said. "Our anniversary is tomorrow. I'm a salesman for American Oil and I have to go to Houston in the afternoon. I've got to have the chair delivered by no later than ten A.M. Otherwise, the whole anniversary will be ruined. I know how hard it is to make immediate deliveries, but in this case I have to ask you for it. If you can't do it, I'll have to buy the chair elsewhere."

"No problem, I'm sure, sir," said the salesman. "We believe in service. Believe me."

The customer gave him the address, 1940 Forest. Wallace Stevens. The salesman wrote up the sales slip, which came to $414.75 including the state's 5 percent sales tax.

"I'll have to give you a commission check," the forger said to him.

"There's nothing the matter with American Oil," said the salesman, taking the check and the customer's identification to the cashier's office. He approved the check, and the cashier gave the customer back $425.25, which he counted carefully before placing it in a slim pigskin wallet.

"Remember," the customer said, "no later than ten o'clock."

"Absolutely," said the salesman. "You have my word on it."

In furniture stores throughout Evanston, Winnetka, Highland Park, and Lake Forest, he repeated the process, never spending less than $300 or more than $400 on any of the chairs. Uniformly, they had high backs and were covered with fabrics in muted browns. In one Glencoe furniture store, the customer left without making a purchase because he couldn't find a chair that he really liked. At the end of the day, he had $4,000 in newly stolen money packed in neat piles in the attaché case.

It amused him to imagine the scene at ten the next morning when delivery vans of ten fine furniture stores descended upon the family at 1940 Forest and the procession of new chairs began. The forger often wished that there was some way he could be present to see how the recipient of his largesse would react to it.

Returning to Chicago, he found himself caught in the midst of a hot summer afternoon's traffic jam on the Outer Drive, where the outward-bound cars somehow occupied two of the four lanes of traffic in the southbound lanes. The nearness of the approaching traffic made him feel uncomfortable, so he turned off the drive as soon as possible, and parked the rented car illegally alongside the inner drive. Removing the box containing the check-writing machine from the trunk, and taking the attaché case, he left the Ford's key in the ignition and the doors unlocked and hailed a taxicab. Since the Ford had been rented with a stolen Avis credit card, there was no particular reason why it had to be returned, and in fact many good reasons why it shouldn't be. A car was simply a tool to be used and abandoned when its function was completed.

Tony felt washed out when he returned to his suite at the Palmer House and wanted to shower and retire for a brief nap before dinner. But the day's activities weren't completed yet. He called the number of the Sheraton-Chicago Hotel, and asked for room 1633. He let the phone ring five times, hung up, and then made the call again. The voice that answered was wary.

"This is Tony from New York," he said. "Does anybody have a message from me?"

"Hey, Tony," said the muscular young man who picked up the phone in the Sheraton. "We been waiting to hear from you." Turning to his older brother, Sammy Goldman said "Tony's in town."

"Listen, Tony, we going to see you?"

"In about 10 minutes, if there's anything to see you about," the forger said to him. "If not, I'll pick up on you guys back in New York."

Sammy Goldman grinned. "Have we got something to see you about! I'm telling you, man. Come on up here."

"Up there?" Tony asked him. "Is it cool?"

"Cool, daddy," said Sam. "Bring cash, huh?"

"Ten minutes," Tony told him.

The Goldman brothers had long razor-cut hair; in their hip, expensive clothes, they looked more like successful rock-and-roll musicians than thieves. They greeted the forger with effusive affection and thrust a bottle of

Schlitz beer into his hand. But Tony's pleasure was cut short when he saw the two orange US Mail sacks leaned against the wall of the room.

"What the hell is this?" he complained.

"Sorry, Tony," Al said. "We just made the snatch at the airport and haven't had the chance to go through everything."

"You guys are too reckless for me," Tony told them. "Somebody could come in here, or be following you, and I'm busted too."

"We didn't mean to tie you up," Sammy said. "Look I said we're sorry. What else can I say? We're *both* sorry."

"You're crazy," Tony said. "What do you have?"

"Traveler's checks," Sammy told him.

"The price?"

"Twenty cents on the dollar," Al said.

"Since when are you charging twenty percent?" Tony said. "The price is always ten percent."

"I know what the price always *has* been," Al said to him, "But we've been thinking about this. On traveler's checks, guys like you make full price. We've been giving away a fortune."

"I've got expenses," Tony told him. "Do you know how much I have to spend on identification? One set, and it's four hundred right out of my pocket. Travel expenses, hotel bills. Besides that, I take all the risk when I'm cashing them, while you guys have the money free and clear."

"Look at the risk *we* take," Al said.

"That's your business," Tony said. "You take the risk, but you make it all in one pile. I go out every day, like a traveling salesman. It's none of this easy life for me."

"Well, I don't know," Al said doubtfully.

"I don't know, either," Tony said. "I've brought the cash with me. I came here to buy. I'm ready. Nobody called me up and said, 'Tony, the deal is all different now.' "

"We didn't know where you were, Tony," Sammy said.

"Who you told the new price to in New York?" Tony demanded. "You told Bananas? You told any of Raymond's people? I haven't heard a word about it."

Al shrugged. "We just thought of it. We got a right to charge *something*."

"We all got rights," Tony said. "But they don't begin with me. I say, the hell with it. I can get traveler's checks in New York for ten cents on the dollar, and I don't have to fly them with me on the airplane."

Al was doubtful. "I don't know," he said finally. "Maybe it depends."

"Sure it depends," Tony said. "Everything depends. But I want a hundred thousand dollars' worth."

Al coughed. "A hundred grand? That's a good buy."

"It is at ten percent," Tony said. "At twenty percent, it's no buy at all."

"Where's the money?" Al asked him.

"Where's the checks?" Tony said. "I want to see them first."

Sammy Goldman pulled a box from under the bed, removing from it stacks of freshly printed $20 and $50 American Express traveler's checks. The forger knelt beside the box, and removed random checks from the stacks, examining them against the light.

"What are you doing?" Al asked him, offended.

"Just checking," Tony said. "Been a lot of forgeries around."

"Not from us," Al said. "All we have is the legitimate merchandise."

"Sure," Tony said. "We'll do it like this. I'll count out my checks. You double-check the count, and then I'll go through it again." Counting carefully, the forger placed on one side twelve hundred $50 checks. In a second series of stacks he laid down two thousand $20s. "Count them," Tony said.

"Ah, forget it," Al said to him. "I trust you, Tony. You never burned anybody that I know."

"Never," Tony said.

Opening his attaché case, he removed ten piles of cash of $1,000 each. "I know you'll want to count that," he said with a smile.

The two thieves broke the bank seals and counted the money, finding it correct. Tony put the traveler's checks into his attaché case and snapped it closed.

"If you guys don't get busted, I'll see you back in New York," he told them.

"We're going out to play tonight down on Rush Street," Sammy said. "You want to come along?"

"Not a chance," Tony said. "You guys are known thieves."

                        The jet passenger planes came in low over the roof of the International Hotel at Kennedy Airport. They were keeping Tony awake. He had arrived from Boston at 11:00 P.M.; too tired to travel anymore, he had decided not to leave for Manhattan until the morning. But now that he was in bed, there was no sleep. He was bored.

Dressing in a pair of black wool slacks and an off-white wool sweater, he went to the hotel's bar for a nightcap. The Saturday-night crowd was good, and the room was filled with airline pilots and navigators, traveling men, stewardesses, hookers, and even wives and girlfriends. Nobody danced, but many of the revelers kept time to Hank Steng's driving organ music by clapping their hands together, or rapping their glasses with swizzle sticks.

Tony edged his way to the bar, and ordered a Chivas and soda. Turning to find a place to sit, he noticed a table at which sat five stewardesses, one of whom he knew as Kathy. The short-haired blonde flew with Swissair and dated one of the believers he knew in the city, a man named Richard Lazarro. Tony called wiseguys like Lazarro "believers" because they made believers out of people who disputed them, or didn't pay their bills, or who tried to cut into somebody else's territory. He couldn't understand why a fresh-looking girl like that Kathy would hang around with a beast like Lazarro, but he accepted the fact that some women especially liked violent men. All women like a hint of danger, he believed—the viper behind glass, the gun in its holster. But some of them he thought of as degenerates for danger—turned on most by what could hurt and kill.

After the second drink, he began to notice that this girl, Kathy, appeared to be having a thing going with Hank Steng, the organist. He didn't know Steng at all, except that he had been playing a long gig at the hotel, on piano and organ. There were a million guys like him around the East Coast—thirty-five years old trying to pass for twenty-five, a mouth filled with capped teeth, expensive haircuts, an envelope of lukewarm reviews, and a desire to hit the big time with only mediocre talent. Steng might be a slightly better musician than most of the motel losers, and he might have been just a little better looking than the average goof who spent his life's earnings on portfolio photographs, but he was just a guy doing a job for $325 a week when he was lucky enough to get work.

Tony thought that this stewardess chick was getting it on with the organist because the man kept winking at her, and she, in turn, raised her glass before and after each number in delighted tribute. Despite the crowd, the friends, and the slightly out-of-tune organ, it appeared that the couple believed themselves together and almost isolated. Tony deduced that the relationship between them was past the introductory stages. In fact, knowing that the stews frequently stayed at the motel between flights and that Lazarro had been very busy making believers out of people in Manhattan these days due to the war between the Gallo and the Colombo people, Tony suspected that one hell of a lot of hanky-panky had been going on.

The man with the hazel eyes didn't make judgments about people going to bed together, but he did know that it was a very bad idea for some square goof to be balling the girlfriend of a Mafia muscle man. Especially Lazarro, who was a hit man as well as a persuader. Particularly Lazarro, who Tony knew for a fact had scarred the face of a waitress he suspected of cheating on him, and tried to murder her lover.

Tony wondered if the guy at the organ really knew. He figured that the girl had made her own choices. If she wanted to ball Lazarro, who was not only an animal but who looked like an animal, that was her business. But Steng wasn't a very big man physically, perhaps five foot six, no more than 140 pounds. He couldn't defend himself against a lady roller skater, much less a 230-pound bull like Lazarro. Tony was willing to bet that a curly-headed chump like the organist wouldn't knowingly screw a murderer's girlfriend under any circumstances. Why the hell should he?

But Tony hated to interfere with somebody else's life. He ordered a third drink, and nursed it for a while. About twelve thirty Kathy got out of her seat and unsteadily walked to the grinning fool at the organ, touching his cheek with her white fingers.

When she had left for the john, at the end of the number, Tony approached the organist with a drink in hand for him.

"Take this." Tony said. "I like your music."

"Thanks," Steng said to him. "Do I know you?"

"No, I don't think you do," Tony said. "But I want to talk to you for just a minute."

The musician responded cautiously. "What can I do for you?" he asked.

"That Kathy chick who came up here a minute ago," Tony said. "The Swissair stewardess?"

"Yes?" said the organist, as though he couldn't quite place the lady.

"I want to tell you something about her," Tony said.

"Are you her husband or something?" Steng asked. "I mean, if you are, I don't know the lady at all. You know? Never even seen her before."

"It's more important than that," Tony said to him, bending down and speaking to him directly. "She goes with a guy with the organization in Manhattan. His name doesn't mean anything. But he's real. He makes his living by beating people up. He kills people, Mr. Steng. I don't know nothing about you. I don't want to. But I want to tell you this, because it's really important."

"Tell me what?" Steng said, belligerently.

"If you're banging that girl, you could be killed," Tony said to him. "That's all. Just for your own knowledge. You can decide."

"If it's nothing to you, then what I do is my own business."

"That's right, Mr. Steng." Tony shrugged. "But I would feel like a wrong guy if I didn't let you know how things really were."

"Some favor," the organist said. "I gotta go back to the organ now."

"Yeah." The warning hadn't taken. Still, he had tried.

By last call, Tony noticed two things. Kathy had abandoned her girlfriends and was standing at Steng's side, with her hand on the back of his neck, weaving uncertainly to his music. That was an awfully stupid thing to do, because standing just inside the back entrance to the bar was a very large, very hairy man in a lumpy blue sports jacket. The hairy man wore a look on his face that Tony translated as astonishment and rage. Next to him was an even taller, rapier-thin man with no expression on his face, whom Tony knew as the Snake. The Snake was known to be a torturer, a maniac who was employed by the crime over-lords to torture enemies and especially recalcitrant debtors. Tony wished he could stop thinking about what was going to happen soon to the little organist and his drunken little girl-friend.

When the bar closed at two, only Tony, the organist, and the girl remained in the room. Tony saw them take hands and de-part. Sliding a five-dollar tip on the bar counter, he casually fol-lowed them, wondering if he really wanted to know what would happen next. In the motel lobby, the girl leaned her head on the organist's shoulder, and he placed a protective arm around her, pushing open the door and leading the way across the park-ing lot. Tony followed outside, smoking a cigarette.

There was nobody else around. A hundred feet ahead of him, the couple stopped to kiss and embrace. A car started up, and drove up beside them. Two men got out. Tony heard words that sounded angry. He heard the girl speaking in an excited voice, and a little shriek that halted as though she had been struck in the mouth. He heard the organist speaking very rapidly, almost stammering.

He heard the car door slam twice. He heard the organist screaming and screaming and screaming as the car moved out of the parking lot and drove away. He saw lights start to come on in the motel rooms, and in the lobby behind him saw the night clerk pick up on the screams and start to come to the door. He walked around the corner of the building away from the man who was screaming in the parking lot and went to his room and turned on the radio as high as he could. He could still hear him screaming, although he knew that the music was too loud, the distance too far, for him to hear anything outside.

He thought about the organist's fingers, crushed in the car

door; about how the bones were splintered and punctured through the flesh. He looked at his own fingers, and wondered what he would do if something like that happened to him. He didn't know why he felt so sorry for the little jerk. He had warned him. The warning wasn't listened to.

Playing poker the next evening with Philadelphia Charlie, Little Steve, and a hardnose called Nick, Tony had successfully pushed the incident out of his mind. They were playing five and seven card stud poker for the most part, and he was having a hot streak, winning nearly every other hand. He never counted his chips during a game because he was afraid of bad luck, but he guessed that he was ahead nearly $500.

Nick, on the other hand, was losing heavily. Tony didn't think that he had won a single deal all night, and he was growing quarrelsome. Philadelphia Charlie was no pleasure to play with tonight either, because he was hitting the sauce so heavily. Tony stayed sober when he played cards, because he liked to win. Philadelphia Charlie liked to get lit whenever he had the chance, forgetting that alcohol made him angry and pugnacious.

It wasn't even ten o'clock when Nick and Charlie started to get into it. Tony and Little Steve had dropped out of the deal, leaving Nick and Charlie head-to-head with $300 on the table in a game of five-card stud. Charlie consulted his cards, and with his cruel smile said that he would raise Nick pot limit. Nick, who had pairs of eights and queens, couldn't believe it. He had lost every hand all night. Charlie knew that he had been betting the hand heavily, so he must have guessed that he held something better than just two of a kind. Given the kind of lousy luck he had all evening, he suspected that bastard Charlie had three of a kind, and was just waiting to cream him.

"Come on, Nick," Charlie grated. "Are you going to see this bet, or not?"

"The hell with it," Nick decided suddenly, throwing his cards face up on the table. "You've got it. Let me see your three of a kind."

Philadelphia Charlie placed his cards face down on the table, and raked in the chips. "People who don't pay to see my cards don't get to see them," he said.

"Bullshit, buddy," Nick exploded.

Angrily, he reached out and snatched up Charlie's cards and turned them over. He was wild with disbelief when he found that Charlie's hand hadn't beaten his own, and didn't even contain a single pair of cards. He had just been bluffed out of a $300 pot.

"You're a bastard," Nick shouted. "You're a cheat."

"Calm down," Charlie said nastily. "Don't be such a lousy pansy."

"Don't you call me a pansy," Nick yelled.

"How about shit-eating dog?" Charlie asked him. "Does that sound better to you?"

Tony saw the nickel-plated .22-caliber pistol in Nick's hand before Charlie did, because he was concentrating on counting his winnings.

"You goddam well apologize to me for that," Nick demanded, his voice shaking with emotion.

Charlie's mouth dropped. "Don't point that at me, man," he said.

When the pistol went off, Tony pushed himself backward away from the table, falling on his back and rolling toward the door. Charlie still sat square in his seat with an amazed expression on his face, staring at the smoking gun only inches from the end of his nose. Nick, who held the gun, looked just as incredulous. Behind Charlie, on a straight line just to the top of his ear, was a small new bullethole in the fern-colored wall.

They heard from the adjoining apartment a great shouting and cries for the police.

"Bullets. Police. Help, police," a man was hollering at the top of his voice.

"Let's get the fuck out of here," Little Steve said.

Grabbing their jackets, Tony, Philadelphia Charlie, and Little Steve bolted for the door and ran down the back stairway to the alley. They didn't know how long it would be before the police arrived, but they knew they didn't want to be anyplace around.

Philadelphia Charlie pounded his right fist into the palm of the other hand.

"I oughta go back there with my thirty-eight and blow that fucker away," he fumed. "He shot right at me. He coulda killed me."

"Screw it," Little Steve said. "Cops will be all over there."

"I'll get him later," Charlie vowed.

"Let it go," Tony advised him. "You're lucky you're alive. This muscle stuff is crazy. Who ever wins at it, huh? It's dumb to even carry a piece."

"You know so goddam much," Charlie said to him. "What the hell would you do?"

"I'd get out of town," Tony said.

"And leave New York City because of a creep like that?" Charlie demanded to know.

"If I had my way, I'd leave the whole country," Tony said. "There are too many crazy people around."

Chapter 5

The year was ending, and Tony's baptism in crime and rebirth as a forger were complete. He could hardly remember the honest soul that had shared his consciousness before the first day with Philadelphia Charlie and his crew. He had forgotten what it had been like to live from payday to payday as a working stiff, or to ride the thundering subways home after eight hours of gainful employment. The plush silence of limousines overwhelmed all other sensations. The bowed head of the attentive tailor at his knees, folding up the cuff of another custom-made suit, obscured the former vision of himself pushing Hotpoint stoves on reluctant customers. The frosted hair of gaunt, sophisticated women resting against his chest brushed away the memory of an unfaithful wife.

As December once again chilled New York, Tony was wrapped against the wind in the finest English woolens and a navy-blue cashmere overcoat. He went from the warm lobby of his expensive apartment tower to the comfortable Cadillac limousine with only enough exposure to the wind and cold to bring a spot of pink to his suntanned cheeks. When he wanted to fish these days, he didn't throw a line into the gray Atlantic waters befouled with the garbage of New York, but leased a fishing boat under the Miami palms and pushed out into bluer waters for sport with great marlin. With the black homburg set squarely on top of his bald skull, he looked as naturally prosperous as the president of an old-line Eastern bank. With thousands of bad checks, he had burned enough conservative banks to know how a bank executive ought to behave—quietly, easily, with the self-assurance of the hereditary rich.

The forger's take over the past ten months was more than $500,000, almost all of which had been squandered by feeding and inflaming his taste for luxury. The cache in Tony's tasteful apartment held approximately $25,000, and his wallet and pockets held another $5,000. He kept no money in the bank, held no investments, owned no property except for the gold watch on his wrist, the diamond ring on his finger, the furniture in the apartment, and the expensive clothing that filled his closets. But his real fortune lay in the trick of his nervous system that enabled him to become, at will, somebody else. There was no Peter Milano anymore, except as the memory of a childhood friend lost in the flux of time. Tony Bartolini, the chalice that held all the other identities, was almost as insubstantial. The forger had no certain name for himself. He was simply *the self* that wrote names on paper and received piles of negotiable paper in return, *the self* that laughed through the night as securely as a baron in the moated protection of his ancient castle, *the self* that chose and held women as easily and as indifferently as a young child takes new toys from a department store shelf.

The forgetfulness, however, had nothing to do with getting the job done. Always careful, even meticulous about the details of work at hand, Tony had become a perfectionistic forger. When he chose to work with Philadelphia Charlie or other check-cashing crews, he refused to deal with men whose judgment he questioned, or whose nerves were weak or whose habits were bad. When he worked alone, he insisted that the credit cards he used for identification were freshly stolen and hadn't been previously used. He never left checks, the typewriter, or the check-writing machine in hotel rooms where inquisitive chambermaids could find them. All his airplane travel, all his hotel bills, restaurant tabs, and other expenses—except for rented cars—were paid for by cash, because he intended never to be arrested for the careless use of a credit card when the risk wasn't worth it.

Tony also had begun to use disguises in bank chains where he had operated before. The bald head made it easy to alter his appearance; he had a full set of expensive, natural-hair wigs cut in long styles and short, blond, brown, black, and white, that made him look like a completely different person. With the wigs and the changing color of his hazel eyes, he changed in an instant from a vigorous blond Swede with steel-blue eyes to a dark Mediterranean with black eyes. But his favorite disguise was the white wig, which gave him a dignified, professorial air that always created strong feelings of trust in his victims.

The strangest thing was that as the parts of his personal identity became scattered and fragmentary, his adopted personas became stronger. From reading and conversation, he had gathered enough information about law, engineering, banking, the arts, the military, and even medicine to assume the conversational gambits of almost any occupation for several hours, an invaluable trick when chatting with a bank officer or a store manager while cashing another check. And finally, despite his striking appearance in any disguise, his way was so mild, his personality so innocuous, that the swindled executive could never quite recall the person who had taken him for a ride.

The police files in New York, the entire state of Connecticut, New Jersey, Miami, Chicago, and dozens of smaller towns, were filled with reports of bad checks that had been passed by the professional forger. But even the FBI, which much sooner than Tony expected had been alerted to his activities, had no idea who the phantom forger might really be.

On this December morning, as Tony relaxed against the gray wool upholstery in the shadowed back seat of the limousine and impassively watched the flakes of snow adhere to the tinted windows, he had nothing in the world to worry about. He was going for a meeting with John Bannanos at the Hotel Dixie, in his room rather than in the restaurant because the openness of the dining room made Tony nervous.

John, who was in shirtsleeves, greeted Tony with the deference naturally accorded a successful forger, who throughout the underworld is considered prince of thieves.

"You look prosperous," John said, shaking his hand.

Tony permitted himself a smile. "Just getting by," he said. "Because you've been so good to me."

John waved away the works of appreciation. "I've got a nice little Christmas present for you, Tony."

The bald forger raised one of his thick eyebrows.

"A new scam," John told him. "This is something really extraordinary. Do you know anything about US Treasury bonds?"

"Nothing," Tony admitted. "I've heard of them. But that's all."

"Treasury notes are bearer bonds, payable upon demand to whomever presents them," John said, sitting down in one of the blue plastic armchairs. "They're not like stock certificates, which are worth one thing today and something else tomorrow. These are backed by the government of the US of A. Institutions and rich people buy them because the interest isn't bad, and the security is one hundred percent. And we've been getting a lot of them lately from one source and another."

"The government?" Tony asked him.

"The government *mails*, sometimes," John said. "But sometimes, our people on Wall Street steal them, and give them to us to pay debts, or whatever. There are lots of ways to get them. But we haven't really known what to do with them."

"Why not cash them?" Tony asked him.

"I think there's too much risk in that," John said. "The denominations of these bonds are ten thousand dollars and up."

Tony whistled. "High amounts."

"Real high. Too high to take into a bank and cash, without somebody checking on the ownership. Unless, of course, the guy at the bank is one of our people, or into us for debts. But we've been working out another scam, that I think is going to work real good."

"How would that be?" Tony asked him.

John smiled. "Nobody will cash these things without checking," he said. "But almost any bank will make a loan against them automatically, using them for collateral. You can't get one hundred cents on the dollar. No way. But you can go sixty-five percent, maybe seventy, without arousing anybody's suspicions."

"What kind of angle do you use?"

"Almost anything will do," John said to him. "Say you're a businessman, and need some working capital. You put down the ten-thousand-dollar bond as security, and the bank loans you sixty-five hundred. You take the cash, and just forget about

100

it. One of these days the loan is in default—ninety days or so—and the bank takes the bond and tries to cash it to make the loan good. By that time, you're long gone."

"I like it," Tony said. "What does the mover get out of this?"

"It depends. We can buy these things from the fences for about ten, maybe fifteen percent of face value. I figure that ten percent of face value is a fair deal for a mover."

"That's only one grand in ten for me, for a lot of aggravation," Tony said. "Is that a good deal?"

"It shouldn't take very long," John said to him. "I think the risk is minimal. Besides, if this works, we've got some other ideas for much larger amounts."

Tony wasn't about to commit himself. "It's something new," he said. "I don't know how profitable it is."

"Listen," John said strongly, "this scam is right at the beginning. We've tried to move some here and there, but nothing really massive so far. But we will, I'm telling you. You're one of the best movers and forgers in the business, Tony. Your reputation is outstanding; I don't mind telling you that. You're a real class guy. You've got no record, and you take good care of yourself."

Tony listened impassively, aware that John was working on him but enjoying the compliments nevertheless.

"I want to tell you something, Tony. There's this guy that you oughta know. You know who Jack Mace is?"

"Diamonds?" Tony guessed. "Is he in jewels?"

"Same guy," John said. "Jack Mace is the biggest fence on the East Coast. Maybe in the world. He's a Jewish guy, real old, but he's bigger than anybody. Honest to God. He's bigger than any of the New York families. They couldn't live without him. He's got it up here." He tapped a forefinger against his skull. "Brains. Nothing but brains. It's Jack Mace who's the center of all of this. It's his plan, if you have to know the truth. But it sounds good to us. You know?"

"I suppose," Tony said. "What do you want from me?"

"I want you to give it a try. Nothing big the first time out. It'll only take you a morning. Nothing else. I've never given you a wrong deal, have I?"

"No, you haven't. I'm not crazy about something that sounds so experimental. I'll try it. But I'm just doing it as a favor to you, John."

"I appreciate that," John said to him. "Believe me, Tony, you'll find out this is a favor to you, too."

"Where do I get these bonds?" Tony inquired.

John cleared his throat, and looked embarrassed. "Mace doesn't know you, see?" he faltered. "I mean, I don't have them, and they have to come from him."

"Where do I find him?" Tony asked.

"That's going to be a little bit unusual," John said to him. "You don't meet him, in the beginning. You gotta go to this place, and some people there will have the bonds."

"Where do I take the money after I got it?" Tony asked.

"You take it back to the place," John said.

"What if I just take the money, and split?"

John smiled broadly. "You know all about that, Tony. We're not worried about you bringing the money back home. Now here's what the program is. I want you to go by this little news-stand at Fiftieth and Broadway. You just tell the little old guy there that you're Tony. Then you go to the bar across the street, Jack Dempsey's, and wait. Then in a little bit somebody will come by and tell you to go to the drugstore right there on the corner, and you'll get the bonds."

"That drugstore?" Tony questioned. "Is that connected to the organization?"

"Sure," John said. "Why?"

"You know, I've gone by that place a million times," Tony said. "They cash checks in there, and I've always thought about popping in there and floating some paper. I don't know why I never did, but I guess I never really felt like it. I'm glad I didn't, now."

"Anybody could make an honest mistake," John said.

"Anybody can get their arms broken, too," Tony commented dryly. "Thank God I got a sixth sense about these things. Keeps my fingers whole."

"When are you going over there?" John asked him, walking Tony to the door.

"I thought I'd go now," Tony said, "if it's all right with you. I might as well get this over with. I wasn't going to work today, anyway."

It wouldn't look right to arrive at a midtown newsstand in a chauffeur-driven limousine, so Tony paid off the livery service and took a cab to 49th. The sidewalks were slushy with salt and snow, and he winced as the corrosive mixture ate into the bright polish of his cordovans. He was mentally subtracting the cost of the shoes from the hypothetical $1,000 he would make from passing the Treasury bond, and the cost of the taxi fare, and the cost of the wear and tear on his nervous system. He decided that even though John Bonnanos was his friend, the deal probably wasn't worth it.

Almost deciding to back out of the arrangement altogether, Tony hesitated as he neared the wooden newsstand at 50th, feeling ridiculous. But he approached the little newsdealer, who wore a corduroy windbreaker and a *Daily News* apron, cleared his throat, purchased a newspaper, and introduced himself as Tony.

Giving the forger change from a dollar, the little man didn't change expression, or remove the soggy unfiltered cigarette from his lips.

"Well, I'm expecting you," he said. "Knew you'd be by. You wait here for just a minute, buddy. Watch my newspapers. I'll be back in a minute."

Feeling wholly out of place as he gave a *New York Times* to a man who looked like a stockbroker, and watching the bustling back of the newsdealer as he disappeared into a liquor store two doorways down, Tony finally decided that the situation amused him. Here he was wearing several thousand dollars' worth of clothing and jewelry, with five grand in his pockets, and he was taking in nickels and dimes for a newspaper seller who couldn't be worth $1,000 if all his assets were gathered together.

"Extra, extra, read about it," Tony sang under his breath, puffing steam out into the cold gray air. "Top forger busted for selling *New York Times* without a license. Madness."

"A *Cosmo*," said a young woman in a fur hat.

"Huh?" Tony asked her. "A *what?*"

"*Cosmopolitan,*" she repeated, pointing to a cover. "That one."

"Sure," he said. "Compliments of the house."

"What?" she said. "You mean it's free?"

"Absolutely," Tony said to her. "But you've gotta give me your telephone number."

"No thank *you,*" she told him, turning her back.

Newsdealers don't do very well with women, Tony reflected as he watched the girl disappear in the crowd.

His feet were getting cold, and he snorted and stamped in the slush, cursing the newsdealer for abandoning him with the goddam newspapers, feeling like the victim of a practical joke. Eventually, a very dignified man came out of the liquor store, leading a small, curly-haired dog on a braided leather leash. The dog jumped up against Tony's leg, causing him to move quickly back. The dignified man smiled.

"Please come on into the drugstore," he said to Tony. "Everything's ready."

"Sure," Tony replied. "What do I do about this newsstand?"

The man with the dog smiled and shrugged.

The hell with it, Tony thought, following him into the rear of the drugstore. In a small room, the dignified man introduced him to a rough-looking character he called Pete. The dog barked several times, and the dignified man left the way he had come.

Pete held out for Tony's inspection a sheaf of papers; the engraved American eagles were parodied by an eagle tattoo on Pete's forearm. There were $5,000, $10,000, $20,000, and $50,000 bonds with perforated coupons at the bottoms.

"Ever seen any of these?" Pete asked him.

"First time," Tony said, inspecting them carefully. "I don't even know what they are."

"These are bearer bonds, Treasury notes, and negotiable securities," he said. "This is the merchandise that we're talking about. I understand you've got a very excellent reputation for moving this kind of stuff."

"I never moved this merchandise before." As he held the

bonds he felt interest and greed begin to stir. "But I'm interested."

"We've got a lot of it." Pete scratched a tattoo of a nude woman entwined by a snake on his other forearm. "You can't believe how much of it we got."

"Who's we?" Tony handed back the securities.

"This belongs to Jack Mace," Pete told him.

"So I was informed," Tony said. "What's next?"

Pete handed him one Treasury note for $10,000. "Start with this one," he said. "Here's some identification. But if you're burned, you never saw me, or anybody else. I suppose you know that."

"What the hell kind of a guy do you think I am? I'm a professional."

"No offense," Pete told him. "I just wanted you to know you're operating on your own."

"I always do. It's safer that way."

"Good," Pete said. "When you've got the money, bring it all back here, and I'll give you your share. That's one grand on the ten."

"Yeah," Tony said. "I'll be back here this afternoon."

He called the limousine service for a Cadillac to drive him to Teaneck, New Jersey, where from the Yellow Pages he had selected a small bank. Before he set out, he stopped in the Horn and Hardart, where he purchased a letter of credit proving that Mr. Bryce Wapshot was a responsible businessman. Other correspondence indicated he was planning to open a hardware store in Teaneck. As a further precaution, he bought a phony driver's license, a social-security card, and a New Jersey voter-registration card.

At the bank he told the limousine driver to wait. Going through the polished brass doors, he went to an unoccupied loan officer in a main-floor area enclosed by a low walnut fence.

"How are you today?" Tony said to him. "I'm Bryce Wapshot. I'm in hardware. I'm planning to open a new store here in Teaneck, and I'd like a ninety-day loan for inventory."

"Certainly, Mr. Wapshot," said the vice-president, adjusting his gold-rimmed eyeglasses. "What do you have for collateral?"

Tony felt the familiar shot of excitement and dread run through his system as he removed the Treasury note from a plain white envelope in the inside pocket of his jacket and put it on the desk in front of the bank officer.

"I have this ten-thousand-dollar note," he said. "I thought I'd borrow about sixty-five hundred against it, if that's all right."

The vice-president carefully looked at the note. "This is quite sufficient," he said.

"Good," Tony said, relaxing. "Here's a letter of credit, if that's necessary. I don't want to pay high interest rates, if I can help it."

"I think we could arrange that," said the officer. "That would be six and one-half percent."

"Fine," Tony said. "Can we make that payable in ninety days, interest and principal?"

"Of course," said the banker. "Whatever is easiest for you. How do you want the money?"

"My main supplier says he wants cash," Tony told him.

"I'll give you a cashier's check which you can cash," the banker told him, filling out the papers for a loan application. "Would you sign here?"

Tony signed the name of Bryce Wapshot in the lines indicated by the banker. He waited patiently while the cashier's check was being drawn up, shook hands with the banker, and went directly to a teller's line to turn the check into bills. When he walked out of the bank and got into the rear seat of the limousine, the whole transaction had been completed in just over thirty minutes. This isn't such a bad deal after all, Tony thought, riding back to Manhattan—$1,000 profit for thirty minutes' actual work, plus the getting-ready time. The risk appeared minimal: the bank wouldn't even look at the Treasury note for ninety days, until the loan was past due, and then it would be thirty days or more before it discovered the note had been stolen in the first place. Meanwhile, he had his money, and no record of his involvement in the scam existed anyplace. There were no photographs, no fingerprints, no way in the world of linking the deal back to him.

Pete was sitting in the back booth of the drugstore, smoking a very long, very expensive cigar in a green wrapper.

"Fast work," he said, leading the way to the back room.

Tony grinned. "I told you I'm a professional," he said, handing over the $6,500 in $50 and $100 bills. Pete quickly counted the money, and handed Tony back $1,000 plus another $200.

"What's this for?" Tony asked him, holding out the extra money.

Pete removed the cigar from his mouth. "Expenses," he said. "We understand you have up-front costs."

"I like the way you and Mr. Mace do business," Tony said. "Let me know when you need my services again."

"We will," Pete said. "Nice working with you, Tony."

Phillip Chapis was in trouble. He was in very serious trouble, and the fear of what those big men had promised to do to him if he didn't pay up the loan made it impossible for him to sleep at night. But how to return the money, Phillip didn't know. He made only $80 a week as a messenger for a big brokerage house, and of that money he hardly cleared $60. A $5,000 debt was much more than he was able to handle. The $500-a-week interest was overwhelming. He didn't know why he got himself in this position in the first place, except he was desperate to pay off the gambling debt because the man who ran the craps game said he was going to cut off his testicles unless he got his money immediately.

Phillip never thought about how hard it would be for him to repay the principal $500 weekly "juice," but it was impossible. Phillip never thought ahead that much in the first place. He lived at home with his parents, paying them for room and board, riding the subway to and from work, going out only occasionally to a movie. He saved what was left until he had $200 together, then went and bought himself a woman. At those times, he also drank hard liquor and joined a craps game until the last of the hard-earned escape money was all gone.

The last game had been his undoing. Flushed by unexpected winnings early in the game, Phillip started to do what he had heard was a way to win a fortune—double each succeeding bet. The winnings turned into losses, and he found himself writing out an IOU for $5,000. Quickly, his uncomplicated life became a horror. He couldn't go to his parents for the money, because they simply didn't have it. Fat Maximillian, who ran the craps game, suggested that Phillip stick up some liquor stores in order to get the money, but the frail young man didn't have the courage for that. Now, he didn't know what he was going to do, although suicide seemed more attractive every day.

What he dreaded now was the order from a gruff-voiced man to meet "the boys" at a diner on West Street during lunch hour. There was no way he could refuse, because they knew where he worked and they knew where he lived, and Phillip was $1,500 behind in interest with absolutely no chance of ever being able to pay for it. *I never had anything my whole life, and now I'm going to get killed,* he thought.

Phillip could hardly force his trembling legs to carry him into the diner. Every composed face he saw filled him with hate and rage. None of them were facing murder.

The diner was filled with working men, mostly truckdrivers and a few longshoremen. Although Phillip didn't know what the men he was ordered to meet looked like, he guessed that the two large fellows in overcoats were there for the appointment. Phillip stood trembling by the booth, desperately clearing his throat.

"What do you want, buddy?" asked Vito Carruchi with a snear.

"I'm Phillip Chapis."

"So you're the guy," Vito said, not unkindly. "Well, sit down, kid."

Phillip nodded and sat on the edge of the orange plastic seat. "You call me Vito. This is Carmine. You owe me a lot of money, don't you, kid?" Phillip nodded again and swallowed, his Adam's apple bobbing up and down like a Yo-yo. "How much he owe, Carmine?"

"As of today, he owes seven thousand," Carmine said.

"That's one hell of a lot of money," Vito told him. "Do you know that you're in trouble?"

"You're going to kill me," Phillip said, blinking back the tears. "I don't have the money. I'll go with you. Would you do it fast?"

"What the hell?" Vito said. "What's this?"

Carmine sneered. "What a punk," he said. "He's been watching too many movies."

"Stop sniveling," Vito ordered sharply. "You're gonna have people looking at us."

Phillip tried to stop crying. But he was too afraid.

"I'm not going to hurt you," Vito said irritably. "You can't go around acting like that. What the hell a simp like you gambling for in the first place?"

Phillip shook his head in ignorance.

"They shouldn't let jerks like this play craps," Vito said. "Somebody ought to have some kind of standards."

"There should be a law," Carmine agreed.

"I don't want to gamble anymore."

"Shut up," Vito said. "I'm thinking. You can't get the money, can you?"

"No," Phillip said, tears falling again.

"Don't do that," Vito told him. "Don't sniffle. We won't hurt you. It ain't worth it, hurting you. You're too fucking dumb to get the message, anyway. You work as a messenger, right?"

"Yes, sir," Phillip said.

Carmine picked up the conversation. "What do you carry?"

"Everything," Phillip said. "I carry stock certificates to different offices, and pick up things at the stock exchange. Sometimes I even carry money."

"You ever carry securities—like Treasury bonds, and that kind of stuff?"

"Yes, sir," Phillip told him. "Sometimes I even pick up things right from the vault."

"Right from the vault?" Carmine asked. "How much are these bonds worth that you carry?"

"I don't know," Phillip said. "Lots, sometimes."

"Here's what you're going to do to get yourself out of this jam," Carmine suggested. "The next time you carry the bonds, look at them, and find out how much the bonds are worth. Can you add?"

"Sort of," Phillip said.

"Great." Carmine sounded sarcastic. "Try. When you have

more than, say, fifty thousand in bonds, call up this telephone number and tell me what you got. Then I'll come over and take them from you."

"Then what will I do?" Phillip asked in a panic. "They'll say I took them."

"Listen, stupid," said Vito. "You say you were robbed. And that would be right, see? We'd even have somebody put a gun on you, so it's all legitimate."

"Then I don't have to pay back the money?"

"As long as you don't describe the people who robbed you. How does that sound?"

"That sounds wonderful," Phillip said with a smile.

"When do you think you can make this telephone call?" Carmine asked him.

"I think this afternoon." Phillip felt relief wash over him. These weren't bad fellows at all. He liked both of them. "Maybe about three."

"We'll have somebody waiting," Vito said. "Let's go now."

At 2:45 P.M., the head teller called Phillip and signed him out with securities to go to the New York Stock Exchange. The securities were put into an unmarked canvas bag, which Phillip placed in his cheap attaché case. But this afternoon, instead of simply walking briskly from the brokerage house to the exchange, he ducked into a men's lavatory. Placing the attaché case on his knees in the toilet stall, he opened the bag and counted the securities. There was a lot more than $50,000 in the bag. So much more, he couldn't even add it all. But just one of the US Treasury bonds had $50,000 on it, and there were at least a dozen more in denominations of $10,000 and $20,000. His heart thumping with excitement, Phillip stopped at a pay telephone in the lobby and called the number Vito and Carmine had given him.

"I got a lot of them bonds," he said, without introducing himself.

"Who the hell is that?" answered the voice.

"Phillip Chapis," the messenger said, filled with self-importance.

"For chrissake," the voice complained. "Any of you guys know a Phillip Chapis?"

"Give me that fucking phone," said Carmine's voice. "Is this you, Phillip?"

"Yes, sir. I have those bonds I told you about. I don't know how much there is, but one of them is for fifty thousand dollars, and I got a lot of others."

"I'll be goddamned," Carmine muttered. "Where are you, and where are you going?"

"I'm in the lobby. I'm on my way down to the stock exchange."

"What street are you going down?" Carmine asked him.

"Nassau Street," Phillip said.

"Go there, then," Carmine said. "Don't worry about anything, understand?"

"No, sir," Phillip said. "Am I going to get off now?"

"Probably," Carmine said. "Just as long as you walk slow."

Tunelessly whistling, Phillip ambled down Nassau toward the stock exchange, looking to his right and left at every corner and stoplight for the robbers. He was disappointed as he neared Federal Hall that he hadn't yet been held up. He never heard the step of the stocky man in a blue wool shirt who came up behind him and clipped him on the back of the skull with the butt end of a .45. He was already unconscious when a second man with long blond hair took the attaché case from his fingers and the pair of robbers disappeared into the crowd. Few of the passersby saw the robbery, and nearly everybody walked over or around the unconscious body of the frail little man lying on the sidewalk.

Eventually, two high-school girls came to the man lying on the sidewalk, and noticed blood on the back of his head, and reported to a traffic policeman that a man was lying bleeding on the sidewalk.

The policeman attracted a small crowd, who stood in a gawking semicircle when the police wagon arrived to take Phillip to the hospital. Only when the sergeant at Beekman Downtown Hospital's emergency ward was filling out his report did he discover that the little man had been robbed. It wasn't until nearly 6:00 P.M. that police discovered the messenger had been carrying $325,000 in US Treasury bonds, negotiable securities that were nearly untraceable.

Phillip was grilled by police, company officials, and the insurance agent for the next two weeks, but all he could truthfully report was that he was walking down the sidewalk and didn't remember a thing. He even passed a lie-detector test, having already forgotten the meeting with Vito and Carmine and the gambling debt.

Three months later, Phillip, drinking whiskey after his whore, was even willing to play craps once again, but was barred from the game. "Guy's got no brains," said Fat Maximillian, tapping his forehead. "He don't learn nothing."

Six months later, his employers gave Phillip a $25 bonus for having stood up to the still unidentified robbers. Phillip couldn't really remember the incident at all.

"This is going to be a special deal," the man with the tattooed arms told the forger in the back room of the drugstore. "This one is going for some real money —sixty thousand."

"I don't know," Tony said. "Will the banks accept that much without checking on bond ownership?"

"This will be different," Pete said to him. "The banker you'll be dealing with is obligated to us."

"How's that?" Tony asked him.

"I think this guy's a fruit case," Pete said. "Likes little boys. Somebody got some pictures, and he doesn't want his wife to look at them."

"But what if he's gone to the police?"

"Too late for that," Pete said complacently. "He's already helped us on a couple of things, so he's in too deep to do himself any good."

"This banker will be contacted ahead of time?"

"That's a promise. I'm out on a limb in this, too," Pete told him. "If you get busted, it goes right back to me. I'm taking a chance, too."

"What about Jack Mace?" Tony asked him. "How come he's never around?"

"A man likes to be careful," Pete said.

"So do I."

"I understand how you feel," Pete said. "I promise you. After this one, you'll meet Jack Mace."

"Will I?"

"Yes. And you'll really be into something."

"What?"

"You'll see."

"After this one."

"Yes. Here are the bonds. The bank is the First Garden State Bank of Newark. The banker's name is Leon Goodiron. Vice-president. Your name for this will be David Zipprodt."

"That's a dumb name," Tony said. "How in the hell do you spell that? When am I supposed to cash these bonds?"

"Tomorrow morning," Pete said. "About ten thirty."

"Zipprodt," Tony said. "I'll be up all night trying to write a name like that."

Tony wore a gray wool suit with a thin white shadow stripe, a white shirt, and a blue tie striped with white to the First Garden State Bank. He carried the US Treasury bonds in a manila envelope inside his brown leather briefcase.

"I have an appointment with Mr. Leon Goodiron," Tony told the receptionist. "I'm Mr. Zipprodt. He's expecting me."

Leon Goodiron was a tall, fat man with thinning gray hair. He didn't look like a faggot, but he certainly did look like a man with something serious troubling him. Judging by the flush in his cheeks, Tony guessed he had been hitting the bottle lately. There was a quaver in the banker's voice as he played out the charade with the forger.

"Yes, sir," said Goodiron, smiling falsely at Tony. "You're Mr. Zipprodt, are you?"

"That's right," Tony said to him. "I'm new in town, from Washington, D.C. I'm planning to open up a new pancake house, and I'd like to borrow some money to purchase the land and begin the construction."

"Oh, my, isn't that interesting," Goodiron said mechanically, alternately smiling brightly and frowning pensively. "How much did you want to borrow, sir?"

"Sixty thousand dollars," Tony said to him.

The banker was surprised. "I thought it was forty," he said.

Tony realized his mistake. "That's right," he said. "I have collateral for sixty, and I want to borrow about forty thousand against it."

"Right. Let's get this business over with as quickly as possible. Give me the fucking bonds. I've got the papers all filled out. You sign them. The loan is for a hundred eighty days. Let me look at the fucking bonds."

"Hey," Tony said. "You don't have to talk to me like that."

"How in the hell should I talk to you?" the banker asked him. "You're just another one of those goddam gangsters, aren't you?"

"Well, mister, I don't fuck around with little boys."

The banker flushed. "Please," he said. "I can't stand up under all this. I've got a family—my whole reputation to worry about. Can I see the bonds?"

"Here they are," Tony said, handing them over. "They're all good."

Goodiron looked at them carefully. "They are real, aren't they?" he begged.

"Of course they're real," Tony said. "You're not being ripped off."

"Aren't I, now?" Goodiron asked him. "You people are like leeches. Once you start on a person, you never get off."

"I'm just doing my job, nothing else," Tony explained. "If you've been having a hard time, it has nothing to do with me."

Goodiron put his hands over his face. Tony looked around, and put a hand on the banker's arm. "Don't cry, mister," he said. "It would look real bad, you know? Let's just get this transaction finished, and you'll never see me again."

Goodiron put down his arms, his face a stern mask. "You're right. Here's the cashier's check. I'd appreciate it if you wouldn't cash it here. Take it someplace else, would you?"

"I'd be glad to," Tony said to him.

"We're all finished then," Goodiron told him. "Tell me one thing, if you could. Do you know where these bonds originally came from?"

"No idea," Tony said. "I can't answer questions like that."

"I don't want to know, anyway," Goodiron decided.

Tony cashed the check at Newark's First National Bank, and brought the $40,000 to Pete in the drugstore. Pete handed him his $6,000, plus another $1,000 for expenses.

"What did you think of the banker?" he asked him.

"A creep," Tony said. "He was scared to death. I was afraid he'd blow it. I'm not going to do that kind of thing again. Guys like that are too dangerous."

"You won't have to," Pete said to him. "You're going to be going overseas now, if you want to. You've been doing good work. Mr. Mace said to tell you."

"I'm not going anyplace until I meet Mr. Mace," Tony said. "I hope you understand that, Pete."

"It's being taken care of," Pete said to him. "At noon tomorrow, tell the newsdealer you're waiting for Mr. Mace in the bar right across the street. Go there and wait. Mr. Mace will be there soon."

Tony was satisfied. "Where am I going to go?" he asked.

"I don't know," Pete said. "From now on, you take your orders from the old man himself."

Bill Woolsey's stomach felt like it had a pin in it. He couldn't put another forkful of Henrietta's casserole into his mouth, and he finally pushed aside the dinner plate. His baby son was oblivious to his distress, but Henrietta, his pretty rose-cheeked Dutch wife, was concerned about the way Bill was acting.

"Is it something I've done?" she asked him, cleaning off the dining room table in the Levittown tract house.

"It's nothing you've done," he said, throwing down the newspaper and peering out the front window.

"Are you having trouble at work?"

"Leave me alone, Henny," Woolsey told his wife, closing the draperies and pacing across the beige living-room rug.

"You're in trouble," Henrietta concluded, approaching Woolsey and taking his hand. "Is there anything I can do to help?"

Woolsey stopped pacing when he heard the sound of a car in their gravel driveway.

"Yes," he said quietly, the large blue vein in his forehead pulsing. "You can find me ten thousand dollars."

"We don't even have a thousand in the bank," Henrietta said.

The doorbell rang. Woolsey stood transfixed. The bell sounded like the signal for an execution.

"Shall I get it?" Henrietta whispered to him.

Woolsey shook his head. He couldn't make his feet move. The bell rang again, more insistently, and the person outside rattled the doorknob.

"Who is it?" Henrietta asked her perspiring husband.

"Open this fucking door, Woolsey, or I'm going to kick it in," the man outside demanded. Woolsey walked to the door on rubbery legs. He closed his eyes as he unbolted it. Four olive-skinned men ambled into the living room: Tuna DeScala, his brother Joey Legs, Milwaukee Phil Scappone, and Sam Trafficunte, an older man whose protruding, round stomach hung six inches over his belt.

"You don't open the fucking door very fucking fast," Trafficunte said to Woolsey. "You trying to bullshit us?"

"No," Woolsey said in a quiet voice, closing the door behind the four menacing intruders. "Let's go in the back and talk."

"So your wifey here won't listen?" Trafficunte said. "Bullshit, buddy."

"Nice-looking piece," Tuna DeScala said, going up to Woolsey's wife and putting his right hand on the back of her neck.

"Leave me alone," the young woman asked, moving away from him. "Bill, tell him to leave me alone."

"Sure, I'll leave her alone," Tuna scoffed. "Give us the money, Woolsey-baby."

"That's right," Trafficunte said. "Keep your fingers out of her box, Tuna, because Woolsey, the crapshooter here, is gonna give us the ten grand. Ain't you, Woolsey?"

"I don't have the money," Woolsey said, wanting to vomit.

"You shit," Trafficunte stormed. "What the fuck you mean, you don't have the money?"

"I don't have it," Woolsey said. "I can't get it. I don't know what to do."

"I'm going to break your legs," Trafficunte told him. "Get the baseball bat from the car, one of you guys. I'm gonna break this bastard's legs."

"Sweet Christ," Woolsey implored. "Give me a chance. I'll find it someplace."

"You already had one week," said Joey Legs. "You were supposed to be at the farm with the money seven days ago. I think he's bullshitting us, Sammy."

"I thing he's bullshitting us, too," Trafficunte said.

"What are you hoodlums doing here in my house?" Henrietta shouted hysterically. "Get out of here! Get out of here!"

"Shut up, cunt!" Tuna DeScala said. "Close your trap or I'll stick my prick in it."

"That's the idea," said his brother. "You like that idea, Phil? You think she's a good piece?"

Joey Legs took the young wife's head between both hands, and struggled to kiss her, pushing out his lips in an exaggerated pucker. Henrietta fought him off, and Joey laughed.

"She wants it," he said. "I can tell. She's tired of this asshole bookkeeper."

"I'm tired of this asshole bookkeeper, too," Trafficunte said. "You have really fucked up, Billy-boy."

"Just leave my wife alone," Woolsey pleaded.

"Get the baseball bat," Trafficunte demanded.

"God, don't!" Woolsey pleaded.

"Why the fuck not?" Trafficunte said scornfully. "What you ever done for me, punk?"

"Anything you want," Woolsey said. "I just can't get the money today. Anything you want."

"That's reasonable," Trafficunte said. "I'll tell you what I want. Tomorrow at the messenger window, you're going to hand one of my people a hundred thousand dollars' worth of Treasury bonds."

"Where do I get the bonds?" Woolsey asked him.

"From the safe!" Trafficunte told him. "You go into the safe just like always, and you pull out a hundred thousand dollars' worth of Treasury bonds. Then, when my man arrives, you give him the bonds just like you do for delivery to other brokerage houses, and you fill out a delivery slip. There's nothing to it, Woolsey," he said insinuatingly. "And then we don't break your legs—tonight."

"That's stealing," Woolsey protested.

"That's not my fucking problem," Trafficunte told him.

"I don't want to do it."

"I've been trying to be reasonable," Trafficunte exploded, frightening Woolsey's baby son, who set up a yell. "I'm tired of this dicking around with an asshole. Goddam you, Woolsey, I ain't gonna break your fucking legs. I'm gonna come back here in sixty minutes with ten of the biggest, blackest niggers you've seen in your life, and every goddam one of them is gonna fuck your wife. Got that? And you're gonna sit there and watch them do it."

Henrietta sat on the couch and began to sob. The baby lay on the floor, screaming in terror. Woolsey looked around at his family, and looked at the four men who stood around them, grinning with pleasure.

"Tell me how I can tell the messenger's the right guy," he said numbly.

At noon Tony stopped at the 50th and Broadway newsstand for a brief conversation with the little operator, who then scurried away up the street. Tony crossed the street and entered the tavern on the ground level of the Hotel Taft.

The bartender brought him a bottle of Rheingold beer, which Tony drank without unbuttoning his coat or removing his black leather gloves. Soon, a short but distinguished elderly gentleman appeared, leading a small black dog with white spots. The portly man's skin glowed with good health.

"Ah-ha, so, you are Tony?" asked the elderly man, peering closely at the forger's face. "We have met before, I would say."

Tony was surprised. "Yes," he said. "You brought me into the drugstore."

"I am always curious about my business associates," said the old man. "I'm Jack Mace. My real name is Malish. I don't know how I picked up the nickname, but even I use it now. And you are Tony," he said, waving a finger at the younger man, "the man with many names, and many signatures. Your reputation has preceded you, my friend."

"That's nice to know," Tony said to him. "Look, Mr. Mace, if we're going to talk business, maybe we'd better sit down at a table. Can I buy you a drink?"

"Oh, no, no. I don't drink anymore. When I was younger I liked to drink. But then, I liked to play around with the ladies, too. Now I'm too old to do anything but walk my little dog and play with my grandchildren. I suppose that you're too young to have grandchildren?"

"Yes, I am," said Tony. "Actually, I'm not even married."

"You'll want to take care of yourself in that regard," the old man lectured him. "Grandchildren warm an old man's heart. Would you hold this leash?" Handing the leash to Tony, the old man struggled out of his overcoat. Finally successful, he folded the thick wool coat on his lap, and placing the terrier on top of its silk lining, stroked the little animal's head.

"Have you ever been to Europe, Tony?" he asked.

Tony blinked. "In the service I was stationed in Germany for a while."

"I want you to take a trip for me to Switzerland," said Mace. "Are you interested?"

"I might be," Tony said to him. "What is the action?"

"The action, as you call it, is movement of securities." From an inside coat pocket he extracted a gray envelope which he placed on the table in front of Tony, tapping it with a long, yellow fingernail.

"In this envelope are one hundred thousand dollars' worth of US Treasury bonds. I want you to take them to Switzerland, to a banker we are in contact with. You'll find that things are much more open there in some ways, because nobody cares where the bonds come from. The federal government will back the bonds in any case, so no bank can lose money making loans against them, nor will any banker get into trouble."

"The banker's involved with the organization?" Tony asked him.

"It doesn't make any difference," said the fence. "He will be doing business with us. How much he knows or doesn't know is none of your regard." The old man scratched the dog's ears and sighed. "He's just an intermediary. After you have the money— sixty-five thousand, in this instance—you'll go back to your hotel, and another man will call you to make arrangements to get the money. On your return to this country, you'll contact me once again through the newsdealer, and I'll pay you your share."

"Ten percent as usual?" Tony asked him.

"That's right." Mace nodded vigorously.

"What about my expenses?" Tony asked him.

"I forgot," Mace said, reaching into another pocket. He handed Tony an envelope, which Tony tore open and shook out twenty $100 bills, all new.

"If your expenses go higher for any reason, just let me know, and I'll make up the difference."

"When do I leave?" Tony asked him.

"In two days," Mace said to him. "You'll have things to do to get ready."

"I sure will," Tony said to him. He opened the first gray envelope, and counted through the ten $10,000 Treasury bonds. Placing the bonds back in their envelope, Tony put them into his leather attaché case.

"We're set," he said.

"Good," Jack Mace told him, holding out a liver-spotted hand. "Good luck. Have a pleasant trip."

He set down the terrier, put on his overcoat, and followed the yipping dog out of the bar.

Tony sat at the table for several minutes, mentally preparing an itinerary. When he left, he took a taxi directly to the Horn and Hardart across from Grand Central, and sat down with a fence named Shamrock. Shamrock, who carried a large fleshy knot on the back of his neck, was the younger brother of a Connecticut judge known for his honesty. He fingered the tumor constantly as he talked.

"Shamrock, I need a birth certificate," Tony said to him. "I need a birth certificate, and a complete set of identification, just as soon as you can get them for me."

"Do you want prime stuff or second-rate stuff?" Shamrock asked. "The price depends."

"I want the best stuff you got, and I want it within four hours. I'll pay you five hundred for the lot in cash, half now and half on delivery."

"Give me three hundred up front. You won't be sorry. I guarantee this merchandise."

Tony reached in his pocket, and took out three of the $100 bills. "By four thirty," he said. "I'll see you right back here."

Shamrock nodded, and ducked out of the cafeteria. Tony finished his cup of coffee, then went to get passport photos. He impatiently came back to the cafeteria at 4:15, chain-smoking cigarettes and drinking coffee until Shamrock appeared about a quarter to five.

"Sorry, sorry, sorry," said the man with the tumor. "I just couldn't go any faster."

"I want the identification," Tony said to him, "not excuses."

Shamrock put on the table for Tony's inspection a blank birth certificate from Coney Island Hospital, along with a driver's license, Diner's Club card, social-security card, and voter-registration card all made out in the name Roman Paris. Tony was irritated about the blank birth certificate.

"This is key to everything I want to do," he complained. "Now I have to take a chance with a phony certificate?"

"I got an idea 'bout that," Shamrock said. "Here's a stamp which was lifted from the hospital, so it's authentic."

He laid down on the table a rubber stamp about three inches long that read "DUPLICATE."

"This is the real thing," Shamrock told him. "You fill out the certificate and stamp it with this, and everything will be absolutely fine. I mean, no problems."

"You got a pad?" Tony asked him.

"Yeah, yeah, yeah," Shamrock said. "It'll be an extra fifty for the stamp and pad."

"That's robbery," Tony said to him, methodically trying the stamp on a white napkin. "Here's another two-fifty and we're even. You're a thief, Shamrock. Did anybody ever tell you that?"

"Listen to who's talking," Shamrock said to him. "You go through more identification than anybody in this city. Did anybody ever tell you that, Tony?"

"Look at all the mouths I feed. You oughta be grateful."

"I'm grateful. What do you want the birth certificate for, Tony?"

Tony pocketed the identification and stamp. "None of your business," he said levelly. "Do you know what that means?"

"I'm just curious. I don't mean nothing."

"Stay curious," Tony said to him. "If I wanted ten more birth certificates, could you get them for me?"

"Two hundred apiece," Shamrock hazarded.

"One hundred," Tony said. "And that's robbery."

"When do you want them?" Shamrock asked him.

"Next week, sometime."

"Five hundred up front."

Tony gave him five more $100 bills. "You burn me, Shamrock, and I'll have your ass pinned up against the wall."

"What makes you so suspicious, Tony?"

"Common sense," Tony said to him as he left. "How can you trust the brother of a judge?"

"That ain't my fault," Shamrock called after him. "You can't hold me responsible for what my brother does."

That evening, Tony filled out the birth certificate in the name of Roman Paris, making him twenty-eight years old. He imprinted the birth certificate with the rubber stamp and black ink: "DUPLICATE."

First thing in the morning, he went to Swissair and purchased a round-trip ticket for Zurich. He took it to the US Passport Agency in Rockefeller Center with the identification.

"I've got an emergency in Switzerland," he told the clerk. "I've got to leave as quickly as possible. Is there anything I can do to get an emergency passport?"

"Yes, sir," the clerk said. "Talk to the supervisor."

The supervisor was an angular, nervous woman in her early forties with a perpetually perplexed appearance. Tony gave her a shot of his highest-octane charm.

"I'm Roman Paris," he said, deep in his throat. "I'm a consultant in electrical engineering. I've been called by the City of Zurich on an emergency job that involves the city's escalators. But I have to leave for there tomorrow, or I'll lose the commission. Can I get an emergency passport?"

"Oh yes, Mr. Paris." The supervisor smiled at him and

blinked her eyes. "We have the special twenty-four-hour passport."

"Is it as good as a regular passport?"

"It's the same thing, except it doesn't go through Washington. We process it right here in our offices, and you can pick it up tomorrow morning at ten." She handed him a form. "Fill out this application. Do you have your birth certificate?"

"Yes, I do," Tony said, giving her the forged duplicate. "Do you need anything else?"

"Passport pictures."

Tony handed several over.

"Two is sufficient. I'll handle this myself."

Tony took her dry hand in his own and pressed it. "I certainly appreciate your help in this," he said. "You're a good person. You've been a real help."

"We're here to help our citizens," she said.

Tony completed the application form and handed it to the supervisor.

With the extra passport photographs, he went to the American Automobile Club office on the ground level, and filled out the application for an international driver's license, just in case he needed it.

All night long, Tony awakened at half-hour intervals, wondering where to hide the bonds. The suitcase seemed to be too obvious, the attaché case too dangerous, the pockets of his suit too simple a plan to escape customs agents. He wasn't quite sure that the Zurich authorities would mind the importation of US Treasury bonds, but he couldn't take a chance of declaring them, knowing that the information would be to Interpol within hours, even if he wasn't arrested for bringing them into the country.

In the airport lobby at noon, he made his decision. Buying an *Esquire* magazine, he slipped the bonds inside the pages. The idea wasn't brilliant, but it calmed his apprehensions. And it worked.

Chapter 6

Milano checked into the Luzern Hotel near Zurich's Bahnhofstrasse, curiously examining the bidet in his two-room suite and grinning at the partial rails on the side of the bed.

"They make me feel like a little kid," he joked to the bellman, a white-haired man with short hair, short nails, and curt responses. Turning down the covers of the bed, the bellman had no idea what the American was talking about, but hanging up the guest's suits in the wood-paneled closet, he surmised the bald man was a wealthy eccentric, possibly a Texas oil millionaire. The five-dollar tip made him sure.

Milano slept with the *Esquire* under his left pillow.

In the morning, Zurich's winter fog bound its many church spires in mufflers of gloom. Tony didn't want to call the contact too early, so he spent the morning climbing the city's hills, window-shopping the rich stores of the Bahnhofstrasse. He felt sad and out of place. He thought that Zurich, despite its unpolluted air and its immaculate streets and sidewalks, was the most depressing place in the world. He longed for a loud American voice, instead of the French and German murmurs its retail clerks reserved for rich foreigners. A group of laughing children passed by, but the overwhelming ambience remained funereal.

"My goddam funeral," Tony thought, patting his pockets to make sure the bonds were there. It would be hell to die in a place like Zurich, far from everybody he knew. It would be even worse to land in jail here. He tried to concentrate on the fog-bound city's ancient architecture. His father would have loved it. Tony hated it.

125

At 11:00 A.M., Tony called the number Mace had given him, asking for Herr Brummer.

The very polite male voice that finally came on the telephone spoke English as though the language had a painful edge to it.

"You certainly had me in a dither," the Swiss banker said calmly. "I've been wondering if you might have missed your plane, or if plans had been altered."

"Nobody gave *me* any time schedule," Tony said testily. "I just didn't want to wake anybody up."

"But I arise at five," the banker said, slightly surprised.

"I didn't have your home number. Where do I come for this transaction?"

"Why don't we meet for lunch?" the banker suggested in his modulated tones. "There's a lovely little French restaurant called Marcel's on Fraumünsterstrasse. I'll make reservations if you like, and we can make arrangements for the transaction."

"I'll meet you right now," Tony said.

"How about one?" the banker asked. "I can't get free until then."

"I'll see you then," Tony said, furious at the delay. The deal was wrong. Tony didn't know a damn thing about the Swiss, except that he disliked them intensely. He had no idea how Swiss banks worked, and no clue how a Zurich banker could tie into Jack Mace back home.

But at the same time, it didn't figure that he would be given $2,000 cash and $100,000 worth of bonds just to be set up for a fall in Switzerland. Tony couldn't think of any Mafia chieftains he might have displeased, unless one of them had grown jealous of his successes. He was worth money to them.

Finally, Tony's didn't *feel* any outright danger. If he couldn't trust the sixth sense that had kept him from danger this far along the way, he ought to get out of the business. Tony decided that the Zurich winter was just too foreign for him to feel comfortable.

Walking briskly back to the hotel, he put on a new double-breasted suit of blue wool, re-counted the bonds and put them in his attaché case, and arrived at the restaurant precisely at one.

Marcel's wasn't exactly to his taste—too heavy and sober, like

Zurich itself. The air was very still and chill. As Tony removed his overcoat and handed it to the tuxedoed host, he saw a man hardly more than five feet tall approach him swiftly, with his right hand thrust out in front of him.

"Mr. Milano, glad to see you," the little man said, smiling broadly under a thin mustache.

Tony didn't return the smile. "How do you know that name?" he asked him, speaking in a very low voice.

The banker blinked. "Do I have the wrong person?"

Tony sat down across from him, memorizing his appearance. "How do you know who I am?"

"A tall, bald man, well dressed, with hazel eyes," the banker recited. "Peter Milano, born in Brooklyn, New York, a courier for Mr. Mace."

"That's a lot of information for somebody to have in Switzerland," Tony said icily. "I don't like it."

"Let me order some good wine for us," Herr Brummer said in clipped but soothing tones. "We Swiss are known for our perfection. It's a national character trait." He smoothed his slick raven hair against his small, well-formed skull.

"No wine for me. I don't drink wine. Just a cup of coffee."

"Yes," the banker said, "You are known to get right down to business. Tell me, how do you like our city?"

"I don't like it at all. I'm not in the mood for small talk, either."

The waiter brought to the table a brown bottle of German Moselle and a silver pot of coffee. Puzzled but unruffled by Tony's manner, Herr Brummer poured coffee for the glowering American and then filled his own glass. "Then business it is," he said. "You have a package for me?"

"Yes, I do."

"May I see it?"

Tony removed the envelope from his attaché case and placed it in the center of the table. The banker put it on his plate as if it were something he was about to eat, opened the seal, examined the corners of the bonds, checking their denominations, and making a little clicking sound with his tongue against the roof of his mouth.

"Fine," he said. From beside his chair, Brummer picked up a

soft leather case and opened its silver buckle. He handed Tony a fat brown envelope.

Tony looked inside. It was filled with American money. He put the envelope in the attaché case, locked it, and sipped at the bitter black coffee.

"Don't you want to count it?" Herr Brummer asked him.

"I don't like counting money in restaurants. It's a little obvious."

"Then you do trust me after all?"

"No I don't," Tony said. "But if it's not all here, I know where to find you. And I will."

"It's there," the banker said coldly. "We survive because we are perfectionists. I hope you enjoy your stay in Zurich."

"You're going to be here a lot longer than I am," Tony said, rising and dropped a twenty-dollar bill on the table.

"Please," Herr Brummer said, handing back the money. "My treat."

Tony left without saying good-bye.

In the hotel suite, Tony shook the money out of the envelope onto the bed. There were sixty packages of new $20, $50 and $100 bills, each bound in a thick gray rubber band. The packages were marked with small squares of paper on which $1,000 was written with a perfect hand in black ink. Tony counted each package. Everything was in order.

He sat down on the edge of the bed looking at the $60,000, hating it almost as much as he hated the swirling fog outside the window. When the telephone rang, he picked it up without saying anything.

"Tony?"

"Yes?"

"May I come up?"

"Please do," Tony said.

There was a knock at the door as he was returning the money to the heavy envelope. He completed the task before admitting the visitor, a very tall man in the most outlandish brown pin-striped suit he had ever seen. The man's carefully shaved face looked dignified and serene, but his tie was a loud, abstract silk in bright oranges, yellows, and reds. Now that Tony had seen some bright colors in Zurich, he wasn't sure he liked them.

"I'm pleased to meet you," the man said in a heavy and unplaceable accent.

"It's nice to meet you," Tony said politely.

"I hope to see you again, after this trip." He sat in an easy chair.

"I hope so," Tony said.

"Give me the money."

Tony handed him the envelope. The man touched the tips of his fingers to his lips and counted through the bills faster than anybody Tony had ever seen before, the money moving in a steady blur like a deck of shuffled cards. Just as quickly, the man slid the money back into the brown envelope and dropped it into his briefcase.

Jumping to his feet, he said in an easy tone, "Thank you very much."

"Wait a minute," Tony demanded, moving ahead of him to the door. "Aren't you going to give me a receipt?"

The man stopped, looking at him strangely. "A receipt? We don't give receipts."

"What do you mean, you don't give receipts?" Tony's temper was rising. "How do they know I gave you the money?"

"They know," the man said to him. "No problem. Don't worry about it."

"I don't even know who the hell you are. Do you have a name?"

"No name. Are you going to let me out of here?"

"I'm not certain," Tony said. "This could get me killed."

"I thought you were supposed to be very cool."

"That was before I came to Zurich," Tony said. "What the hell am I going to do now?"

"Don't worry. This is how we operate." He nodded his head at the door. "May I?"

Tony stepped aside, with a bad taste in his mouth, watching the man leave.

He was certain now that he had been set up. Fear, which had never bothered him in the United States, took over. His legs were trembling, and sweat ran down the back of his neck. Tony picked up the telephone to call New York but was afraid to; he thought it would be listened to by an operator, or the police. He composed a telegram to Jack Mace—MERCHANDISE DELIVERED, RECEIPTS PICKED UP BY MAN IN BROWN—which he tore to pieces and flushed down the toilet. Frantically, he called Swissair; a return flight to New York left in two hours.

Tony began drinking scotch the moment the airplane took off from Zurich-Kloten Airport, and drank without stopping until the plane landed at Kennedy at nine that night. The alcohol couldn't stall his racing thoughts. He was stone sober and still terrified when he went into the first open telephone booth and called the drugstore, saying, "I'm on my way in."

He grabbed the commuter helicopter from the airport to Manhattan, left his bags in a locker, and took the first cab to 50th and Broadway.

There was nobody he knew in the drugstore. But an elderly man with pure white hair and heavy black-rimmed glasses told him to wait at the bar across the street.

Tony hastily downed a double Chivas and had ordered a refill when Jack Mace entered, this time without his dog, and sat down beside him.

"Don't worry about it," he said in comforting tones. "Everything is all right."

Relief hit Tony in a flood, and suddenly the hours of alcohol made his head swim. "What do you mean?" he asked dizzily.

"I should have told you not to expect one," Mace chuckled. "You can't ask somebody in this business to give you a receipt. It's not what I would call a formal transaction."

Tony put his forehead down against his arms.

"You weren't very friendly in Zurich," Mace said. "But you did fine."

Tony lifted his head, trying to focus on the old fence's grandfatherly features. "What about *my* money?"

"Certainly." Taking an envelope, Mace shoved it inside Tony's double-breasted jacket and patted his hand. "We'll see you again soon," he said, turning to leave.

Feeling ashamed of his panic, thoroughly intoxicated, and completely exhausted, Tony slumped at the bar until closing time when he staggered into the street and took a taxi to the suite he kept at the Waldorf Hotel. Without undressing, he stretched out on top of the bed and fell deeply asleep, dreaming of a squad of tall men in ugly brown suits with wild ties who robbed him, bound his hands with thick rubber bands, and held him captive until a grandfatherly figure with white hair came with a revolver.

"Where is the receipt?" the old man demanded.

"I didn't get one," Tony protested.

"Then you will die in Zurich," the old man said, his face twisting and the gun exploding and the thick cold fog coming down.

Tony didn't awaken until after noon, fighting for consciousness through the clouds of nightmare into a steady, drumming hangover that twisted his stomach with nausea. His clothes had soaked through with a sour sweat, and the bedcover and blankets were twisted around him. He lurched into the bathroom and vomited bile into the toilet bowl. He stripped off his clothes and, barely making his shaking body stand, lurched into the steaming shower.

Keeping the water as hot as he could bear, Tony remained in the shower until the nausea left and the pain subsided in his head and neck. His hands and legs were still trembling and he was so hungry that his stomach knotted. Dimly remembering his conversation with Jack Mace, he tore through the piled clothing and found the envelope. Inside, in new bills, was $10,000.

Without knowing why, Tony was enraged with Mace. Picking up the heavy lamp on the desk, he threw it against the opposite wall. The sound of the smashing white porcelain brought him momentary calm. He was able to dress before the rage moved in again. He fantasized about buying a gun and murdering the old man. Instead, he shoved the money into the pockets of his tan raincoat and left the Waldorf in search of something to eat.

At a nearby restaurant, Tony drank four glasses of V-8 juice and devoured three cheese omelettes. He was uncertain what to do next. He was lonely, and New York reminded him uncomfortably of a filthy Zurich, with tall buildings instead of Alpine rises, and brutal people instead of sullen ones.

The rootlessness of this life had gotten to him. Tony had

come to an abrupt turning point. He needed to get someplace to think for a few days. Remembering a coed he had met the month before, he called her at Cornell, asking tentatively if she was doing anything for the weekend. Bored with her studies, she was pleased to hear from the wealthy man with whom she had spent a weekend in Miami, so she invited him up.

Tony stayed at the girl's apartment for five days, buying steaks and expensive wine for the girl's friends, and cooking for them like a hired chef. He went to the first college football game of his life, to a crowded student pub, to the campus library where he stood amazed at the thousands of books, and for walks through the tree-filled campus over paths winding through the snow.

Nights, he slept chastely with the girl, holding her close to him the way a child holds a beloved toy. The girl found him very quiet and moody, emotionally fixed someplace thousands of miles away. Tony bought her presents every day—a set of gold bracelets, a dozen bottles of Arpège, half a dozen cashmere sweaters, a television set, and finally a fur coat. She reluctantly accepted them, feeling both cherished and degraded.

On the fifth day of his visit, after Tony had come into the apartment with the large silver box containing the mink coat, she fixed her blue eyes on his face and asked him what he was trying to do.

"I hardly know you, Tony," she told him. "I met you a month ago, and we had a good time for a weekend. You appear here, and spend thousands of dollars buying me presents. I like you. But I don't know who you are, or what it is you want."

"Would you believe me if I told you I didn't know that, either?"

"Yes, I would. Are you in trouble of some kind?"

"Not that I know of." Tony looked at her and then looked away. "Maybe I am. Maybe I'm not."

"Do you have any family?" she inquired. "What do you do, Tony? Are you just a bored rich man playing around in life?"

"I'm looking for something, I think."

"Where is it?"

"Zurich."

"*What* is it?" she asked.

Tony shook his head. He stood up, packed his bags, and put on his overcoat, giving the girl a kiss on the forehead. "I'll tell you what it is," he said at the doorway. "It's my nerve."

The following Monday, with a new passport and a new identity, Tony left for London on BOAC with another $100,000 worth of bonds. More cautious this time, with the feeling that he had passed a particularly painful initiation, a rite of passage into another style of life, he disguised himself in a long white wig and horn-rimmed glasses.

His London contact was a director of Barclay's Bank named Andrew Neville-Phillips, a large, round-faced man who asked him to come to his paneled private office.

"Sherry?" the ruddy-cheeked man asked him. "Mister . . . ?"

"Wondershire," Tony said. "William Wondershire. I will have some sherry. Thank you."

"What is your business, might I ask?" Neville-Phillips asked as he poured the sweet wine into cut-crystal glasses.

"I'm a textile manufacturer," Tony said, playing along. "There's a small plant here along the Thames that I'm interested in buying. I'd like to borrow sixty-five thousand dollars. I have collateral, of course."

"Of course," Neville-Phillips said, making a wry face. "You realize that this—ah—transaction is a bit unusual. As a director of the bank, I have a certain amount of discretion in situations like these. I think it would be best for all of us if I made the loan from my personal account."

"Very fine sherry," Tony said smoothly, unable to tell one sherry from another. "Whatever arrangements you want to make are fine with me. I hope that we can get our business completed today, if possible."

"That's hurried," Neville-Phillips told him, sitting down behind his huge desk. "I think I could make the necessary arrangements by about five."

"That would be fine with me. Should I come back here then?"

"No, no," Neville-Phillips said, shaking his jowls. "There's a nice little pub called the Ha'penny, two blocks from here. Why don't I meet you there? We can share a spot of whiskey, and get to know each other more informally."

"I'd be glad to," Tony said. "I'm not much of a socializer. But I've never been in a British pub."

He entered the Ha'penny shortly after five, carrying the bonds in a magazine. Neville-Phillips stood facing the door, leaning against the bar. Two glasses of scotch rested in front of him. He lifted one for the man he knew as Wondershire.

"Listen, I'm in a bit of a spot," Neville-Phillips said without preliminaries. "Everything is arranged. But I can't get my hands on the cash until I have proof of the bonds. Sorry about this; it's a complication I didn't foresee."

"What do you call proof?" Tony asked, downing the whiskey.

"Why, the bonds themselves."

Tony held up a finger, and ordered two more drinks. "Now that's quite a little risk, isn't it?" he said, neatly imitating Neville-Phillip's high voice. "My goodness chap, they're the same as money. Suppose you should decide that being a banker is too much of a chore for you, and you'd rather be lying in the sun in South America? Then what would I do with my pockets empty and my face covered with egg?"

"I realize that, my boy." Neville-Phillips looked worried. "But I'll tell you. My Bentley is parked outside. I'll give you the keys for it, and take a taxi to where I have to go. The car must be worth something to you."

"Not sixty-five thousand dollars."

Neville-Phillips puffed up his cheeks, looking like a blowfish. "Then I don't know what I'm going to do."

"Take me with you," Tony suggested.

"Quite impossible. My wealthy friend must remain *totally* anonymous. Nobody can know who he is."

"It puts me on the line," Tony said. "But I think I believe you, Neville-Phillips. I'll give you the bonds. But if you skip, we'll find you. And when we find you . . ." He smiled and put his index finger to the Englishman's temple. "Bang."

Neville-Phillips looked both startled and relieved. "You've helped me in a tight spot. I won't forget it."

Tony handed him the magazine. "Page sixty-five is worth a hundred grand. How long will you be, Andrew?"

"No more than ninety minutes." The banker's round face was wreathed in smiles. "I'll bring the money right back."

He handed Tony the keys to his car. "It's the silver one, right outside the door."

Tony waved them away. "You'll be back," he said with a shrug. "Or you won't be back. I don't like cars with the steering wheel on the wrong side."

Neville-Phillips finished his drink and hurried out with the magazine tucked securely under the elbow.

Tony ordered a pint of stout, and looked around the pub. It reminded him of a New York tavern trying to imitate a London tavern. He wasn't particularly interested. Nor was he especially intrigued with the tailored businessmen socking down ale and beer. But he was curious about a pretty young woman with long hair who sat at a small booth across the way, talking excitedly with a large-nosed man wearing a black and gray Harris tweed sport coat. Both had American accents.

Picking up his glass, Tony ambled over.

"Excuse me," he ventured, displaying his brightest smile. "I couldn't help overhearing your voices. You sound like home to me. I think that you're American. In fact, I think you're from New York. If I'm wrong, I'll buy both of you a drink. If I'm right, I'll do the same thing."

The couple looked up, pleased to find a fellow American.

"Sol Gordon from Brooklyn," the man said. "This is my wife, Phyllis. I guess you owe us a drink."

"Two of them," Tony said. "Tony Wondershire. I'm originally from Brooklyn myself. It's a long way from home."

"Sit down with us," Phyllis suggested.

Tony looked at the narrow bench. "Can't fit."

"I'll slide over," Sol said. "Phyllis's ass is too big."

Tony appraised the woman's figure as he sat down next to Sol. Her large breasts fought to get out of the open coat on her shoulders. If her hips were large, it appeared that her waist hardly measured anything at all. From the gold earrings and the diamonds on her fingers, it was apparent that the Gordons had plenty of money. What interested Tony more was her flawless complexion. The good-humored expression on her face, slightly tipsy, and her excited, glowing cheeks attracted him. Not until the barmaid brought their drinks did he begin to realize that Phyllis was a truly stunning beauty. Her slightly exotic features reminded him of a Semitic Elizabeth Taylor.

Sol, who chewed an expensive cigar, looked only like a prosperous New York Jew. But as the rug merchant talked and wisecracked, Tony found himself laughing with a man he felt could be a friend.

Neville-Phillips reappeared precisely at six thirty, looking winded and puffing up his cheeks. Excusing himself, Tony joined the banker at the long bar. Neville-Phillips tapped a satchel, grinning.

"It was a bit of a trip, but I made it. The bonds are good. No problem."

"Of course the bonds are good," Tony said raising an eyebrow. "Is the money good?"

He opened the satchel and looked inside. It was filled with loose bills.

"You certainly are a messy packer," he said.

"But it's all there," Neville-Phillips said. "Do you want to join me for dinner?"

"Some other night. I've met some old friends from Brooklyn."

"Then I'm off," Neville-Phillips said to him. "Hope to be doing business with you again, old chap."

Still puffing, he hurried out of the bar. Tony carried the satchel over to the booth and put it beneath the seat.

"You could have brought your friend over," Phyllis said with an exaggerated pout. "He could have sat down next to me."

"Not a chance," Tony said to her. "If Sol doesn't mind, that's a privilege I'm reserving for myself."

"If she gives me one day alone in Soho, you can sit next to her all night," Sol said.

"Give him the day," Tony said, moving over to squeeze next to Phyllis and taking her hand in mock seriousness. "Can I have this evening on the bench?"

"If I'm lying on it first." The woman blushed.

Tony and Sol shook with drunken laughter.

"I'm going to buy you dinner," Tony told them. "Anyplace in

London that you want to go. Anything in the world that you want to eat."

"We've got expensive tastes." Sol peered merrily over the long cigar.

"That's all right, because I've got a bag full of money," Tony said. "Right under that seat."

"Put it under my seat," Phyllis said. "Maybe it'll bring me luck."

"You think I'm kidding," Tony said to them. "There's sixty-five thousand dollars in that bag the fellow brought me."

"Let me see it," Phyllis squealed.

"Show it to her," Sol dared.

"I will," Tony said picking up the satchel and placing it on the table. "One look apiece, and that's all. Are you ready?"

Sol and Phyllis nodded "Yes." But Tony hesitated. There was too much risk in showing off. "I'm kidding," he said. "There's really nothing in here but French postcards."

Phyllis was disappointed. "I was looking forward to a real thrill."

"What the hell do you do for a living?" Sol asked, perplexed.

"I'm an electrical engineer. I just sold a building here."

"And I thought rug merchants were rich," Sol said. "You can buy us dinner, Tony boy."

"Dinner, hell," said Phyllis. "I want a Ferrari."

Carrying the money, they dined and drank and gambled at a private club until two in the morning, when Tony dropped them off at their hotel.

"I'm at Claridge's, Room eight twenty-four," Tony said. "Give me a call, and we'll go see the Queen tomorrow."

At ten in the morning, Tony was doing pushups on the hotel rug when Phyllis stepped out of the elevator wearing a pair of tight wool slacks and a fur coat. She hesitated briefly at the door, and then rapped her knuckles against it. One hazel eye peered at her from a narrow opening in the doorway and then the door opened wide enough for her to slip inside.

Tony wore a pair of gray cotton sweat pants. Sweat flecked the bare skin on his chest and rippled stomach.

"If you haven't ordered breakfast, I will," she said brightly. "Don't mind me. I'm just an American expatriate wandering around old England, looking up old friends. I don't suppose you like art museums?"

"Hate them, until I've finished my exercises and eaten something. Is Sol bringing up bagels?"

"Good ol' Sol has gone to Soho this morning," she said. "He woke up and asked so nicely that I just had to let him go. After all, when a man pays for twenty-one days in England, at least one of them should be alone, don't you think?"

Tony did twenty-five pushups, thinking about that.

"What's so hot in Soho?" he asked when he finished.

Phyllis had removed the fur coat, and stretched her small, lush figure out on the bed, squinting at him with a hand under her dark head. "Poor dear," she said. "He wants me to think that he's interested in those kinky British callgirls, so I'll be jealous of him and think he's a virile devil."

"Is he?"

"Certainly not," she said, grinning. "He's got me at home, and I think that's quite kinky enough for any man. Besides, good ol' Sol is a devoted father and a loving husband. He's a super guy, really. He'll just wander around looking at things, feeling a little bit free until it all gets to him and he comes running home to mommy like the other kids."

Tony was surprised. "I didn't know you had children," he said, lighting a cigarette.

"Four of the loveliest babies you've ever seen. Aged six to fifteen. Ah, the impassive electrical engineer looks surprised. Do you know how old I am, Tony?"

"I thought you were about twenty-five. But you couldn't be."

"Add ten years to your estimate and you've hit it on the head. I married Sol when I was twenty and he was thirty. I was a ballet dancer, and he was a rich rug merchant. So I had babies and he had scads of money. We've lived happily ever since."

There was no trace of sarcasm in her voice.

"I love him, Tony. That's the God's truth. I couldn't live with another man, ever. We have the only happy marriage that I know about. Kids, house, Temple every week, a big dog, and two furry cats. We travel every year. We don't owe any money, and we spend what we want. Sol might play around once in a while, but that's a man's business. He's good to me, and a good lover. Since I've married him, I've never been with another man, except for my father. That's not the same thing, is it?"

"No, it's not." Tony rested in a corner chair, as far away from her as possible. "Why don't you order bacon and eggs for both of us while I shower and get dressed? We'll go visit one of your museums and maybe watch them change the guard at the Queen's Palace."

"Lovely," she said, reflectively chewing on her bright red lips. "Here I spend all night thinking about this, and screw up the courage to come here wearing perfume all over my body and scanties underneath my slacks, and my reluctant engineer wants to take a shower. Do you want me to take a shower with you, Tony?"

Tony began to feel excited.

"Maybe you'd better not. You know what can happen when two people take a shower together."

"That's the idea, isn't it?" she asked. "I don't know how to do this, Tony. I can see that you're going to be no help at all. Is it because you like Sol so much, or is it because you don't like me enough? Usually, men are all over me."

"I'm not usual," Tony said. "I like Sol. He's a good guy. I think he's going to be a friend of mine."

"I think he is too. So am I. Look." She undid the buttons of the pale pink silk blouse. "I'm taking off my clothes for you. Am I being too forward?"

"You're making me nervous." Tony looked away as she removed the blouse and unsnapped the bikini bra that held her lovely breasts. "I don't know about married people. And I don't know why you're doing this."

"I'm not sure, myself." Phyllis rubbed the nipple of her right breast until it stood out hard and pointed. "I've got the hots for you, Brooklyn boy. When I saw you in the pub yesterday I decided I was going to screw you. But I've got to have some help. Are you such a reluctant dragon?"

"You don't know anything about me," Tony said. His hard cock poked up the front of the sweat pants like the center pole of a tent. "You don't know what I am or anything."

"I know that you're not an electrical engineer," she said. "I know what I think you are. I think that you're some kind of a criminal."

"Why do you think that?" Tony asked quietly.

"Because you carry around bags full of money. And because you are absolutely the most solitary person that I've ever met. You talk. You laugh. You drink scotch. You eat dinner. You might even fuck; I don't know about that. And you're someplace back there inside your eyes, looking out at everything. Making decisions. Taking chances. Testing yourself."

"That doesn't sound very nice."

"But you want me," Phyllis said. "I can feel that, Tony."

He remained immobile in the corner chair.

"Look," Phyllis said, unzipping her slacks and pulling them away from her legs. "Nice body, huh?"

"Yeah," Tony said, looking now, unable to take his eyes away from the dark foliage shadowed by the silk underpants between her legs.

"Now the scanties." Phyllis pulled them down. "Stand up and come over here to me, Tony. I want you, too."

"You're doing the asking."

Tony walked to the side of the bed, looking down at the lovely, naked woman who lay pink and smiling on the sheets.

"That's it, baby." She reached up and pulled the bow of the drawstring that held up the sweat pants. The gray material dropped down to the floor. Phyllis pushed herself up with one arm to a sitting position. With her right hand she encircled his cock, slowly and deliberately pumping it up and down. Resting her head against his abdomen, she licked the tip of his prick with her tongue, and then blew on it, sending tremors up Tony's back.

"Ummmmm," she said, opening her mouth and going down on him. The sensation made Tony's balls contract, and sent a hot flush over his chest. He held Phyllis's head very gently in both hands as she rolled her tongue around his cock, sucking it deeply into her throat and letting it slip back out again. By hurrying and then holding back, she brought him three times to the edge of climax. He could feel her hot saliva running down the shaft and an increasing, overpowering tremor running through her body.

"One of us is ready," she said weakly.

Turning away from him, on her knees with her buttocks toward him and her head pressed against the sheets, Phyllis reached back her hand and guided his cock into her slippery vagina, wriggling slowly against him.

"Reach around and take both of my breasts," she told him. "Like you're milking me."

Tony obeyed, bracing himself flat on both feet and sliding his cock as deeply as possible into her, withdrawing, sliding back again with increasing speed. The interior of her flesh felt as though electrical charges were shooting back and forth over the huge swollen end of his penis. A bright red flush spread over her back and buttocks and tears started to flow from her tightly closed eyes.

"Tell me you love me, Tony," she begged. "Tell me."

"Yes, I love you," he said, for the first time in thirteen years.

A huge taut bow released inside of him and he thought for a moment that he passed out before the sperm burst from his loins and was swallowed up by the powerful contractions of her body. The climax seemed to go on for many minutes, until he could stand no more and fell down beside her on the bed with his teeth chattering.

"Poor baby," Phyllis crooned, pulling his bald head to her breasts and placing a rosy nipple between his lips. "Tony needs somebody to love."

Then, after a while, he fell asleep.

He stayed in London, sightseeing with the Gordons, and making love to Phyllis each morning, for a week. The day they pushed on to Paris, he rolled the $65,000 between blueprints, which he placed in his attaché case, and returned to New York, sailing past the customs agents and certain that his existence was a charmed one. But he didn't plan to be a courier for the cash again, if he could help it.

Instead of blowing the $10,000 right away, he stashed it in the apartment and worked check schemes through the New England states. In four days, he amassed another $12,000 in preparation for a longer stay in Europe. When he returned to New York, the mild-mannered, white-haired old man in the bar at 50th and Broadway gave him $150,000 in bonds to take to Lisbon.

"You seem changed in some way," Jack Mace commented when Tony had the bonds deposited in his well-traveled attaché case. "More sure of yourself."

"I'm always sure of myself," Tony stated.

"Too sure, perhaps," Mace said. "Your travels through New England were very successful last week, my friend."

"I was resting in Aruba last week," Tony murmured.

"There are federal authorities who think differently. That white wig. It has become a trademark."

Tony frowned. "The bald head isn't a bad signal for banks these days, either."

"Why don't you restrict your activities to favors for me?" Mace suggested. "I like you, Tony. You are very dependable. My work has no risk."

"Everything has risk. I don't want to deliver milk in the morning."

"We test ourselves to challenge the gods. But the real challenges are inside," Mace said, smiling and tapping his chest.

"You're awfully sentimental," Tony commented. "Is one of your grandchildren having a bar mitzvah?"

The old man was quiet for a while. "I have a strong feeling," he said suddenly. "Be very careful on this trip. The Portuguese are a strange people."

"The people in Zurich are the worst. Don't put a hex on me, Jack."

"Do you have a gun?" Mace asked.

"I'd never carry one. That's a guaranteed way to get yourself killed."

"There are many ways to get oneself killed in our business," Mace said philosophically. "The surest way is to be careless."

"I get more careful all the time."

"Be most careful," instructed Mace with a touch of bite in his voice. "You'll be getting one hundred ten thousand for these bonds. Lots of money, Tony. You will make contact with Senhor Campos at the Baccarat Casino. Shortly thereafter, the pickup man, a Spaniard named Ramez, will appear at the Hilton and take the money. The casino is the safest place. Don't leave till you have to."

"And if I have to? Say it's necessary?"

"There is a check-off man in Lisbon," Mace said softly. "Only in an emergency. He's very expensive."

"He carries guns?"

"If you have to give the money to him, call the drugstore and leave a message for Spotty. Tell Spotty you can't return on time for the wedding, and send your regrets. Then stay away for a while. Do you have traveling money?"

"Some."

"Here is five thousand," Mace said to him. "The usual ten percent on your return."

"One question. Who is Spotty?"

"The little dog," Mace said with a trace of a smile. "Next week, he is going to be bred."

The ancient city of Lisbon sits on a series of hills on the westernmost point of land of the European continent, where the Tagus River snakes past the old villas and churches and widens into the beautiful Mar de Palla before entering the Atlantic. The port is always crowded with freighters, American warships, ocean liners, ferryboats, and the *fragatas* with their Phoenician silhouettes skipping over the waves on black hulls, under sepia-colored sails.

Near the Praça do Commercio, where King Jose I still rides proudly on a bronze horse, a fat Portuguese man named Julio Campos sat drinking wine in a cafe beside a garden, speaking urgently to a dark-skinned man as narrow as he himself was broad. Both men wore straw hats with broad brims, and white linen suits that could have been copied from gangster movies of the 1930s.

"This American comes to the casino tomorrow," Campos was saying. "I will get the bonds from him outside, by the pool. I'll try not to give him the money then, but I will probably have to.

In any case, when he departs, you and Umberto follow, and—eliminate him. Check him for the money. Allow him no contact with anyone."

"Who is his transfer?"

"I believe it is the Spaniard, Ramez," Campos said gravely.

"There are many risks in this." The dark-skinned man pensively stroked a large scar on his neck. Then he put on a pair of sunglasses and strode away down the bright sidewalk.

The yawning Portuguese customs agent looked at the passport picture of the blond American called Curtis Dall and then at the face of the man standing before him in a silk suit. He motioned him past. He hated monied Americans, especially these tall, handsome young men with fancy magazines and confident postures. But he supposed all Americans were born rich.

The man with the blond hair rode without speaking in a taxi to the Lisbon Hilton, where he told the reservations clerk that he wanted no maid service for two days, because he was expecting a lady for whom discretion was most important. He gave the man a $20 bill and the clerk smiled broadly, moving his head in almost violent affirmation.

The blond man allowed the bellboy to carry his single suitcase to the entrance of the room, where he tipped him heavily and went inside, bolting the door behind him. Removing the blond wig and sunglasses, he opened the suitcase; and from the folds of a clean shirt he removed a long screwdriver with a thick blade. Closing the shades, he took the screwdriver and pried the wooden window molding away from the wall, bending down and looking inside. As he expected, the molding concealed an inch-high space at the bottom of the window casement. Into this space he slid a tightly rolled tube of engraved government securities. With the tip of the screwdriver, he pushed the nails back into the wood, and stepped back to examine his work.

The varnish was slightly chipped, but unless somebody literally tore the room apart, the bonds were safe.

After showering and putting the wig back on his bald head he left the hotel and went to the Baccarat Casino, a sparkling white building set at the bottom of a steep green hill overlooking the Tagus.

In the casino's plush executive offices, Rocco Nucci, a tall, thin gangster from Brooklyn, swung his white patent-leather loafers off the top of the antique wormwood desk when the blond American gentleman came asking for Senhor Campos.

Although the man seemed vaguely familiar, Nucci was startled when Curtis Dall called him by his nickname—Fat Neck. Dall said he had business with Campos and would be waiting for him at the swimming pool in one hour.

When Dall left, Nucci made a telephone call, trying to find out what was going on. Campos was a difficult man to meet, and a dangerous man. Nucci didn't know quite who he was—only that he was a Portuguese and not part of the organization. No answer at the number he thought might give him some information. Many things happened at the casino, but it was his responsibility to make sure there was no trouble that would alert the authorities. Nucci paced his office, and decided that he'd better keep an eye on the pool himself.

At noon, Nucci stepped onto one of the balconies overlooking the courtyard. He saw Dall sitting with Campos. The American and the Portuguese were arguing about something. Campos appeared very tense; for a moment, he seemed about to draw a weapon. The swarthy Portuguese gangster in the white suit threw a roll of money to Dall, stood up, and walked away.

Fat Neck didn't like what was going on. He wanted the blond American out of his casino. As he came down the steps into the main gaming room, he saw two very thin strangers moving over the rugs in Dall's direction. At the entrance, the American broke into a run, and the two assassins sprinted after him.

Nucci didn't like this at all. Neither did the American.

Running up the hill away from the casino, Dall threw himself over a yellow stone fence, landing on his feet on the other side. He heard the click of the assassin's heels ringing on the stone sidewalk coming after him. He dashed up the narrow road that led to the top of the hill, where narrow two-story buildings housed a community of stores.

"Stop, bastard," one of the men called after him.

Dall put his head down and ran as fast as he could, puffing

hard as the hill rose more steeply. He nearly tumbled when he burst over the crest, but caught his footing and flew down the other side of the rise toward an open outdoor cafe. The tourists in the street looked after him curiously, but he thought with the part of his mind that wasn't fighting for more oxygen that he would look a lot stranger with blood pouring out of his back from the slug of a .38.

At the cafe he stopped running. Controlling his breath to a rasp, he ambled through the dining room to the kitchen and confronted the chef, who was preparing squid, cutting the black tentacles with a wide-bladed chopping knife. The chef stopped working at the sight of the puffing stranger in the sweaty suit, and put his hands protectively over the corpse of the squid.

"Yes?" he asked.

"I'll give you five hundred dollars American to hide me and get me safely downtown," Dall told the man. He took five $100 bills from his wallet. "You must hurry."

The chef decided quickly. He stuffed the money into a pocket behind the bloody white apron and led Dall to a shed in the yard behind the kitchen, where he hid him behind sacks of grain, potatoes, and onions. Dall listened for the sound of the chef chopping, and heard men speaking loudly and asking questions in Portuguese and Spanish. Then the voices disappeared and there was only the sound of the chef going about his chores.

Dall crept out of the shed and re-entered the kitchen. The busy cook nodded his head and motioned to him to follow. Dall removed the blond wig and hid it in his pocket. The chef pointed to the passenger seat of an old red Fiat pickup truck. Dall got in, watching the street for the assassins. Pulling up to the Hilton, he had $110,000 in one pocket, $3,500 remaining of his expense money in the other, and his life in his hands. But his feeling was one of tremendous exuberance. He was not dead.

In the privacy of his room he stripped off the soaked suit and shirt, noticing for the first time a long, bloody laceration on his right leg that extended from the knee almost to the ankle. He cleaned the wound as carefully as he could with alcohol, sent the filthy suit to room service, and dressed casually in a pair of plaid slacks and a white La Coste shirt. He telephoned the number of the Madrid contact and told the man who answered that he wanted somebody at his room immediately.

Shortly thereafter, as Dall was balancing the merits of a $15,000 profit versus the demerits of sudden death, the telephone rang. A scholarly voice with a faint Spanish accent announced that he would like to pay Senhor Dall a visit.

The courier who rapped at the door looked like the kind of European banker Dall had come to expect over the past few months. The slight man in the conservative gray British suit introduced himself as Miguel Ramez, and asked if Dall was enjoying his stay.

"Portugal is fine," Dall answered. "But the Lisbon contact tried to set me up this morning, and very nearly burned you on what's coming."

"Let me total it," the banker said politely. He counted quickly through the worn fifty- and hundred-dollar bills; all the money was there.

"Describe to me who caused you this inconvenience," Ramez requested.

"It was Campos at the casino," Dall said. "Do you know what he looks like?"

Ramez nodded.

"He didn't want to give me the money like it was agreed. When I left, he sent two of his assholes after me."

"Who?" Ramez asked softly.

"I don't know who," Dall said, peering out the window at the fishing boats. "Both of them were slight, dark-skinned men, wearing suits with wide lapels, cleats on their heels, and hats with big brims."

"That could be anyone," Ramez observed.

"Yeah, there are assholes everyplace," Dall agreed. "But I'll tell you this—I'm the mover for this part of the world, and I'm not coming back to Portugal. Nothing personal. This business may be important to you, but nothing is that important to me."

"I understand," Ramez said. "You will report this, I presume."

"I'll tell Jack Mace," said Dall. "I'll tell Raymond and I'll tell anybody else that I have to."

"It will all be taken care of, I promise," the banker said. "I'm sorry you are upset. You have done a good job. This will help."

The banker handed Dall five thousand American dollars. "Appreciation from outside," he said with the trace of a lisp. "If I were you, I would relax for a couple of weeks. Have a good time. Find some girls."

"Sure."

"As a man of the world, I would suggest Ibiza," the Spaniard told him. "The most action anywhere. The most beautiful women. The wildest parties."

"That's an idea," Dall said.

"It *is* a good idea," the Spaniard told Dall. "You will thank me for it forever."

Julio Campos sat drunkenly in the lamplight in the cafe near the *Praça do Commercio*, knowing that he was a hunted man. The American Treasury bonds were folded crookedly in the pocket of his sweaty white suit, worthless to him unless he could find someplace to cash them. His two accomplices had fled the country without him.

Campos wanted to run, too, but he knew that no place in Europe would be safe from the men who were looking for him. He felt almost resigned when the black Fiat stopped and two men got out and stood behind him.

"Senhor Campos." One of the men placed a hand on his shoulder. "You made a very serious mistake this morning. Do you have the bonds?"

"Please, sit down, have a drink," Campos said politely. "It tires the legs to be standing after a hot day."

"Please," the man said. "The bonds."

"They are worth a great deal," Campos said to him. "Perhaps they are worth my life, eh?"

"Your life is worth nothing without them," said the man. "We begin after they have been properly delivered."

Sighing deeply, Campos handed over the securities. "They are a little crumpled," he apologized. "But they are intact."

"Now you will please come with us."

With a great show of solicitude, the two men helped Senhor Campos into the rear seat of the little Fiat. They squeezed in on each side of him. Campos' fat knees were pushed uncomfortably together.

"I have a wife and seven children," Campos told the men in the car. "I have been of great service over the years. I have been helpful in many things. This was my only mistake, eh?"

"Yes," said the driver. "Everyone is entitled to one mistake."

"That's right." Campos spoke urgently. "I didn't realize the importance of the blond American. The Americans own everything. We Portuguese must stick together, eh?"

"Oh, we are all friends," the driver said to him. "Are you comfortable back there?"

"It is very tight," Campos said. "I am not a small man. Where are we going?"

"We are going to meet somebody," said one of the men next to Campos. "It is best you do not know where we are going."

"Then you're not going to kill me?" Campos asked hopefully.

"Kill you?" The man turned his large eyes on Campos' flushed face. "You will be punished, of course."

"Perhaps you could just beat me," Campos suggested. "I would prefer that none of the bones be broken."

The man smiled broadly at him. Campos smiled back. "The courier was only an American."

The Fiat came to a gentle stop at an ancient fishing wharf. The sky overhead was bright with stars. Campos heard the creak of the fishing boats as they rocked on the waves.

"Where are we going?" he asked the men who walked behind him.

"There is a boat at the end of the dock. The man who would speak with you is waiting there."

Campos breathed deeply of the air redolent of fish and saltwater. He had grown up near these docks, playing beside the shore, fishing in these same waters with his father and brothers. He felt comfortable. By concentrating on the shadows of the boats beside the wooden dock, he could almost ignore the three pairs of footsteps behind him. There was an unlighted *fragata* at anchor at the end of the wharf. Campos halted and turned to the men.

"This boat?" he asked.

"The man is on the deck," said the one who had driven.

"I see nobody on the boat," Campos said to him.

"Bend down, and look for him," the driver said.

"But there is nobody on the boat."

"You know who is on the boat," the driver said. "He is the companion of God."

"Then I am to die," Campos said.

"Do you wish to pray?" the driver asked him.

"I do," Campos said to him.

The driver motioned with an object in his hand that Campos knew was a gun. Wordlessly he turned his back, and dropped down on his knees at the end of the wharf, folding his hands under his double chin. The ancient dark boat slid forward on the water as though it wished to pull away from its ropes and take to the open seas. Campos closed his eyes, and thought of the bright sun of his childhood burning through the early morning mists and lighting the top of the waves. He thought of his wife, and of his children. He thought of the gardens of Lisbon, and for a moment remembered the blond American in the casino earlier that morning.

When the driver stepped forward, Campos said aloud, "Amen."

He fired five times into Campos' back with a Spanish .38-caliber automatic. The fat man's body fell forward half off the dock. The two other men pulled him back, and the man with the gun leaned over and fired a final shot into the base of Campos' skull.

Chapter 7

           The sunlight baked the skin on the tall man's head as he leaned over the railing of the Balearic Islands ferry and watched the cars drive onto the ship. The sky was unflawed porcelain blue. The Mediterranean was indigo and still, with a shimmering transparent haze between ocean and air. Ship bells rang; behind their brassy clang, the ship's diesel engine started to rumble. Young people with guitars and harmonicas played Spanish flamenco and American blues from the bleached sundeck. Tony watched the gulls trailing the ship through the harbor like an aerial wake, his own body feeling so unfettered that he might be able to join the birds floating on an updraft under the citrus sun.

           The white ferry moved very slowly, as though a magnet drew it toward its destination. The wind rose slightly now, tugging at the Spanish flag and fluttering the pants legs of the tall man perched on one leg at the front of the sundeck. His large eyes were fixed not at the water or the sky but upon the glittering haze in the distance between that seemed to grow more golden during the ship's leisurely progress.

           A fish three feet long broke the surface of the ocean only thirty feet from the leeward side of the ferry. It stared blindly for a split second at the immobile man on the deck before arching back under the water, cutting the sea the way a knife opens a ripe melon. At that signal, the startled man groped for a cigarette in the pocket of the broad-striped red-and-blue silk shirt. Lighting the cigarette, he let a puff of smoke float out between his even teeth; it trailed momentarily in the ship's wake before it disappeared.

151

What had drawn him out of his reverie was not the appearance of the fish but the fragile splash of its tail that sounded to him like the faint tinkle of ice in distant crystal goblets. The silence around him had been overwhelming, and he thought for a while that the engines had stopped, that the ferry moved of its own accord. But he felt the diesel engines' throb through the thin soles of his sandals. He heard a guitar playing a bright but very slowly moving melody from one of the farther decks, the notes vibrating with the deliberate skill of a trained musician exploring the limits of a new composition. The music was unknown to Tony, so unmistakably *foreign*, that the hairs stood up on his arms and a chill ran down his long back. Then the guitarist's fingers moved more quickly and he heard young people laughing as they stood on the tourist deck and began to dance.

The music whirled; the man on the sundeck smiled and soundlessly clapped his hands. Alone on the front of the ship, he danced with extraordinary agility, filled with the joy of being thousands of miles away from home, sailing to a new place that he knew would be vibrant with flowers and oranges. He danced because he had narrowly escaped death in Portugal, and because he was as wealthy as a pirate after plundering the Spanish Main.

"Say, there," a young woman's voice interrupted Tony's singular tarantella. "Pretty hot stuff for an old geezer."

"Eh?" Tony stopped and looked at the black-haired girl who had walked up behind him holding a tall glass of a clear beverage. "Geezer? Where did you learn such an old-fashioned word?"

"I speak English good, don't you say?" the girl asked him, shaking her long hair and smiling boldly at him. She looked like Sylvana Mangano. "My father, he spent many years in America working for the railroads. You dance good for such an old man."

"Ah, come on," Tony said. "Don't let this high forehead confuse you. I'm really only nineteen years old."

"Too young for me," the girl said. "Geezers are more interesting."

"Then I guess you'd better find somebody else. You are—let me guess—Italian. Am I right? I'm a Dago myself."

"From Naples. I go to Ibiza, to visit with my boyfriend. He is a Swede. He has blond curls all over his head. You like the music, don't you?"

"I like it fine," Tony said to her. "Where did you find that drink? Is there a bar on this boat?"

"Certainly. Even those of us who ride third-class are allowed to use it."

"Show me." He appraised her tanned legs and muscular buttocks in the cut-off blue jeans. "I'll buy you another one of those if you do it."

"I knew I'd find a rich American if I came into the first-class section," she told him when they were seated on the bench along the railing of the open bar. "You are Mr. Rockefeller. And I am Letizia. I am what Americans would call a filthy hippie. Do you like me?"

"Yes, I like you," Tony said, sipping at his gin and tonic. "Are you really one of those hippie chicks?"

"All young people are hippies in these times. I work in a dress shop, making clothes for the groovies. Pretty clothes you can have fun in. I drink gin. I smoke marijuana. And I screw the boys."

Tony choked on his drink.

"You do not like women to be so freely spoken?" she asked him. "You do not screw the girls? You are one of the policemen?"

Standing, Letizia tugged at his shirt. "Come with me to the station house. We are going to put you in jail and throw the keys away for the screwing. Come, Mr. Rockefeller-Policeman."

Tony laughed and stood up beside her, hanging his arms out on either side of his body. "I surrender. I'm unarmed."

"But a *dancing* policeman. No, perhaps he is one for the boys. I will find out."

Putting her face upwards towards his, she puckered her lips and pressed them against his cheek. Tony noticed that she smelled of a spicy perfume.

"No, Judge," she said, flinging herself back onto the bench and lifting the glass. "He is for the girls. It is because I am stoned that I am acting this way. Do you think I am a fool?"

"You're delightful."

Letizia shook her head vigorously from side to side. "I am the fool. It is the marijuana that has done this to me. Do you wish to go with me below decks to share a smoke?"

"Below decks? I thought the cabins were up here."

"All the moneybags think that. But the real people travel below the decks, down in the cellar. The dungeon. That is why I am filthy, too. There are no showers down there. And it is *hot*. Do you want to see?"

The Italian girl led Tony downstairs to the third-class section. Bunks hung from the walls of the compartment in five rows of three, barely large enough for a person to lie on his side.

"Do boys and girls sleep down here together?" Tony asked, incredulous.

"There is the screwing and the marijuana-smoking and the music-playing," she said. "It is fun."

"But it costs only a couple of dollars more to go first class," he explained. "I have a whole nice suite."

"*Only* to you is *everything* to me. So. I will take advantage of you, Mr. Rockefeller. I will use your shower."

"Absolutely. I'm not using the room anyway, it's so nice outside. Why don't you take your bags up to my room? I'll carry them for you."

"Yes. The canvas bag, the sleeping bag, the Alitalia bag, and the tennis racket. I will carry my purse and you will be my porter."

Tony loaded his arms with her luggage, and carried it upstairs to his stateroom.

"Here's a clean towel. The shower is there, and there's soap in it. Do you need anything else?"

"A little privacy."

"Yes, ma'am," Tony said to her, nodding. "When you get finished, I'll see you back up on the deck. How long does this trip take, anyway?"

"Twelve hours. It is the slowest ferry boat in the whole world."

When Tony returned to the bar, he paid more attention to the handsome young people walking in their bare feet, drinking wine from goatskins, and playing instruments. He naturally scorned hippies as low-class riffraff when he saw them from the other side of the tinted windows of limousines. In the Mediterranean they looked different, somehow. Even the long hair and whiskers on the men didn't offend him today.

Letizia, her face scrubbed, fresh white lipstick on her full mouth, and her hair wet and shining, sauntered up to him with her hips swaying.

"Now I am clean, Mr. Rockefeller. I am in the mood for screwing."

"You don't have to say that. I don't want anything, just because you used my shower."

"Come on, kid. Give me money for a bottle of wine. And don't keep the lady waiting."

Tony handed her a ten. Letizia bought two bottles of chilled vino blanco, put them in her straw purse, and motioned with her head for him to follow.

Clothing from her bag was scattered all over his stateroom. Letizia picked up a white blouse from the bed and draped it over the flight bag "I was trying to find something pretty. Then I looked in the mirror and thought, Why wrinkle something clean when I'll be taking it off right away anyway? So. Now we are taking off the clothes."

Letizia unzipped her cutoffs and kicked them off her feet. She pulled the short-sleeved blue jersey shirt over her head, and was nude.

"Come, come. Americans are so modest. Is it because you have gray hair down there? Is it bald too?"

She giggled and bounced up and down on the bed.

"Toot! Toot! Toot! All aboard what's getting aboard!"

"You're a crazy kid," said Tony, blushing. He removed his own clothing, feeling as though he was on display before a dispassionate judge of his masculinity. His manhood suffered from being on stage and hung head down like a slain snail.

Letizia smiled sweetly. "The screwing takes the big stiff one," she said. "Tell it to go up."

To his surprise, Tony's penis lengthened and stood erect. "How's that?"

"You are so clever."

Letizia spread her legs and reached out her hand for him.

"Now come on. Let's not waste any time."

They left the stateroom three hours later, Letizia bouncing

over the deck ahead of him and Tony with a serious crink in his back that made it painful to walk.

The sun was falling into the sea, and the clouds reflected lavender, scarlet, and orange when the ferry finally pulled into Ibiza's harbor. The purple hills were set with white houses that had a bluish cast in the twilight. Here and there, an electric light burned. Large bats tumbled overhead. A small crowd of people stood waiting, among them a tall, curly-haired blond boy who stood on tiptoes and shouted when he saw Letizia.

"See," she squealed to Tony, "There is my lover, Kurt. You must meet him."

She led Tony down the gangplank and pulled him over to the handsome youth, whom she embraced and kissed.

"Kurt, this is some rich American I found on the ferry boat. He let me use his shower. He is a nice man."

"How do you do?" Kurt said, taking a step forward. "I am very glad to meet you, sir. I thank you for taking care of Letizia."

"Don't worry about it." Tony was glad that the darkness covered his second blush of the day. "I'd do the same for any lady."

"Yes, thank you, Mr. Rockefeller," Letizia said, giving him a brief hug. "I hope you stay on the island for a while."

Tony took a cab down Ibiza's rough main street to the Don Quixote Hotel in the Figerettis section of town. It was the height of tourist season, and young men and women were camped out on the street corners. The hotel had no available rooms, until Tony handed the owner two $20 bills and a place was found for him.

Stashing his bags, he strode back onto the street to find something to eat.

"Tony. Tony Milano, hey, man," a voice called out to him from the shadows. Tony stopped rock-still and cautiously turned around to find Dick Whitman, an old friend from the States, sitting with a lovely blonde girl under an incongruous umbrella at a sidewalk cafe.

"I'll be damned," Tony said. "Dick, I haven't seen you for so long, I thought you were dead."

Whitman stroked his goatee, laughing aloud. "I saw that goddam bald head and that walk of yours, man, and I said to Inge here, I know that dude, that dude is a friend of mine from Brooklyn. Oh, wow! Wow, man. Come on and sit down with us. I got a whole huge fucking jug of sangria. What are you doing here, Tony?"

"You're growing hair like a lawn, Dick," Tony said, sitting down with them. "You got hair all over you. What's that beard? Is it real? What are you now, a hippie?"

Whitman slapped the palm of a hand against his head. "A hippie. Listen to that, honey. So square. Sure I'm a hippie, my man. I'm into something good. Real good. You know?"

"We'll talk about it."

"Hell, yes. You'll be interested in this. When did you get here? Where are you staying?"

"On the ferry boat. I'm checked in over at the Don Quixote."

"Like a tourist," Dick groaned. "How would it look—my friend staying here like a hick! I won't have it. I've got a villa here, up in the hills; you've got to come and bunk with me, man. I've got room. It's like a palace. Believe me."

"You're doing good?"

"Oh, so good. Listen, Tony," Whitman said, leaning over the table. "This island is *the place*. Everybody who lives here has something going. Guns. Gold. Drugs. Baby, there's a guy here who's into *birth-control* pills. Can you beat that?"

Tony shook his head. "Why the hell would anybody get into birth-control pills?"

"They're against the law," Whitman shouted. "Can you believe it? The broads here are desperate for the damn things. They'll pay ten bucks for a month's supply. The guy's making a million bucks. It's like he's a saint. Christ! Let me look at you. Inge, move that candle over. Look at that bastard—gold. Where did you get so much gold, Tony?"

"It's just a watch, for God's sake."

"A Patek Philippe, twelve and a half grand. Right? A diamond ring. Tony, that's a big diamond. How does a square Dago like you get a diamond like that? All right. Don't tell me. Save it. But I wanna know."

"What's this stuff I'm drinking?"

"Sangria. I told you. Wine and oranges and stuff. Good, huh?"

"Good. Give me another glass."

"You're goddam right. Costs nothing. Seventy-five cents for this whole jug. A scotch and soda, twenty-seven cents American. This is Paradise, Tony. I'm telling you. And the women— fantastic."

"I think I'm going to like it."

"You're going to *love* it. I'll show you the place. Top to bottom. And listen—there is this monster party tonight. You've got to come. You'll love it. You aren't too tired, are you?"

"Hell, no."

"I knew it. You're ready, right? Whatever it is, you'd better get ready for this place, Tony."

Whitman took Tony to his battered green Land Rover and, after picking up his bags at the hotel, he recklessly sped over the rutted road up a mountainside to his white stucco villa overlooking the sea. The house was sparsely decorated with rugs on the red tile floor and heavy Mediterranean furniture.

Whitman leaned back against the bright beaded cushion on a carved chair. "I'm into this fantastic dope thing," he said. "Everybody on this island smokes pot and hash. I pick up hash for ten bucks a kilo, and I turn it over for a thousand. I cleared a hundred thousand last year without even breathing hard. Can you get behind that?"

"I'm glad you're doing so well. It sounds pretty risky, though."

"No risk," Whitman exclaimed, jumping out of the chair and putting a Rolling Stones album on the stereo. "It's just smuggling. Nobody here cares about that. Were you checked coming off the boat?"

Tony shook his head.

"They just don't care," Dick said with a sweep of his hand. "I bring it in. Others bring it to the country where the buyer is. I'll let you in on it, Tony, 'cause you're an old pal."

"You don't have to do that," Tony protested.

Whitman pointed both index fingers at him. "You're right. Because you're into some monster thing. I've heard rumors, I can tell it just by looking at you. Yes I can. Now tell old Dick, because he's your old friend, and he needs to know."

158

"Just legit stuff," Tony said.

"Dick, honey, tell me how this looks," Inge said, coming into the living room. The twenty-three-year-old Swedish girl wore a short tan skirt printed with tropical birds cinched around her small waist, and nothing more. Her slight breasts jauntily jiggled as she walked. "Is this OK for the party?"

"It's pretty," Dick said, walking around her and examining the skirt. "It looks nice, baby. Is it new?"

"I bought it today." Clapping her hands together, Inge scampered out of the room.

Tony raised his wondering eyes to Dick's. "Is she going to the party like *that?*"

"What's wrong?" Whitman asked. "What is it, Tony?"

"I mean, with no top on like that?"

"You'll get used to that. This damn island is made of tits. French ones. German ones. Canadian ones. Scandinavian ones. American, Brazilian, even Nigerian. Tits from all over the world. You get so you don't even notice them anymore."

"*I'll* get that way?"

"Yeah," Whitman commented sadly. "It gets so nothing turns you on anymore." Reaching for a pottery plate, he picked up a small circle of fried dough. "You want one of these pancakes?"

"Pancakes? You eat pancakes before dinner?"

"Hash pancakes," Whitman explained. "I eat them all the time. They keep me stoned around the clock."

"You like to be stoned all the time?"

Whitman's eyes glistened in the candlelight. "Does a bear shit in the woods?"

The Land Rover carried them farther up the mountainside to a large sprawling villa on the top of a hill behind which stretched ancient Venetian graves. Below the villa, shining like fireflies, were the lights of the town. In the driveway in front of the house, several Land Rovers, a solitary white Jaguar, several MG convertibles, and a gleaming Cadillac. The front door of the house was open, spilling light and a loud tangle of music and voices.

Inside the huge living room by a landscaped interior garden, more than fifty incredibly beautiful men and women lounged on the carved furniture and stood about in small groups beside a profusion of paintings, by modern masters from Matisse to Modigliani. Interspersed among them were bright Picassos.

"Is this a museum?" Tony asked.

"Of a sort," Whitman told him. "I'll introduce you to the guy who did them."

He pointed out a short, round-bellied man who wore his gray hair combed down over his forehead like Julius Caesar. The host was dressed in a loose green blouse with printed flowers, soft beige slacks, and open toed sandals. Around his neck hung a huge hammered-gold pendant. Tony, who had dressed for the party in slacks, shirt, and short black kidskin boots felt like a farmer.

"Emil, Emil," Whitman called to the effeminate host. "I've got somebody here I want you to meet."

The man in the green blouse waved one of his thin arms in greeting and, excusing himself from the couple he spoke with, came to them with swaying hips and arms opened to embrace. He threw himself against Whitman, pulling his body close, and giving him a dry kiss on the cheek. He had a similar embrace for Inge, and a coy, appraising, closed-mouth smile for Tony.

"Welcome to my humble dwelling," he told Tony with a Dutch accent, extending his hand in the manner of a rich female socialite at a benefit ball.

Whitman introduced Tony to his host.

"Such a handsome fellow," Emil said, taking Tony's broad hand and holding it lightly. "What do you do, my new friend?"

Tony felt so intimidated by the man's seductive manner that he withdrew his hand and tucked it under an armpit for protection, stammering like a schoolboy. "I'm an importer . . . I mean an exporter. An engineer, I think."

The effeminate man looked at him oddly. "That's all right. We understand on the island."

"Emil is an art forger," Whitman pronounced. "Have you heard of him, Tony?"

"A forger," Tony said happily. "That's great."

Emil preened.

"There's been a whole book written about him," Whitman said. "And he's been written up in magazines all over the world. Do you remember?"

"I'm sorry. I don't read much."

"It's just this wild talent that I have," the round little man said modestly.

"You're the greatest art forger that ever lived," Whitman said. "See all these pictures on the walls, Tony? He did every damn one of them himself. And he sells them all over the world as the real thing. Twelve thousand, even twenty, a painting!"

"How do you do that?" Tony asked professionally.

Emil looked like an elf with a great secret. "You and I will talk together," he said. "My instincts tell me that you're somebody that I could talk shop with. But this is a party. What can I get for you to drink, Mr. Milano?"

"I'd like sangria, please."

"And to smoke?"

"I've got Marlboros."

"*Well*," Emil said, "there's anything here that you could possibly want. Dick keeps us well supplied. But watching your eyes, you devil, it's obvious to me what your interests are. I would say the ladies are very available. And if your taste should meander in any *other* direction, well—" He moved his head close to Tony's ear. "—anyone except that lean lad over there at the buffet. My house guest, you see."

The painter led Tony over to the bar and poured him a large glass of sangria.

"And there's champagne with dinner." The painter indicated the buffet table.

Covering the top of a massive table was a large silver bowl in which hundreds of peeled jumbo shrimp rested on a bed of ice. In two rows extending from the bowl were a hundred bright red lobsters. On either side were silver plates holding a profusion of hot and cold fish, soups, and casseroles. The plates, in turn, were encircled with smaller silver bowls containing a variety of sauces. Flanking the table were dozens of bottles of Spanish champagne, the chilled glass wet with condensation.

Beyond the table opened the villa's inner court, planted with tropical plants and flowers. In the center of the horseshoe described by the two back wings of the villa, a patio lit with colored lights was filled with dancing couples and graceful people sitting on chairs and the garden railings. A large group of men had gathered around the most beautiful woman Tony had ever seen, a languid creature nearly six feet tall with long blond hair and fine, small breasts under a transparent blouse.

Tony whistled. "Who is that?"

"The Baroness Von Pilant," Emil told him. "Competition for her favors is very intense, my friend."

"No doubt about that."

Emil took his hand again. "I like you, Tony. I'm glad to have you here and I hope you enjoy yourself. You're welcome at any time in my house. And we will talk later, about what I suspect are our mutual interests."

Carrying his glass, Tony found Dick and Inge out on the flagstone patio.

"That's some fine gentleman," Tony said, in something of a daze. "I normally don't like gay men but Emil seems different."

"He goes both ways, baby," Whitman told him. "Young girls flock to him because he's so generous. So he goes with girls sometimes and he's into boys, too. But he's a genius, if you know what I mean. So it's all right."

"If he did these paintings, he must be one. Why didn't you tell me what he did before we got here?"

"I figured you'd rather find out first hand," Dick said with a knowing smile. "I know what you're up to Tony. But what I can't figure out is how you're forging here in Europe."

"I'm just vacationing," Tony demurred.

Whitman laughed. "What do you think of the broads?"

"Not a dog in the place," Tony approved. "I never knew there were so many beautiful people in the world."

Tony's habitual reserve dissolved with the sangria and champagne. He floated in a sea of fantasy. The lights, music, lovely women in jewels, diaphanous transparent clothing, and rich perfumes, the self-assured men, and the incessant, bright conversations in half a dozen languages made him feel he had been transported into a technicolor dream. In it he found membership in a unique social order composed entirely of persons who were more than human beings, angels almost, the fictional creations of a baroque imagination.

Free, almost overpowering passion took possession of his body. The availability of the voluptuous skin and come-hither smiles brought him to such a state that even the farthest parts of his body felt openly sexual. His perceptions sharpened. He began to observe that not only couples but groups of three and four and five clustered together and floated *en masse* away from the others, into the further reaches of the villa.

"What's going on?" he asked Dick, who embraced Inge and another woman simultaneously. "Where do they go?"

"Little orgies," Dick leered. "Boys and girls, girls and girls, boys and boys—everybody all together. Back in the bedrooms. They're all set up. Interested?"

"Not me," Tony said. "I'm not into kinky scenes like that. Have you done it?"

"I've been there," Whitman said dreamily, pulling both women closely to him and leading them away.

"Dick—" Tony called after them, tempted to follow, but held where he stood by childhood Roman Catholic training.

Emil saw his new acquaintance reach after his friends and withdraw as they left him, sensing the feeling of abandonment that knocked Tony down from his euphoric cloud. Approaching Tony from behind, he took his elbow and drew him unprotesting into a corner of the patio overshadowed by the leaves of a high palm.

"Sometimes we are lonely in the midst of friends," Emil whispered. "Find yourself a companion, my friend. Which of these lovely creatures here interests you the most? Pick whom you want from my gallery. I guarantee she's yours."

"Just choose somebody?" the American asked with a feeling of wonder. "Don't they mind?"

"Somebody new and handsome is always interesting. And there is such a fragrance of money to you, Tony, that I am almost overwhelmed myself by temptation."

"Wait a minute, Emil—"

"Just joking, my friend. You're too old for my jaded tastes. But look—a gathering of four stunning beauties blooming there, by the orchids. Any one of them."

Tony's attention was directed to a quartet of two blonde and two dark-haired girls who were laughing and animatedly talking together. One of them, taller, fuller-bodied, more aggressive than the others, captured his fancy.

"The big blonde . . ." Tony said.

"Your captive." Emil joined the group of women and parted from them with the large blonde girl in tow.

"Tony, I would like you to meet Karin Nilsson, in my opinion the most beautiful girl in Sweden. Karin, my newest American possession." The tipsy art forger fluttered off once again to circulate among his guests.

Karin's body was exquisitely developed, almost Rubenesque in stature but without a trace of fat, a superbly conditioned form with athletic grace and classical proportions. The ends of her wide lips turned up with a mischievous grin, although her large blue eyes were serenely intelligent. She appeared both sensuous and chaste, passionate and reserved, impulsive and deliberate in her movements.

"What do you do for a living?" he asked her.

"I'm a stripper."

"Really?" Tony was startled. "I didn't think they had strippers in Sweden."

"They don't. I do it outside the country, to send my parents money. They are very poor. I enjoy it. It's a good living. I dance all over Europe." Karin shrugged. "It's a way to make good money. But whenever I can manage, I take a week or two off and come here. Ibiza is my spiritual home."

"Where do you stay?"

She cocked her head, looking at him seriously under long lashes. "Tonight, with you. Tomorrow, who knows? Perhaps with you again, if you are good enough."

"I hope I'm good enough."

"We'll see. Americans are very reserved."

The euphoric, hazy feeling moved through Tony again, making him feel giddy as he danced with Karin through the flowers of the garden to the slow Spanish music. The colored lights, which first appeared so definite in each color, spread and intermingled their auras, forming rainbows that refused to go away even when he closed his eyes. The back of Tony's neck seemed to be touched by a cool hand and his forehead and nose almost felt numb. Pleasant waves of warmth spread in his muscles. The notes from the Spanish guitars came very clearly, each specific, yet linked, in a way he had never heard music before.

Karin's flawless features obsessed him as he looked down at her head resting against his chest, and he was certain that she was the most beautiful woman in the world.

"I feel extraordinarily strange," he told her when his intoxicated brain could find the right word. "That Spanish champagne isn't like anything I've ever drunk before."

Karin kissed him on the mouth, licking the sensitive membrane of his lips, and kissed him on the chest before replying. "You are stoned. There is hashish in all of the dishes on the table."

"Go on!"

"That's true."

"So this is what it's like. I thought it was because you were so beautiful."

"That's true, too."

Tony giggled softly to himself. When he opened his eyes again, Karin was leaning against him, barely moving to the music. There was a bright half-moon overhead. The colored lights were extinguished and in their place, white candles shed a golden flickering light. The band was gone, and Frank Sinatra crooned from hidden speakers. They were alone on the patio. Inside the villa, nude men and women in candlelight moved from one to the other like children telling secrets.

"I don't believe this," Tony said, bringing Karin out of her trance. "Those people have taken all of their clothes off."

"It must be very late."

"I prefer couples only."

"Let's go, then. I do too."

Emil, fully dressed, but arm in arm with his young Italian boy, bade them farewell at the door.

"I'll meet you at the Plaza tomorrow," he told Tony.

Holding hands, Karin and Tony walked down the mountainside to Dick's darkened villa and chose a large bedroom that appeared to be unoccupied. In the warm night, with the moonlight pouring in through the open windows, in a silence as intense as Tony ever experienced, they explored each other and found it good.

Karin slept soundly when Tony awakened to the melodic chirping of a bird, clear-headed and comfortable despite the late night and his first experience with drugs. The air's heat told him it was nearly noon. Tony bathed in the green marble tub, sudsing his body with a great cake of yellow soap scented with oil of evergreen. He smiled at himself in the mirror.

The Plaza was a small restaurant with a large patio on Figerettis Street. Wearing a beret and a masculine shirt, Emil was sitting outside with an aperitif, picking at a plate of cold squid in vinegar. He greeted Tony effusively.

"You won't mind my being forward?" he asked. "Dick already came by my villa this morning. I determined that my initial intuitions are correct. You are also a forger. Dick tells me that you are perhaps the very best."

"I just write signatures, Emil."

"But one artist recognizes another. I just copy other painter's styles."

"You have a lot of ability."

"Not really—I could never do anything important of my own. But your compliments flatter me. Perhaps you would like to join me in my business?"

"How's that?"

"On a contract basis only. I had two partners who cheated me on my paintings. Now I don't have any partners, and I don't want any. I never leave the island these days, except to go to my home in England. I sell nothing by myself anymore, but I make deals with people I trust. I sold the paintings myself once, you know. In the United States especially, where I lived for years."

"How do you move your paintings now?"

"Those girls you saw at the party are part of it. These lovely creatures come from all over the world. When I find one I can trust, I give her one of the paintings, which she carries to someplace else. Acting as though she acquired the work by accident, perhaps found it in an attic or someplace, she takes it into a reputable art gallery and asks if it has any worth.

"Art dealers are thieves, Tony. Believe me. Not a one of them would scruple to let a bargain pass or refuse to swindle a young innocent. The dealers, you would say, fall right out of their socks. For a large Picasso, the dealer might offer the girl twelve thousand, knowing it is worth forty or fifty—if it were real, of course. She takes the money, keeps half, and sends the other half to me."

"Don't the girls swindle you too?"

"I have ways of finding out how much was paid. Sometimes they cheat; there is endless larceny in the human heart, my friend. But more often they are honest with me, because they want more of the paintings, and because I am a generous man. Always, they are more honest with me than my partners were." Emil's mouth turned down in a deep frown, and he looked nearly sixty years old.

"What are you interested in me for?" Tony inquired.

"I am sure that you could move pictures for me back in the United States. I have several exquisite pieces that I know Americans would love to have. I thought that with your contacts, you could make both of us a substantial, quick profit."

Tony thought about the offer for a while.

"I appreciate the opportunity very much, but I would rather not. I'm doing very well. I don't want to get into other people's business because it would complicate matters. But the idea is a good one. I know many people, wealthy people, who would pay very good money for any of those paintings if I just told them it was stolen. Rich people love to buy stolen objects they think are a bargain."

Emil raised his glass to him. "I respect your integrity. I will not ask you again."

"I hope you're not mad at me, Emil."

"Of course not. I told you, you are a friend at my house any time. I mean that sincerely."

Hiking back up the mountainside to Dick's villa, Tony could see across the Mediterranean all the way to the island of Formentera.

Tony and Dick stayed up late that night, Whitman puffing incessantly on a carved Moroccan hash pipe and Tony drinking sangria, mellow and *borracho*.

"I hear those people are killing each other back there in New York," Dick said, rolling a piece of hash into a small ball and dropping it into the pipe. "Do you know what's going on?"

"Business problems," Tony said to him. "I know all the guys, but I don't really know why all the killing is going on."

"What are you doing in with them now?" Dick asked him, holding a match to the drug and inhaling deeply. "You always ran alone."

"I always ran with *them*," Tony said reflectively. "But I was straight, you know? About a year and a half ago, I came over. But I belong to no one. The word all over is *'Il Tony non si tocca'*—Hands off Tony. I am not one of their *velites*."

"*Velites?*"

"Foot soldiers."

"Exactly what are you into, Tony?"

"My business, or my head?"

"What's more important to you?"

Tony thought about that. "What if I told you they are the same thing?"

"I'd say that was unusual, my man."

"How do I explain it? I was square my whole life. But I hung around the edges of the outfit. The guys were my friends. I grew up with them. That does something to your life. I made decent money. I didn't get into trouble. And I wasn't happy.

"When I came over, it was like a bridge that opened up in front of me—like a narrow rope bridge you would string up between these hills. On one side I was safe, because it was so empty. The other side was dangerous, but there were castles on it. I decided to walk over the bridge. One step at a time. Only once I put my foot on it I found out that I was flying along. I was that fellow who touched something and it turned to gold. I was born to be a forger. But I never actually got to the other side. The bridge gets longer and longer. It goes up higher and higher. I'm not afraid of falling anymore. But it's a long, long way down to the bottom. And I'll tell you something, Dick. I know in my heart that I'm not going to be able to keep on going forever. I know it because I can't get much higher."

Dick's head nodded, drowsily. "Man, I can't get much higher, either."

Tony continued. He was speaking mostly to himself.

"Last week I was adding up how much I made, and I've taken in more than a million dollars in the past eighteen months. That should make me a rich man. I *am* a rich man. I'm the richest man in the world. I have everything there is in the world. Gold. Jewels. Women. Limousines. Steak. Airplanes. The whole shot. The money runs through my fingers like sand. I don't get older or younger. The money flows out of my fingertips like ink from a pen.

"I'm not a Catholic anymore. But it's a God-given gift. I wonder, did God give me this talent so I would become a criminal? A thief? I don't know what the answer is to that. Maybe the devil gave it to me. But it doesn't feel like I'm doing any wrong."

"What's it feel like?" Dick asked, momentarily picking up the thread of his friend's conversation.

"It feels like a contest," Tony meditated. "Here I am on one side, by myself, going against all of the established parts of society—the banks, the police, the federal government, the FBI. I don't have a gun in my hand. All I have is what I was born with. My hands. My mind, whatever that's worth."

"It takes guts, too," Dick said, drifting away again.

"Not guts exactly. Something like that, though. It takes will. You have to make a decision to do it, and then make yourself do it, even if you're afraid. Maybe that's what it's all about. What do you think about that, Dick?"

Dick didn't answer, because he was sound asleep.

It never seemed to rain. Tony's skin baked dark brown. His eyebrows bleached blond. His eyes were always green. The sun circled the sky. The stars wheeled. The boats skittered across the blue water. The moon disappeared, and grew full.

"Tony. To-*ny.*"

"Yes, baby."

"I am *wrecked.* Dick and Inge and I. Where are you?"

"On the patio."

"Come here lover. I want to."

"Say, that's a pretty dress. You don't look wrecked."

"Look at my eyes, lover. Weird, huh? Come on. Take off those shorts."

"Are the others coming back?"

"I don't care. Off with them, horsey."

"Where we going to?"

"Shower. You're going to get soaped."

"Don't make it too cold."

"Good for you. Stir you up. Nice Tony."

"Say, that feels good. What's got into you?"

"Mmmmmmm. Now you rub the soap over me. All over me. Lots of big bubbles. Good Tony. Rub me there."

"There?"

"Make it real slippery. Put it *there* Tony."

"You're sure you want this?"

"I want this. Not so fast. Be careful. Now some more. O God. Some more, lover. It feels unbelievable. Oh. I'm going to die. Don't stop. I can feel you. Oh. Oh."

"You ever going to come out of that shower?"

"Course. I'm a fishy. Look at you. You're always ready. That's why I love you Tony. Now do it this way."

"Like this?"

"Wow. The way you Americans say."

"I'm still a little bit horney, I'd say."

"Incredible."

"Wake up, you little devil."

"Be careful. He's getting sore."

"I'll fix that."

Darkness. A large moth against the cypress wall, its shadow huge in the candle light.

"You finally woke up."

"Oh, yes, I have. I had the most amazing dreams. They were all cartoons."

"What the hell had gotten into you? What were all of you doing that turned you on like that?"

"Dick has some opium. We smoked it out on the boat. I felt like somebody put a bomb inside me."

"You ought to smoke that shit all the time. You're too much."

"Let's do it again, Tony."

"Christ, no. Dick! Dick, are you out there? Would you please come in here and help me take care of this broad?"

"I hear you Tony. Go to hell. I've got my own problems."

Laughter.

"I've got to be heading back to the States," Tony informed Dick a month later, as they rode in a small power boat back to Ibiza from a picnic on Formentera. "After this long, nobody will know me back in New York."

"You're crazy to leave this place, my man. Where are you ever going to find skies like these?"

"I've got to keep the money coming in." Tony moored the boat and helped Karin and Inge onto the dock. "But I want to get a place here of my own. Is there anything available?"

Dick grinned fondly at his big friend. "The big place up the hill next to Emil's is coming up. Want to live in style?"

"Why not? It'll be nice to have a villa of my own to come to when I visit the island. Would you check it out for me?"

Karin left Ibiza that day to make some bookings in France. The following morning, Tony flew to Madrid and took a plane back to New York. He moved checks and money orders throughout the Midwest for several weeks, made a fast trip to Paris with $100,000 of Treasury bonds, and went to Ibiza to look at the home. Not as elaborate as Emil's palatial lodgings, it contained a mammoth living room, three bedrooms, a large dining room, and a spacious veranda. He leased it for two years, paying the money in advance, and went to meet Karin in Copenhagen for a weekend.

By the summer of 1967, Tony was established in his Ibiza retreat as a footloose American of independent means. He kept his apartment in Manhattan, and had rented a small apartment in Sheepshead Bay, in which he seldom stayed, but where he kept checks, check-writing machines, typewriters, and other necessary equipment for his profession. His forging activities had expanded throughout Pennsylvania, Ohio, and Illinois, Nevada, and even into California, in addition to his established hunting grounds in the New England states and down the East Coast.

Phyllis, the wife of the rug merchant he met in London, became his lover in the United States. Their passionate affair continued without Sol's seeming to notice it. Karin was Tony's steady companion on the continent. He flew her in to meet him in Zurich, Paris, London, Copenhagen, Madrid, wherever his frequent trips to Europe carried him. Tony never carried less than $100,000 worth of bonds for Mace or other members of the crime syndicate, and sometimes as much as $500,000 in a single trip.

In late 1967, Tony made his first contact in Beirut, Lebanon, where he accidentally ran into Dick Whitman and Inge in the Saint George Hotel on the Mediterranean.

"This is one hell of a thing," Whitman exclaimed, dragging Tony to the bar with him. "It's like you're everyplace, my man. What in the hell are you doing here?"

"Just meeting somebody," Tony said to him.

"I'll tell you what I'm doing here," Dick said. "I've got some hash to pick up in Baalbek, up in the mountains. Inge and I are driving there today. Want to come along for the ride?"

"Not if it's dangerous," Tony said.

Whitman shook his thin hands back and forth. "The safest thing in the world. Come on along. It'll be a nice ride."

Whitman, Inge, and Tony got into the old rented American Ford. The day-long ride up steep inclines and over roads gnawed away by weather and rock slides finally brought them to a high, stony area strewn with boulders as large as houses.

As they passed beside a towering black stone, an Arab man wearing a long dark robe and a burnoose swung an ancient long rifle at them, keeping them captive with their hands raised in the air until two other Arab men also wearing desert garb came and ordered them released.

The shorter of the Arabs, a dark-skinned man with sinewy

172

muscles, directed them to a large adobe farmhouse. Next to the house was a shed guarded by a fourth man, carrying a machine gun.

The leader, Ali, spoke very little English, although he appeared to understand Dick's conversation. His speech was translated by a young Arab in Western dress, who had been educated in England. Ali and Dick had done business together many times before.

"I am glad that you have come and I welcome you and your friends to my home," Ali said through the translator. "Your trip has been long. Perhaps you would care for something to quench your thirst?"

Tony, who stood beside Dick outside the adobe house, noticed that Inge had inconspicuously returned to the car, away from the business of the men.

"My thirst would best be extinguished by fire, not waters," Dick said ceremoniously.

Ali spoke to the guard at the door of the hut, who went inside and returned with a heavy rectangular object wrapped in dirty burlap, about the size of a house brick. Ali put it on a piece of rough cut board which was supported at either end by rusted oil barrels, and unwrapped the burlap covering. Inside, an approximate kilo of pure hash, almost black under a surface layering of straw, looked to Tony like a package of so much damp clay. Ali took out a large, very sharp knife and pared one of the corners of the brick. Picking up a long-stemmed pipe of hammered silver, Ali squeezed the slivers of hash into a ball the size of a marble and dropped it into the bowl. He lit it with a wooden kitchen match, explosively intaking a powerful breath of smoke and air, letting the blue smoke slowly ease out of his lungs between his yellow teeth. Whitman followed suit.

Ali offered the pipe to Tony, who demurred.

"He doesn't smoke," Whitman told the Arab in slightly superior tones.

Ali went into the house and brought out a small stone cup containing a brownish liquor, which he handed to Tony. It tasted like a medicinal scotch, very strong and very bitter.

"What is the price for this straw?" Whitman asked Ali.

173

"Twenty-five dollars American for a brick," Ali told him.

"Such offal is worth no more than five dollars a brick," Whitman told him.

Ali appeared to get very angry. "It is the finest hash grown in these mountains. Mohammed himself has given it his blessings. You are an American fool. Twenty-three dollars a brick and not a penny less, on my honor."

Whitman sneered, picking up a sliver of hash between thumb and forefinger. "It contains rat droppings," he said. "It is entirely adulterated. It is worthless, and unwanted except by maniacs and fools. Seven-fifty, and I am being bankrupted by thieves."

Ali looked as though he had been poisoned, the way he tugged at the front of his robes.

"Hear me, Allah," he groaned. "I open my arms in hospitality to the mannerless Americans who come like dogs to my door. And for thanks, I am insulted in my pride and reputation. I swear that I will die before I accept anything less than twenty dollars a brick. I think I have gone mad."

"What?" Whitman cried, pierced to the heart. "Does this mean that my generous offer of nine dollars a brick has been thrown out along with eternal vows of friendship? Slay me now, for my creditors shall surely murder me later in my poverty."

Ali spun around on a heel and stomped away. At three yards he wheeled around, shaking a finger at Dick's head. "My grandfather's bones are crying in the wind. 'Such generosity is taken for being a fool,' his spirit cries. At eighteen dollars a brick the starving bellies of the children will bloat and burst asunder."

"Ten dollars—and not a penny more," Whitman shouted.

"Aghhhhh," Ali screamed, tearing at his burnoose. "Sixteen." He ran up to the hash; snatching it protectively from the board, he held it to his chest.

"Fifteen," Whitman roared, laughing and coughing and pounding himself on the leg.

"My friend," Ali said somberly, reaching out and taking Whitman by the hand. "One hundred bricks?"

Dick winked at Tony. "Only fifty bricks today."

"I thought we were discussing the hundred-brick price," Ali said, raising an eyebrow.

"I thought," Dick said, "we were discussing how much you would pay me to throw it away for you."

That made even the other three Arabs laugh.

From the trunk of the car, Whitman withdrew two large Second World War flight bags and put twenty-five bricks into each one. Paying Ali his money and giving each of the Arabs his warmest farewell, Whitman motioned Tony to get into the car and they drove away.

"I really like that fellow," Whitman said. "Arabs are the greatest people."

"Why did Inge have to stay in the car?"

"They're not much into broads," Whitman told him. "But Jews are different, baby." Turning around to receive a quick kiss from the Swedish girl, Whitman pressed on the accelerator and the car rattled and bounced down the mountain on the rutted road.

In their hotel room, Whitman and Inge packed their clothing amid and around the hash in the Army-green bags, doing such a bad job of concealing the bricks that Tony got nervous looking at it.

"How in the hell can you expect to take anything as obvious as that through customs?" he wondered.

"It looks pretty good to me," Dick said to him. "I'll carry one and you can carry one for me, Tony."

"No, no," Tony said. "I'm not touching it. I want nothing to do with that."

"Don't be so uptight," Whitman said. "What's there to worry about, Tony?"

Whitman refused to depart for the airport until it was nearly time for the plane to take off. When they arrived, he slipped a porter a five-dollar bill and handed him both the flight bags. The porter carried the bags to customs.

The customs inspector took one of the bags, a look of surprise on his face when he felt how heavy it was.

"Good-bye, baby," Tony said softly, walking away from Dick and Inge and passing alone through customs and onto the airplane.

175

But a few minutes later, Whitman and Inge climbed aboard and sat across the aisle from him. Whitman rubbed his fingers together. "You've just got to grease the way," he said. "It's easy, Tony."

The plane took them to Copenhagen, where for $1,200 Dick purchased a battered, five-year-old Volkswagen. In the back of a rented garage, Inge cut the stitching of the car's seats and they laid the hash inside, replacing the springs with the bricks of drug and covering them with foam rubber. Finally, very carefully, Inge restitched the seams of the seats.

Whitman explained to Tony that the VW would be shipped to New York on a Moore-McCormack steamship, which Inge would meet in three weeks.

In October, when they met again in Ibiza, Dick told him that he had cleared more than $50,000 on the deal, finally giving away the VW after unstitching the seats and removing the hash.

"It's a hell of a good way to make money," Whitman said.

"It's even a better way to go to jail," Tony said to him. "Dick, I think you gotta be nuts."

For dinner that night, he invited Dick and Inge, Emil, and dozens of other island regulars who had become his friends. His villa was decorated with colored lights. The heavy Mediterranean furniture was polished to a hard shine by the two maids and the mosaic tiles on the floors were cleaned and waxed. Tony cooked a huge Italian feast himself. He invited fifty people to the dinner, and more than a hundred showed up.

As he relaxed and enjoyed himself in Ibiza's serene climate, he had no idea that in New York, the FBI finally had put together enough information to begin moving against him and had sought warrants charging him with interstate crimes in checks, credit cards, and traveler's checks.

The dinner was a huge success.

Chapter 8

Two FBI agents rang the doorbell of Sol and Phyllis Gordon's Brooklyn home, trying to run down the trail of the forger named Peter Milano. Politely, they showed Sol their identification, and he invited them into the living room.

"We hate to bother you, Mr. Gordon," said one of the short-haired agents in a conservative dark suit. "We're trying to locate a man we suspect has been passing bad checks in Connecticut and other parts of the country. I would like you to look at this picture, and tell me if you recognize the man in it."

He handed Gordon a grainy black-and-white eight-by-ten blowup of a picture taken by a hidden 16mm. camera. Despite the picture's fuzziness, it clearly showed the man Sol knew as Tony Milano.

"Yes, I know the man," Sol said, shaken. "But he's an electrical engineer."

"He may use that as a cover identity," said the second agent. "But we think that he's one of the most active check-passers in the country. Do you know where we could find him?"

Sol thought for a moment. "No. I don't see him very much," he said, hating the feeling of lying to the FBI. "Sometimes he calls, or stops by for a visit, but we never know when."

"How long have you known this man?" the first agent asked him. "Did you know that he was involved in criminal activities?"

"No, I had no idea," Sol said. "I don't know if I believe it, either. He's a very nice man, very well-mannered and polite. He has been a good friend to us. He even came to my son's bar mitzvah not long ago. I can't believe he's been breaking the law."

"There may be a number of things that you don't know about," the second agent said. "I don't know how to tell you this, Mr. Gordon, but we have information that this man is having an affair with your wife."

"I don't believe that," Sol exclaimed, visibly shocked. "Phyllis would never do anything like that. He's more my friend than hers, anyway."

"You may think so," the first agent told him. "But you've been lied to. We found out about Mrs. Gordon through two men who were arrested by the Connecticut police last week for passing bad checks of their own. They had been taught how to do it by this Milano fellow. They provided the police with your wife's name and said she is Milano's girlfriend. I don't think there's much doubt about it."

"This is incredible," Gordon said to them. "It couldn't possibly be true. We have four children, a happy marriage. I don't believe it."

"You ought to believe it," the second agent said, speaking with slow, heavy emphasis. "Here is that professional criminal having an affair with your wife. Don't you want to give us his address now?"

"No, I don't," Gordon said. "I don't have it. I don't believe you. I don't understand why you come here into my house, and say these things to me."

"Where is your wife?" the agent asked him. "We ought to ask her about what the truth is."

"She's at the grocery store."

"We'll wait," the first agent said.

"No you won't." Gordon stood up. "No sir. I don't like the way you're talking to me and I don't want you dirtying up Phyllis with your crazy charges. I want to ask you to get out of my house."

"You should watch the way you talk to the FBI," the second agent said.

"I pay my taxes. I'm an honest man. I want you to get out of my house. I don't know anything about what you're talking about. And I don't believe a word of what you have to say. Leave now."

"All right," the first agent said, standing. "It's your funeral." For the first time, he smiled. "That's only a figure of speech," he said, putting on his coat. "If you change your mind, please call me at this number."

He handed Gordon a white business card imprinted with the FBI seal. "Call anytime. If we're not there, we'll get right back to you."

When they had left, Gordon sat in the living room trembling, rising when he heard Phyllis's key in the lock. He helped her bring in the groceries from the car to the kitchen, and then turned to confront her.

"Phyllis, I have to talk to you." There was a quaver in his voice.

"What's the matter, Sol?"

"The FBI was just here, looking for Tony Milano."

"Whatever for?" she asked, puzzled. "Is he in trouble of some kind?"

"They say that he's a professional check-forger."

"I don't believe it," she said positively.

"Phyllis, they said something else."

"There's a funny look on your face. What is it?"

"They said you and he are lovers."

"Are what?"

Phyllis sat down in her coat on a kitchen chair. "They said that we are *what*?"

"Lovers. Screwing each other. They told me it's been going on for a long time."

"What a terrible thing to say," she snapped. "Do you believe them, Sol?"

"I don't know what to believe. Maybe it's all true."

"What did they want from you?"

"They wanted to know where they could find Tony. They said I should tell them, because of what you and he have been doing together."

"Did you give them his address?"

"No, I wanted to find out from you if what they said was true. I wouldn't turn him over to the police anyway."

Phyllis was white-faced, sick with worry. "We should tell
Tony about this. We ought to find out what the real truth is. I'll
call him."

"What if the phones are tapped?"

"I don't know," she said. "Could they be tapped already?"

Tony got up from the Saturday-afternoon college football
game to answer the ringing telephone.

"This is Phyllis Gordon," he heard her announce in a constricted voice. "Tony, the FBI was here this morning, looking
for you. They told Sol that you're a check-forger and they have
warrants for your arrest. They also told him that you and I have
been having an affair to get him to talk."

"Did he tell them where I am?" Tony asked.

"No."

"Did you admit the affair?"

"No."

"Good. Let me talk to Sol."

Tony listened to the sounds of a cheering crowd as one of the
teams made a touchdown.

"Hello?"

"Hello, Sol. This is Tony. Phyllis just told me about the FBI.
She said the agents told you she and I were having an affair."

"That's what they said."

"Tell me *exactly* what they said."

"They said they got Phyllis's name from some check criminals who were arrested in Connecticut. They told the police she
is your mistress. The FBI said you and Phyllis have been having an affair for a long time."

"Do you believe that kind of crap?" Tony asked him.

"I'm not sure."

"Do you believe that that wonderful wife of yours is having a
thing with an old bald-headed bastard like me? Do you think
that she's that kind of a woman, Sol?"

"I never thought so, no."

"Because you're right, Sol. Not a bit of it's true. They just told
you that to find out where I am. You didn't tell them, did you?"

By turning his head, Tony could see the bright red and white
jerseys of the football players running into each other on the

color TV. From across the room, the players were abstract scarlet and pale forms that streaked and collided against a green background. The crowd's cheers and the announcer's forced enthusiasm seemed to be totally devoid of sense or content.

"No, I didn't say anything," Sol's voice came thinly over the line.

"I'm glad of that," Tony said sincerely. "You're a very good friend, Sol."

"But what about the rest of it?" Sol asked him. "They said you were a check-forger. Is that true? Is that why they want you?"

Tony hesitated before replying. A scarlet jersey was dashing across the green field. It was cut down by a streak of white. He heard a pop, as though something had broken.

"I have to tell you the truth," Tony admitted. "They are right. I'm not an engineer. I am a forger."

"Tony, I wish that wasn't true," Sol's voice was anguished.

"I'm sorry. I'm really sorry," Tony said. "But that's true."

"I don't know what to do," Sol said. "We can't have you coming here anymore. There are the kids that I have to think about."

"I understand that," Tony said sadly.

"I still like you Tony, even knowing the truth. But the kids— what would they think? I have to raise them the right way."

"Sure," Tony said. "I won't come by anymore, Sol. I won't embarrass you and your family."

"I wish you'd told me before."

"Maybe I should have," Tony said. "Believe me, I'm sorry, Sol."

The line went dead. Tony returned to the television set. The football game didn't make the slightest bit of sense to him. He turned the dial to a news interview on another channel. Nothing made any sense at all.

Deciding that New York City was too hot, Tony fled to New Orleans to forge checks and await the delivery of two hundred blank money orders from an East Coast contact. He checked into a hotel under the name of Peter

Mitchell. Feeling pressured and pursued, he drank as much as he worked.

On the third day, sipping scotch in the hotel cocktail lounge, he heard the bellboy come through calling: "Paging Peter Mitchell. Paging Peter Mitchell."

He was signing the bar tab with the name Peter Mitchell. The sound of the name meant nothing to him, except an irritating cry breaking through his concentration. The bellboy came through half an hour later calling again for Peter Mitchell, and for a third time shortly after that.

"Goddammit," Tony said angrily to the bartender. "I wish that guy would answer the page."

The bartender hesitated for a very long while, looking at him strangely.

"What's the matter with you?" Tony asked belligerently.

"What's the matter with *you?*" the bartender demanded suspiciously. "Ain't you Peter Mitchell?"

There was a darkness in his mind. Tony's first thought was a question about who he was supposed to be. For a brief moment he couldn't even recall his real name. The bartender saw the angry face of the bald man turn into the frightened features of a child lost in the woods and quickly transform into a smiling, sophisticated gentleman filled with reassurances.

"I've been so worried about my business that I just wasn't listening," Tony said to him. "Excuse me. I was a million miles away."

Nodding his head apologetically, Tony handed the bartender a twenty-dollar tip and ducked out of the room. Waiting for him at the desk was the package containing the two hundred unsigned money orders worth $20,000. In his room he filled them in, and began cashing them all over New Orleans, waiting for the roof to fall in.

When it came on the following day, it took an entirely unexpected form. The hotel fell in *under* him.

At 6:00 A.M., sitting at his desk signing the money orders, the foundation pilings of the hotel—weakened by years of truck traffic on the street—let go. Tony thought New Orleans had been hit by an earthquake. His bed slid all the way across the room, and the chair he sat on followed as the hotel lurched sideways at a crazy angle. The check-writing machine and hundreds of checks followed.

Panicked, Tony scrambled over the tilted floor, stuffing checks and equipment into his suitcases. Going to the door with the suitcases to make a quick departure, he found the door frame had been bent out of shape. He was locked inside. Tony was positive his life depended on getting out of the room as quickly as possible. He picked up the chair on the floor and threw it out the picture window. Still in his undershorts, suitcases dragging behind, he crawled out onto a ledge that ran around the building.

Tony's escape was halted by the hysterical screaming of a woman in an adjacent room who stood in nightgown and hair curlers madly beating on her door. Tony heaved one of his suitcases through the woman's window, went inside, and led her outside to the broad ledge.

It was obvious that he was the only person with enough presence of mind to climb outside for safety rather than batter fruitlessly against the wedged hotel doors. Feeling ridiculous in his undershorts but caught up with excitement, Tony rescued six people from their rooms, and led them in a line to a New Orleans Fire Department ladder, which they climbed down to safety.

The street was packed with policemen and firemen, hotel guests in their nightclothes, news reporters, and television cameras. The cameras surrounded Tony, and the reporters zeroed in on him for an interview. Tony covered his face with a hand, mumbled that he didn't know anything, and pushed away through the newsmen.

The guests were taken to the Sheraton Hotel. They were trailed to the new lodgings by a second army of reporters. Tony fled to his new room, wondering how many FBI agents around the country would see his bald head on the evening news and come roaring after him.

The knock at the door didn't help his confidence. The man who wanted to come in identified himself as a lawyer for the hotel. He was trying to make settlements and get signed releases from hotel guests before they filed suit.

"There are a lot of people calling attorneys and suing," he

said. "I'd be glad to make an immediate settlement for any inconvenience. "If we give you your room for nothing, will you sign a release?"

"Definitely," Tony said. "Hand me a pen."

He began signing his name "Peter Milano" before he realized what he was doing. Turning the "Mil" in Milano into "Mit" for Mitchell he signed the release and pushed the lawyer out of his room.

That day he flew out of New Orleans for Miami. Deep-sea fishing, yellow sand, and Miami's beautiful young girls would straighten him out, he hoped.

Tony checked into a hotel as Peter Watson, depositing $2,000 cash to cover his stay. He was put off immediately by the irresponsible kids, the pretty young men and women who had come down to the sea in search of one another. He couldn't get over the openness with which they smoked marijuana and dealt in pills, LSD, hash, and other drugs. He felt his role as a wealthy businessman was being compromised by their activities.

After partying in the hotel bars up and down the Miami Beach strip, Tony returned at 3:00 A.M. to the hotel and found an urgent message in his box from New York. Coded, it said that the delivery of two hundred additional money orders had been detained indefinitely.

"Listen, I've got to send an important telegram," Tony said to the desk clerk. "Can you help me?"

"This switchboard closes at midnight," the clerk said smugly.

"You're telling me that I can't make any kind of a call from this hotel until the morning?" Tony asked. "You're nuts."

"Screw yourself," the clerk said. "I just work here."

"Listen you asshole. Open up that switchboard," Tony demanded. "You know how to run it. All you have to do is move the jacks."

The clerk straightened up from his newspaper and sneered. "Who the hell are you?"

Tony exploded. "I'm going to break your goddam head in two seconds if you don't open that switchboard! I'm going to destroy you, you sonofabitch."

"Help, Angie, help!" the clerk shouted to a security guard at the entrance. "This guy is causing trouble."

The security guard was an ancient retired policeman who hadn't seen action of any kind for more than a decade. Hobbling to Tony, the old man tried to throw a hammer lock on him.

Tony shoved him away. "I'm going to take that gun from you and shove it up your ass and pull the trigger," he ranted.

The guard backed away. Tony stomped out of the hotel, searching for a pay telephone so he could send his telegram to New York.

Within a block, a police car sped up with its light flashing. The two patrolmen got out and approached Tony on the sidewalk.

"OK, buddy," a policeman said. "What are you up to? What are you trying to do at that hotel?"

Tony turned on the charm. "I'll tell you exactly what's happening. I'm a guest at the hotel down the block. I've got an emergency telegram to send to New York, and the clerk told me that I can't make any calls from the hotel from now until tomorrow morning. I'm very angry about it. I've got a two-thousand-dollar cash deposit with that place, and I think I should be treated with some respect."

"We'll check out your story, sir," one policeman said.

They gave Tony a ride back to the hotel. The clerk smirked when he saw the bald man enter with the policemen.

"This man says that he's a guest here, and he has a two-thousand-dollar deposit with you," one policeman said. "Is that true?"

"How the hell would I know?"

"Check it," the policeman suggested evenly.

Sullenly, the clerk looked at the records. "That's right," he admitted.

"And you won't let him use a telephone?" The policeman shook his head in wonder. "Are you nuts, mister?"

"I made a mistake, that's all," the clerk whined.

"I'll say you made a mistake," Tony said. "I want my deposit back right now, and I want to get the hell out of this hotel."

"I can't give your money back," the clerk said.

Tony's fury returned. "Are you planning to steal my money now, you bastard?"

"Calm down," a cop suggested. "Why can't you give him his money back?"

"It's in the safe. Only the manager can do that."

Tony pounded his fist on the counter. "What kind of place is this?"

"You're right to complain," one of the policeman said soothingly. "But do me a favor and do yourself a favor, and wait until tomorrow to get your money back. You're fighting a losing battle. He doesn't have the money, and we can't force him to open the safe."

"OK," Tony agreed.

Getting his bags, Tony rode a taxi into downtown Miami, where he sent his telegram to New York. Tony noticed that a police car followed his cab from the Western Union Office to the Newport Hotel. At the entrance, he approached the police car and leaned in to address the cop at the wheel.

"What can I do for you guys?" he asked.

"Are you Mr. Watson?" the policeman asked him.

"Yeah."

"We were informed of your troubles and were just making sure everything was all right," the policeman said. "We want to see that you're taken care of."

"If I can buy you a drink sometime in thanks, let me know," Tony said.

Courteously, the policemen helped carry Tony's bags into the hotel lobby. The doorman and bellboys were suitably impressed. Tony deposited $3,000 in cash on deposit at the Newport, and at the room tipped the bellboy $30 to get him a bottle of brandy and a bottle of Chivas Regal. He had one drink before he fell asleep as the sun rose over the ocean.

Tony vowed to enjoy himself no matter what it cost. Tipping only with tens and twenties, he set out to make himself king of the hotel. Services were lavished by employees scrambling after the flurry of money: His suite was a profusion of flowers; fresh ice appeared hourly; the chefs prepared special meals; his shirts were perfectly ironed, the rooms spotlessly cleaned.

Two nights later, Tony was sitting in the Newport's cocktail lounge with two gangster friends from New York, Al and Morris, men instrumental in the acquisition of bonds and transferable securities. Tony bought drinks for the entire room for more than two hours, and handed the guitarist a hundred-dollar bill, requesting the musician play his favorite songs. Tony's confusions began to evaporate as he basked in the admiration of the tourists.

But at a nearby table, two athletic young men were offended by the flashy show of prosperity. They showed their appreciation for the five drinks by a stream of increasingly loud insults.

"Who the hell does that bald creep think he is—King Farouk?" the long-haired sun-bleached young man asked his friend.

His dark-haired friend had the large raw-boned frame of a college football tackle. "He's buying the whole joint because he's some kind of freak," he said, making sure Tony caught the words.

"I think that people who throw their money around like that are a piece of shit," said the blond youth.

"Listen to that," Al said to Tony. "You going to put up with that stuff?"

"I'm ignoring it," Tony said. "I'm not going to let them bring me down."

"I understand old bastards like that spend money because they can't get it up anymore," the raw-boned youth said, turning to look at Tony.

"Probably a tourist." His friend had a smirk on his face. "Has to be a Jew dress manufacturer."

Tony sat rigid in his chair, trying to ignore their taunts.

The tall youth turned around and spoke directly to him. "Listen, you old fuck," he jibed, "why don't you just leave us young guys in here with the broads?"

Tony smiled, as though he had been paid a warm compliment. "Eh?" he asked. "I'm sorry. I have a little hearing problem. What was that again?"

Leaning forward, with his hands on his knees, the young man moved his face close to Tony's and began the insult again.

"Listen, you old fuck," he enunciated clearly and loudly, "why don't you—"

Tony's right fist swung in an uppercut that landed under the man's jaw. The blow brought him out of his chair, back over the table, crashing to the floor. Tony picked up his chair and swung it against the blond youth, who staggered sideways into another table, and fell to the ground in a cascade of broken glass. Screams and shouts electrified the room.

Al and Morris moved ahead of Tony like bodyguards with their hands under their suit jackets on the handles of their guns, motioning for onlookers to stay out of their way. The bartenders ran forward holding bat handles.

"What's the trouble, sir?" they asked Tony.

"Nothing," Tony said. "You got two wise guys here. They're trying to hassle me."

Four bouncers ran into the room. They seized the two young men, who were painfully picking themselves up from the floor, and dragged them out of the lounge.

"God, I'm sorry about this," the hotel manager said to Tony. "I personally apologize for the way you were treated."

"Forget it," Tony said. "I can take care of my own problems."

Tony's moods were unstable, and he alternated between depression and recklessness. The following night in the Seven Seas Lounge, Tony ran into a Philadelphia gangster he knew named Mario Ilano. They took a table on the left side of the horseshoe bar.

At a nearby table, a bleached-blonde prostitute with the drawn but still attractive face of an aging model began to argue with her dapper pimp, a slight fellow at least ten years her junior.

Without warning, the woman stood up, knocking over the little cocktail table, and pulled a tiny .22 pistol out of her sequined purse. The barrel of the gun, aimed at her pimp's head, also stared directly into Tony's startled eyes. He saw a dagger of fire jump from the gun she fired. Shoving Mario to the rug, Tony lunged over the tables at the homicidal whore as she pulled the trigger again and again, the weapon popping in a deadly salute. Tony slapped the gun out of her hand and whacked her to the floor. A dozen waiters and bartenders descended upon the woman and her pimp like dogs on a fox, pummeling them into unconsciousness.

Tony helped Mario to his feet, giving him a shot of brandy. The manager hovered at his elbow.

"What are you going to do about that dame?" Tony asked. "If you're going to call the cops, let me know, so we can get out of here."

"No, we don't call the cops here," the manager said. "We'll handle it our own way."

"What kind of joint is this?" Tony asked. "Is this a bust-out joint? I thought it was a fancy restaurant."

The manager wrung his hands. "We seldom have this," he said.

"*Minchia!*" Tony said. "Once is too often."

"You saved somebody's life," the manager said. "Dinner is on me. Anything you want is yours."

"Anything but peace and quiet," Tony said.

Tony left Miami Beach, picked up a quarter of a million dollars' worth of bonds, and went to Copenhagen to cash them and meet Karin.

"But you are so jumpy, Tony," Karin complained to him after dinner. "What is the matter with you? Why don't we go to Ibiza for a couple of weeks to calm down your nerves?"

"Something bad is coming down the road for me," Tony said. His face had aged; in the candlelight of the Danish restaurant, he could have been a man in his fifties. Karin picked up one of his hands.

"I have never asked you your business," she said, kissing his fingers. "Is there anything about it you want to tell me?"

"There's nothing I can tell you. Too much information would be dangerous for you."

"I can keep secrets."

"Nobody can keep secrets," he said. "Secrets are the interesting stories that pass from person to person. Private information is what has no other place to go."

"Who wants no place to go?" she asked. "Who wants a life that cannot be let out? Not me, my love. You are more fun, Tony, without this 'private information.' "

"But it pays the freight."

"I know what you are," she said to him, lifting a yellow rose from the bud vase and smelling its center. The wet stem made a mark like the shape of a dog's head on the linen tablecloth. "You are a spy. A dangerous double agent, who flies from country to country with plans for armies. Sometimes when you are away, I wonder where you are. I think of you in secret briefing rooms, receiving orders from generals and premiers. Then, zap, you are behind the Iron Curtain, armed with weapons, walking through the night on lonely roads. Is that a true story?" Her smile was dazzling.

"The only secret installations I'm interested in are yours," he said. The *bon mot* failed to go over. Karin had caught his pensiveness.

"I might be afraid of you," she said. "You are deep, but impossible to look into. You say there is something coming down the road to meet you. And that something frightens me. You are a wild animal, and there are hunters looking for you."

"Are they armed?" he asked.

"They have nets and cages. I worry about what will happen to Tony when he is captured."

"I don't think about that." His voice was so still that she could barely hear the words.

"Tony!"

"No, no. There is nothing for you to worry about."

"Then come to Ibiza. You have plenty of money. Buy a little villa. You have enough money. I know it. We will live there. I will have little babies with eyes of hawks and we will never grow old."

"After a while, I'd get bored. I need more action than that."

"Then smuggle," she hissed. "Your friend Dick Whitman smuggles. Everybody does it on the island. You could do it too."

"It's against the law," he said, smiling slightly at his words.

Karin raised an eyebrow. "Everything is against somebody's law," she told him. "Taking off my clothes is against the law in some countries. But—" She shrugged her shoulders. "—by *my* law, my poor old mother and father should have enough to eat, and warm clothes to wear. It is not against the law for them to starve and wear clothes with holes in them. No, never that. The law is a club to beat the poor, to grind the copper out of their souls. I like my laws better."

"I never thought about it that way before," Tony said to her. "I think about the law as the rules of a game on which two sides play. There is the side protected by the law, and there is the side that is not protected by the law. And then, there are the police."

"And the police. What are they?"

"The soldiers of the rich," he said. "The hired guns. They work for the highest bidder on either side."

"That's unfair to the poor."

"Everything's unfair to the poor. That's why it's better to be rich."

"But there are natural laws."

"Such as?"

"You shouldn't murder. You shouldn't take food from the starving. You shouldn't injure the weak."

"The golden rule," he said. "But the law has nothing to do with any of that."

"I have no respect for such a fool's order," Karin said bitterly.

"I do," Tony said. "Perhaps I shouldn't. But I think about it all the time. It has to do with how my parents raised me."

"I never knew you had parents," Karin joked. "I thought you were born out of a dreamer's forehead."

"Nice parents. Nice people. Hard-working. I haven't seen my mother for three years."

"Tony," Karin said. "That's not the right way to be. She must be old. You must go and visit her."

"I support her," Tony said. "I send her money."

"But mothers need love more than money," Karin said positively. "What if she died, Tony? Think how you would feel . . . Bad, eh?"

"Yes. That would make me feel bad. I think I know what I want to do."

"What?"

"Visit Momma in Philadelphia . . . right away."

"No Ibiza," Karin sighed. "I should keep my mouth shut. It would be better."

"I'll be back in two weeks," Tony promised. "I'll send you a ticket, and we'll meet on the island."

"Promise, Tony."

"I swear."

After buying an intricate gold necklace, the next afternoon Tony flew to Philadelphia by way of Montreal, where he telephoned his mother and said to expect him in two days. Before the reunion he had a favor to repay Philadelphia Charlie, who had fallen on hard times. Charlie desperately wanted to put a crew together to burn the Philadelphia banks, and get a stake together for a new start in a square life.

Tony met Philadelphia Charlie and his crew—Fat Louie, now a shambling alcoholic hulk, and a man he didn't know named Jersey Joe—at the Philadelphia Hilton. The crew looked bad. But they worked well together, and hit two dozen banks that day for more than $12,000. Returning to the hotel that night, Tony was surprised to find Fat Louie's girlfriend from Manhattan, the black-haired hooker Francine, had come down with them. She and Louie were staying in the second of the two connected rooms rented by Charlie.

After changing for dinner, Tony, Philadelphia Charlie, and Fat Louie went downstairs for a drink. Two hours later, Jersey Joe and Francine hadn't come to join them, so they rode the elevator back up to see what was keeping them. Fat Louie barged in first.

Over the obese man's indignant back, Tony saw Jersey Joe's skinny shanks stop their rhythmic motion between Francine's spread legs. Making little piggish grunts, Fat Louie rushed at them, picking Joe up entirely from the bed and throwing him like a pillow against the wall.

"Wa ya dun ta ma broad!" Louie shouted.

"Hold him, Tony, before he kills that asshole."

Philadelphia Charlie slammed and locked the door.

Charlie lunged on the heavy man's back as he moved towards Jersey Joe's pantless body, which uncoiled from the floor on hairy legs and lunged toward his jacket. Tony sensed that Joe was moving for a weapon, and tried to stop him. Fat Louie bolted in his way, and the three of them fell in a tangle of arms and legs while Jersey Joe rooted through his suit pants. Fat Louie's weight crushed the breath out of Tony.

He saw the huge man rise, with Philadelphia Charlie still hanging onto his back with his arm crooked under his neck, trying to stop his furious charge. He didn't see the knife that Jersey Joe plunged into Fat Louie's chest until Philadelphia Charlie and Francine began screaming at the same time.

The pearl handle of the knife stuck out of the middle of the fat man's shirt. With a rush, an incredible amount of blood jetted out of the torn white shirt and poured onto the floor. Fat Louie wore an incredulous look on his face. He touched the pumping blood and examined his bloody fingers, as though he wasn't certain that the fountain came from his body.

"What did you do to me?" Fat Louie asked plaintively. "Joe?"

The question brought a gush of blood out of his mouth and he coughed, spraying blood across the room.

"I'm sorry, man," Joe said, his face looking more tortured than the stabbed man's. "I thought you went crazy."

Francine hid her face under the pillows, screaming.

"Shut that fucking broad up," Tony ordered Philadelphia Charlie. "You get out of here," he told Jersey Joe.

The assailant pulled on his pants and shoes and ran out into the hallway with shirttails fluttering and his jacket over a shoulder.

"I'm really sorry," he called as he ran away towards the elevators.

Tony slammed the door shut. Louie had sunk down to his knees, his head drooping like a broken flower, a trail of blood coming from his mouth and more blood still pumping out of his chest. The floor was covered with blood in a pool now nearly three feet wide, dark and crimson and glistening.

"Stop screaming or I'll strangle you," Philadelphia Charlie hissed to Francine, his mouth next to her ear. Her sounds of terror turned into wracking sobs.

193

"Get me towels," Tony requested.

He put an arm around Fat Louie's shoulder. "Can you hear what I'm saying?"

The wounded man's head barely moved.

"Is it in the heart?"

Fat Louie's head turned upwards to look at Tony. His lips were spread, exposing the worn yellow teeth coated with blood. With his eyes open, his head fell backwards. The blood still came.

Philadelphia Charlie handed the white towels to Tony, who pressed them to Louie's chest around the protruding knife handle. "Is he dead?"

"Don't know. We've got to get him to a hospital."

"How the hell can we do that?" Charlie was full of worry. "He weighs a ton."

"We can't let him die. Help me pick him up."

"Goddam you Tony. He's a dead man. Let's clean our stuff out of here and get away before we're held for murder."

"Get the car, Charlie. Go get the car right now. Bring it around to the back. Come up the service elevator. We've got to get him help."

"You're fucking crazy."

The pupils of Tony's eyes were the size and color of lead pellets. "Don't get me angry now, Charlie," he said. "Move quickly."

Charlie hurried out of the room.

Tony bent over Fat Louie, pulling the knife out of his chest and pressing down on the wound as hard as he could with a wadded towel to stop the blood.

"Francine, get your skinny ass off of that bed. Tear the sheet into strips one foot wide. Fold them lengthwise twice and bring them to me. Hurry up."

"Did that bastard kill Louie?" Francine whispered.

"Please hurry up," he said. "I don't know if he's dead or not."

Taking the bandages, Tony wrapped them as tightly as he could over the towel compress on Louie's fat chest. No matter how many layers he wound over the incision, the blood still soaked through. Taking a deep breath, he heaved Louie's three hundred pounds onto the bare mattress and raised him to a sitting position.

"Get me his coat, Francine."

The naked hooker carried Fat Louie's gray wool topcoat from the closet and Tony put his loose arms into the sleeves.

"It's Charlie," he heard from outside. "I got the elevator waiting."

Holding the unconscious man's arms over their shoulders, Tony and Philadelphia Charlie dragged the heavy body down the hallway and into the service elevator, which they rode down to the loading dock. The car's motor was running, and the back doors were hanging open.

"Use your head," Tony said. "We can't lift him out of the back. He goes in the front."

Charlie took the wheel. Tony sat beside him, holding up Fat Louie's body. "Philadelphia General Hospital," Tony said.

"I don't know why Joe did that," Charlie complained as they neared the hospital's emergency room "He never did anything like that before."

"He never got caught screwing Francine before," Tony said, tiredly. "Where was your head, letting Louie bring along that damn broad? You know you can't work with broads in the way."

"I screwed up," Charlie said. "That's why I wanna get outta this kinda life."

"Alive, if possible," Tony said. "At the emergency room, I'll pull Louie out and put him down against the wall. You ring the emergency bell. Then drive like hell."

Charlie brought the car to a quick halt just outside the aluminum and glass doors of the hospital's emergency entrance. Charlie slid from behind the wheel, and Tony swung his legs out after him and ran around to the passenger door, jerking it open and catching Louie's body as it fell out of the car. He didn't seem to notice the inert man's weight as he carried it, heels dragging, to the yellow brick wall.

"Somebody's coming," Charlie hollered in warning. Tony dove head-first into the moving car, which careened with screeching tires down the driveway to the street. Charlie was making unusual sounds.

195

"Don't cry," Tony said. "It won't do any good."

"I liked that guy," Charlie said, tears running down his cheeks. "We worked a long time together."

"Yeah."

"He was my best friend."

"Charlie, you go back to the hotel and help Francine clean up that room. Get every bloody thing out of there. Wash the floors until they shine. In the morning, give the cleaning lady a hundred bucks and tell her you and your wife got drunk and messed up the room. Do you understand me?"

"Sure, I understand you," Charlie said. "What are you going to do?"

"Visit my mother."

"I didn't know you had a mother."

"I do. I just *feel* like a sonofabitch."

"Momma."

"Petey. Petey. Look at you. Let me hold you. Give me a hug and a kiss."

"You're looking wonderful, Momma."

"I feel okey-dokey. Where have you been for so long?"

"I've been traveling, Momma. Overseas. You got my letters, huh?"

"A friend reads them to me. Come here by the light. Your hair is all gone. You look wonderful, though."

"You look good, too, Momma. But you're thin."

"I'm an old lady. I get thin missing your father."

"I'm glad to see you. I've thought about you a lot."

"I've missed you, my son. You look so wonderful, Petey. Are you rich?"

"Yes, Ma. I'm rich. Look. I brought you a present."

"What is it?"

"Open it."

"What is this? A necklace? Is this gold?"

"Yes, Momma. Eighteen-karat gold. I got it for you in Europe."

"Petey, what's an old lady like me going to do with a gold necklace?"

"Wear it courtin', Momma."

"Petey, you shouldn't talk like that. My, you're so thin. Have you been eating?"

"Sure, Ma."

"You're wasted away to nothing. You're too skinny. Have you eaten dinner?"

"No, Ma."

"Let me make you some spaghetti, the way you used to like it, with meatballs. You like that, Petey. With the meatballs?"

"Yes, Momma."

"And we'll have some wine with dinner. But I forgot. I don't have any wine."

"I brought some, Momma. From Italy."

"From *Italy*. It makes me lonesome for the old days. But I'm glad you're rich, Petey. The apartment, I like. You take good care of your old mother. You are a good boy. I'm proud of you. You make Momma happy."

"I'm glad, Ma."

"Sit down on the chair there. I'll take care of things. How long are you here in Philadelphia?"

"Just tonight."

"Just tonight? Where are you staying?"

"I'll get a room in a hotel."

"You won't stay with your Momma? For just one night?"

"Sure I will, Ma."

"I'll fix up the couch with clean sheets."

"Wonderful."

"Let me look at you, Petey. You look so skinny. You're nothing but bones. Have you eaten dinner?"

"Not yet, Momma."

"I have an idea. I'll make you spaghetti, the way you used to like it. With the meatballs. But wine, Petey. I don't have any wine."

The handsome bald man in the dark suit took the frail old lady in his arms and kissed the gray hair on her head.

"Did you miss your Momma?"

"Yes, very much. I have an idea."

"What's that?"

"Let me make dinner," he said.

"Spaghetti?"

"Sure, with the meatballs. And the wine."

In the morning, Tony put $10,000 into his mother's living account and checked into the Drake Hotel to wait until doctors at the hospital could determine whether Louie would survive his stabbing. He had just hung up his suits in the closet when there was a knock at the door.

Two men in identical blue suits stood outside, offering their identification.

"Federal Bureau of Investigation," one said. "Don't move."

Tony froze in the doorway. "Fine," he said. "Come on in."

One of the men stood at the opened door and the second one came into the room and patted Tony down for weapons, finding none. He searched the dresser drawers and suitcases, but the forger was clean.

"It doesn't make any difference," the agent said to him. "We're going to nail you to the cross. You're a tricky bastard, Milano."

Handcuffing Tony's hands behind his back, they led him through the hotel lobby to the light-green unmarked government Plymouth parked at the curb. Tony was humiliated by the experience. The handcuffs were so tight they caused pain to shoot up his arms. One agent got in the back seat of the Plymouth with the captive. The other took the wheel.

"Man, would you please loosen these handcuffs?"

"Nope," said the agent beside him. "Not a chance."

"Where are you taking me?"

No answer. The Plymouth went to the US Court House on Chestnut Street, and the agents brought him immediately before the federal magistrate for arraignment. Events were moving too quickly for Tony to sort them out, but his head was clear and his emotions were calm, almost placid. He was charged with flight to avoid prosecution and there were federal warrants from Virginia, Pennsylvania, New York, Connecticut, Florida, and New Jersey. Each bad-check warrant carried four charges— forgery, uttering (a legal term for putting counterfeit into circulation), accepting money under false pretenses, and transporting a forged certificate. The total was forty counts.

"Your honor," the FBI agent told the magistrate, "don't let this man out on the street. He's a menace to society."

The federal prosecutor agreed. "This man is a professional criminal, an extremely dangerous threat. He has eluded capture by the federal government for nearly a year."

"Do you have anything to say to these charges?" the magistrate asked Tony.

"Yes, sir," he answered respectfully. "What he's saying isn't true. I'm not guilty of any of that."

He tried to project an image of concerned sincerity, of a respectable citizen accidentally caught up in baffling government webs.

"Where does your family live?" the magistrate asked.

"Churchville, Pennsylvania," Tony answered him.

"If I let you out on bail, will you stay here?"

"Of course, I'll stay here," Tony said.

"What does the state have to say?"

"A criminal this elusive shouldn't be released on bail," the prosecutor told the magistrate. "If the court feels that he should be, we request that bail be set at seventy-five thousand dollars."

"In view of the fact that the accused has no previous record," said the magistrate, "and has family living in the area, I think that five thousand dollars should be sufficient."

Tony could barely suppress a grin. The disappointed FBI agents and prosecutor groaned aloud, to the magistrate's irritation.

Making things even easier, the magistrate decided that Tony had to put down on the bond only 10 percent of the $5,000—$500. He immediately posted the money, and left the courtroom as soon as the necessary arrangements could be made.

One of the FBI agents came up to him in the hallway. "I'm going to get you, Milano," he promised. "You've really gotten a pass so far, but I know all about you. You're a bad guy, and I'm going to make your life hell until you're safely salted away in the penitentiary."

"You don't have any evidence against me."

"We'll find the evidence," the agent said.

The agent flinched in the split second before Tony blinked his eyes and smiled. He wanted to arrest the forger for the unbridled rage in his eyes, because it made him afraid.

Tony was equally afraid; he knew the agent would have no qualms about planting bad checks or drugs in his suitcases if he couldn't rearrest him soon for other reasons. The two men, filled with mutual loathing, stood smiling at each other in the courthouse corridor.

"I intend to be as cooperative as I can possibly be," Tony said smoothly. "Believe me, I don't want any trouble."

"I'm encouraged by your positive attitude," the FBI man said, taking Tony's proffered hand with a strong impulse to twist the fingers and slam the forger up against the wall. "We'll be watching your movements, you know that."

"I'm a legitimate businessman," Tony said, removing his hand from the agent's. Two blows, he calculated, would lay the smug bastard out on the marble floor with his nose in a puddle of blood and chipped teeth. The problem was that assaulting a fed was a federal rap, and he didn't want any more of them against him. "We'll be seeing each other around then. I'll watch for you in the rear-view mirror."

Watching the forger's broad shoulders pass through the door of the courthouse, the FBI agent thought, "That bastard is never going to appear in court again."

Tony was of exactly the same mind. He had no intention of every appearing again in Philadelphia. Switching cabs rapidly, shuffling the cards so that the feds couldn't stick to his trail, Tony finally disappeared into a department store, where he purchased a trimmed black wig. Putting it on in the men's lavatory and adding a pair of dark horn-rimmed eyeglasses, he meandered out another door, into two more taxicabs, and to the Philadelphia Airport. One hour and forty-five minutes after leaving the federal magistrate, Tony was on an airplane back to New York. If they captured him again, it wouldn't be in the City of Brotherly Love.

Now that Tony was formally a fugitive with the FBI some-place behind sniffing at his tracks, he no longer worried about being caught and brought to trial. There was something exhilarating about being chased, a sense of playing a game in which every additional day of freedom added points to his side.

"But maybe you could have beaten it," said the black man to Tony. Sy was a forger, an expert on criminal proceedings. "If the feds didn't have any hard evidence against you, they couldn't have done much. I think they were just trying to get you to cop a plea and bargain out some time because they couldn't make any real charges stick."

"I don't trust those Philadelphia FBI agents," Tony said. "I thought the FBI was supposed to be the best, but these guys were low-lifers, threatening me like a bunch of organization goons. How can you respect somebody like that? The one prick promised he was going to nail me to the cross. It was too big a risk to take."

"Now if they got you again, it'll be worse."

"It's another roll of the dice. Maybe they won't get me. Maybe I'll disappear."

Sy rested his dark eyes on Tony's face. "You're my friend. But you don't look to me like a man who's about to retire."

Tony grinned. The black man and the white man, both wearing tan raincoats, leaned against the bar, waiting to be served.

"Say, you," Tony called to the bartender. "We're waiting for you."

"Just a minute," the bartender called. "I'm getting it ready. What do you want to drink?"

"He's getting it ready?" Tony snorted. "What? Does the fella brew his own beer?" He held up two fingers.

The bartender carried over two draft beers in glass mugs. In his pocket was a white paper envelope. He folded it in half, and slipped it into Tony's hand before walking away.

"So, he hands me a love note," Tony said, opening the envelope. It contained two $20 bills. "What's this money for? Am I to believe that jerk likes my face so much he comes over here and hands me forty bucks?"

Sy laughed, slapping his leg. "That dummy thinks that we're cops in here for our weekly payoff. And that's it." Sy pointed at the money, tears running from his eyes.

Tony broke up too. "There's going to be some pretty damn pissed-off cops in here in a few minutes," he said, handing one of the bills to Sy. "Come on, my man, before we get into some *real* trouble."

The wayward payoff seemed to mark the end of Tony's run of misfortunes. He felt good. He was back on top—the shadow that the police would follow but couldn't find. He was the rich international businessman who traveled from country to country under a constantly changing variety of disguises and identities. He was the sophisticated American expatriate with a lovely villa on Ibiza, the companion of European royalty, the lover of the continent's most beautiful women. He was the exquisitely tailored gentleman who was chauffeured through New York City's crowded streets in gleaming limousines, who *now* lived in four different apartments in Manhattan alone, and had permanent suites at the Waldorf-Astoria at the top of the heap and the Essex Hotel at the bottom. He was a member of the exclusive club that rode the helicopter to the airports, that flew to the Bahamas for a birthday party, Aruba for a cocktail, Los Angeles for a premiere, Houston for a football game, the Keys for fishing, London for breakfast, and Paris for lunch.

Charming, quiet, rich, he was a man of respect from whom Mafia dons requested instruction in the fine arts of forgery, check-passing, altering credit cards, and the international movement of bonds and securities.

He was the greatest forger in the world.

Chapter 9

There was nothing very special about Bill's Lounge on 41st Street near Times Square, which is why on an occasional afternoon when Tony was kicking around New York City he liked to stop in for a quiet drink. Knowing that the government had been on his trail since he jumped bail in Philadelphia one year before, Tony had grown more solitary in his movements than ever before.

The sense of being pursued wasn't the heart-thumping, short breathed, constricted feeling that a rabbit feels before the snapping jaws of a dog. It was different from the burst of fear you feel when a man you are with is shot down beside you in the street and the man with the gun turns in your direction. It was much more leisurely.

Mixed with fear that never quite went away was another almost sensuous sensation. Because he knew that he was a wanted man, because the awareness of being pursued never could be quite forgotten, Tony had almost come to enjoy the fact that he was *desired* by the system he had so cleverly eluded. It was as though the FBI, the Justice Department, the attorneys general of the various states, the postal authorities, the duped bankers, the retail merchants, the various forces of law and influence and wealth, had assumed a single, beckoning presence. Tony began to develop a reciprocal desire to surrender to that embrace, even though giving up meant not fulfillment but destruction. Even humiliation. Certainly ruin. But if he were brought, stripped and shamed and manacled before the blind presence of justice, he would also be the subject of a particular kind of tribute awarded to only a few.

For there was no question in Tony's mind that the continuation of the system depended entirely upon men like him to excite it and justify its vast apparatus. The system existed entirely to regulate, govern, order, marshal, punish, police, and kill. Without his clever tricks, false identities, forgeries, without the fox coming in the early morning after the flock of honking geese, there would be no reason to maintain the fences and the dogs and the shotgun over the fireplace. Without him, the system would not exist at all. While he didn't create it, he perpetuated it and refined its internal moving parts, its schemes, and even helped order its future direction.

Tony was certain that the bartender here at Bill's Lounge, a puzzled look on his face, had no way of knowing that the four men approaching him in step from behind were his angels of doom. The mirror reflected the four identical men in gray hats and gray coats and white shirts and black ties, mass-produced cherubs. Their bleached white features were so ordered and serene, their sense of direction and purpose so perfectly triangulated to the exact spot where he sat with an amber glass of Chivas Regal and soda, that it did not seem polite to reject their advances—which, he knew, were inevitable.

With an eerie sense of unreality, he knew he should not lift his hand to touch the drink and bring the liquor to his lips for a final taste of freedom, because the four, who had separated to surround him, might be frightened and scatter like birds by a sudden motion. And then, of course, they might find the guns inside their coats and shoot him down from the stool as he turned, a smile on his face, a drink in one hand, to express his appreciation of their punctuality. *Because they were exactly on time.*

The first time, in Philadelphia almost exactly one year before, had been the wrong time, a gaffe, a foolish blunder. This was so much more appropriate. 3:30 P.M., November 13, 1968, had been waiting for all five of them—six, counting the mute and uncomprehending bartender. This moment had been waiting for him his entire life, carrying him here to a silent cocktail lounge where the ice slowly melted away in a glass of untasted scotch. Waiting for introductions was socially embarrassing. Nobody knew how to speak first. But one of the forger's gifts was silence, so he waited.

"Just quietly put your hands behind you and don't make a move."

The FBI agent who spoke behind him struck exactly the proper tone of respect, the way a junior officer requests the last junta's general to walk into the yard for execution. Tony folded his hands behind him like a bird settling its wings.

He was surprised by how perfectly the steel handcuffs fit around his wrists. The cool chill of the polished metal felt as silky as gold bracelets. How many other policemen stood behind these four waiting for this quarry? The policeman who received the informer's telephone call. The superior who initiated the final thrust of the long hunt. The dispatcher, the clerk, the interrogators waiting impatiently in their offices for the first sight of his face. Four men are an extraordinary number to send after an unarmed figment of his own imagination.

The FBI agent at Tony's right hand apologetically wavered over the change from a hundred-dollar bill on the walnut counter, dipping and picking up the bills, careful not to wrinkle a single one.

"Leave five dollars there as a tip," Tony requested.

The bartender's face, which Tony now noticed had a pinched, worried expression, opened as though it had been fed by his generosity.

"Thank you, mister," he said as Tony slowly turned away from him and stood flanked by the men in gray coats.

One of the agents indicated the doorway with an outstretched arm, and like royalty leading a small army of retainers, Tony pushed through the swinging door. Tony intuitively knew their transportation for him would be waiting unobtrusively around the corner, legally parked, with twenty-five minutes still showing on the meter.

The nondescript green Chevrolet four-door sedan resembled the rented car that Philadelphia Charlie had arrived in that first day moving checks three years before. It even had that smell of newness, rubber and plastic and freshly milled metals. But Tony couldn't help comparing the thin foam rubber stretched uncomfortably over the driveshaft in the center of the back seat where he sat between two agents with the broad luxury of a new limousine. In the limousine, he could stretch out in comfort as far as he wished across three feet of unobstructed floor warmed by thick rugs. Here his knees were jackknifed up to eye level because of the driveshaft hump. American sedans forced a man to sit with his view blocked by his own knees. Unfortunately, moreover, the agents were not all identical, and the two fattest crowded in on Tony from either side. These six-passenger sedans really were designed for a maximum of four, and while Tony wouldn't complain, he was uncomfortable.

His bladder was full, sending urgent signals for release. Tony recalled a particularly ostentatious Mercedes limousine he had hired in Berlin; it even had a small chemical toilet. Tony pressed his knees tighter together, spitefully deciding that these silent smug robots deserved to have their smugness unsettled by a stream of hot piss into their car seats. If he weren't wearing a new $500 mohair suit . . .

The fat red-haired FBI asshole had, in shifting position slightly, passed a disgusting cloud of gas, and now sat in his own fumes, self-satisfied and serene. Men like this had no business representing the government of the United States. The other agent looked at Tony, annoyed, and sniffed loudly, the end of his nose twitching. *I didn't do it, you damn creep.* The agent rolled down his window several inches, and the red-haired *fart* smiled gratefully at him. Mr. High and Mr. Low. Tony was figuring out their roles.

Their silence was undoubtedly a technique for wearing down his resistance. Or else, discouragingly, they didn't even care. Maybe these guys don't talk to each other at all. They get computer cards in the morning, which they feed like tapes into their mouths. Automated policemen, marching down the street, scanning the people on the street for post-office mug shots. Did their eyes light up and bells ring when they spotted someone they sought? What the hell is the kick of being a government cop? It must be like brushing your teeth. You don't like it very much, but you'd feel like hell with a dirty mouth.

"Excuse me," Tony spoke up. "Will we get someplace soon? I've really got to use the bathroom."

"We're going to the headquarters," the driver said, pleasantly enough. "We're almost there."

Riding upstairs in the elevator, Tony contemplated flight rather than facing the depressing monotony of the FBI headquarters.

> *In a short, violent struggle, the captured man, using his feet like fists, laid low four FBI agents. Bursting from the elevator, hands still cuffed, he slid down a back stairwell, leaving bloody carnage behind. Reporters fighting to get to the scene. Television broadcasters. A general sense of wonder. The fugitive was reported fleeing the country dressed like a Roman Catholic bishop, en route to Rome. A tricky bastard. Too clever for me.*

"What are you smiling about?" the red-haired agent asked him.

Tony scowled. The elevator doors opened onto a scene worse, smaller, dirtier, and more cluttered than he had imagined. The steel desks were gray. The secretaries belonged in city high-school offices or city halls, waiting in hate for the public. A small 1969 calendar from a bail-bonding firm, fixed by a paper clip to the outside of a metal in/out basket. 1969. *They're already processing next year's arrests*, he thought. Now he belonged to statistics already being compiled. Tony stood, head down, looking at his shoes. *Show some class*, he urged himself. He lifted his head, yawning. Signed in, the four agents moved him inside a small room with two bare metal desks and two metal chairs.

"How about the bathroom?" Tony asked again.

Scowling, they showed him a small john, standing outside the partially opened door while Tony relieved himself. Small blessings.

"Mind if I smoke?"

The agents pointed to the chair with a rip in the green plastic seat and the stuffing showing. They took his coat, his wallet, checked through his pockets. They took the change from the hundred-dollar bill from his jacket pocket, and the roll containing $5,000 from his pants pocket, whistling, "Look at that."

From his wrist, they took the brand-new gold Rolex chronometer, one of the seventeen expensive timepieces he had collected over the past few years. They put his possessions on top of one of the desks, the expensive alligator wallet containing no identification of any kind, the money, the $2,100 watch, gold cufflinks studded with half-karat diamonds, and examined them, envious. They reminded Tony of farm boys bending before the Tiffany windows. Tony was starting to understand that these men saw him differently than he saw himself. They didn't have the vision to understand how unique he was, how exotic his world compared to theirs. They could never comprehend his vision of eternal social retribution that had enlightened him at the moment of their entrance into Bill's cocktail lounge. Common clay. Well, he didn't give a damn.

"Where do you live, Milano?" asked the red-haired agent, whose name was Mulligan. Mulligan, a badly seasoned stew.

"Live?" The forger awakened from his meanderings. "New York. Here and there. Why?"

Mulligan's lips compressed like two flat tires. "Live, dammit. Where is your house? Your apartment? What's your address?"

Tony permitted himself the luxury of a superior smile. "In hotels," he said. "Whatever appeals to me for a night."

"Ah, come on," Mulligan complained. "I won't accept that. You've got to live someplace, mister."

Tony folded his arms, ignoring him. "I want a lawyer."

The agents groaned, as if the request was terribly unreasonable.

An agent named Ripley said, "It'll be easier for you, Tony, if you cooperate with us, huh? This form here that you oughta sign says you're releasing us to use anything you say that might be held against you." Ripley set down the long form in front of Tony, and handed him a pen.

Tony gently brushed the pen aside. "No. No way I'll sign that. Do I look like an idiot or something?"

"You're a fucking wiseguy. You've been ripping off the world, and you've been getting away with it." Mulligan's voice was very loud and emotional. "We're going to bury you, Milano. I'm personally gonna bury you, and bang your goddam head in."

"Go fuck yourself. I've been hit before."

The fat FBI man threw up his hands and stalked away from him, muttering to himself. The other three agents looked away.

It was 5:00 P.M. by the round clock on the wall above the door. Ninety minutes down, twenty years to go, Tony calculated. Time was passing so slowly, he was going to live a long, long time. Might as well be nice, even though the FBI didn't live up to its reputation.

"No offense intended," he said to Mulligan. "Come on, you guys know what the rules are supposed to be. You're not really going to knock me around like some precinct flatfoot, are you?"

The driver, whose name was Markowitz, looked over at Mulligan, who appeared a bit ashamed of himself.

"Aghhh," Mulligan said. He scornfully cleared the desk of Tony's money and jewelry, brushing it all into a manila envelope. He licked the flap and closed it, writing in large letters "Peter Milano: Forger" underlining the occupation with the intensity usually reserved for child-molesters.

"What's up?" Tony wanted to know. "I'm not heavy enough to deserve all this attention. Tell me, what in the hell are you doing, sending four guys down after me?"

"We understood you carry a piece." Markowitz lit a cigarette, handing it to Milano. "We didn't want to take any chances."

"You make mistakes like that by talking to the wrong kind of people. You listen to all the rat assholes who come to you, everybody's John Dillinger."

"Dillinger didn't hit as many banks as you did, Milano," Mulligan told him. "Dammit. We've got sixty-eight counts against you from Connecticut alone. God knows how many states want you. You've burned hundreds of banks. And I don't think we know the half of it."

"How do you get stories like this?" Tony acted incredulous.

"We got dozens of pictures," Mulligan exaggerated. "And we got friends who tell us things that we should know."

"You guys can't do it without using informers." Tony had a native scorn for stool pigeons. "I'm the one who keeps you in your job." Tony felt sad and philosophical. "You wouldn't have a job if it wasn't for me."

That made the agents laugh.

"Come on," Mulligan urged him. "Will you answer our questions?"

"No, I won't. You can do what you want and you can keep me here as long as you want, but I'm not saying a thing until I get a lawyer."

"It's getting late," the most silent agent observed. "My wife's going to have dinner ready for me."

"We have to take him to the US Commissioner's office," Markowitz said. "You might be late."

The silent agent grimaced.

"Take me there. It beats sitting here." Tony wanted to be on the move.

At least the commissioner's office had a touch of class. The cut-crystal ashtray, Tony recognized, came from Dunhill's. The commissioner's secretary, fat red lips, fat round boobs, just had to be Queens. What happens to federal officials who get caught screwing in their offices? *This might be the last decent-looking woman I see in years,* Tony reflected. He could feel on the palm of his hand the silken smoothness of her underpants. He wished he could get close enough to her to smell her perfume. Just a trace of it wafted in his direction. *Tonight I'll be in jail.* Holding her would comfort him. But no more dolls.

"This is *the* Peter Milano," Mulligan said to the commissioner. "He's been a fugitive for a year, since he jumped bail last year in Philadelphia."

"Interesting." The commissioner looked at Tony, appraising the cut of his suit. "Is that true?"

"No comment."

In other circumstances, Tony and the commissioner might have sat aboard ship in the Caribbean, playing bridge, amusing each other with stories about human foibles. The man looked like somebody who appreciated Barbados dark rum, a splash of tonic, heavy lime. He had just bid two spades.

Tony smiled. Three no trump.

"Can you post bail?"

Was that a game bid in clubs? "That depends on how much it is."

"At least thirty-five thousand dollars." A small slam, at least.

Tony shrugged. He wasn't in a position to do anything but make a strong defensive play.

"Welcome to the Federal Detention Center."

West Street by the docks. Bricks. Soot. Bars, slamming iron doors ringing through the cold misery of the night. Sweat smells. Fear. Urine. Headaches. Heartbreaks. I'll be a song writer when I get out of here. "Good-bye suit. Good-bye fancy clothes. Hello prison clothes. I don't wanna cry. I don't wanna die."

But the prison orderlies who helped with the processing patted him on the back, giving him shirt and trousers that fit. Old-home week. Half of Canarsie was here. The half that wasn't black. A million guys in the prison Tony knew. Well, six. Word spread through the cells. Tony Bartolini. The forger. No shit, where? Coming in, sooond floor. Big bald guy. A millionaire, honest to Christ. Met him with Joey. Fast with his fists. Nice guy. Keeps his mouth shut. One of Frankie's guys. Belongs to Raymond Met him in Chicago, for chrissake, two years ago. Yeah? I met him in Miami with two broads, one on each arm. How'd he get busted? The word is the Ciferelli brothers ratted on him. Victor had been talking. What the hell, you gotta take a fall sometime.

Holding his head gravely, his chin raised, he measured his steps past the open recreation room and the cells, ignoring the shouts but nodding to men he recognized. He was accompanied by two guards. *Monday, I should be en route to Aruba*, he meditated. His new lodgings were in a grimy four-man cell already filled with seven prisoners, Tony now being the eighth. Four on bunks, four on the floor to shit in. *Unh-uh. Hell no. Three fairy queens. Black junkie sick, yellow-eyed. No-account nobodies.*

"Nice bod, lover," one of the drag queens shrilled, eyes blackened with match charcoal. "You can bunk with me."

Tony stared at the tall, thin, effeminate man. With a shock of black hair standing on end like a cock's comb, the man was licking his cracked lips around his yellow and decaying teeth. The homosexual was sitting on the edge of one of the bunks. Taped to the wall above his mattress was a beefcake photograph of a weightlifter. Tony gazed at the fag the way a cat looks at a mouse with its head pointing curiously out of a bag of garbage. He was ready to strike.

"What are you looking at, sweetie? Like what you see?"

Several moments passed, and the faggot was beginning to feel uncomfortable. The others in the cell sort of edged away against the side wall, the fags enraptured and afraid.

"Who are you more interested in, lover, the bunk or me? Can't have the bunk without Lacy, dearie, not without me. I'm a part of this bunk. My ass is a permanent fixture. Ask anybody in here. Isn't that true, darlings?" Lacy made a throwing motion with his bony right forearm. "Tell the dear boy that I'm the queen of 3-D."

Tony had never liked fags, his Italian Roman Catholic boyhood combining with Mafia machismo rage. There were no hidden lusts or confusions about the scorn: homosexuality was beneath contempt. It was not to be dealt with. It was an abscess in a person's head best drained by cracking the skull. He wasn't about to tolerate one single night in a prison cell with a long-armed pederast like this one even near enough to brush a single scummy fingernail against his skin. Nor was he about to lie on the floor amid somebody's puke. For the sake of his personal pride and the years he saw ahead in prison, he would begin now to impress his natural superiority and authority on this pack of mangy losers.

"Say." The drag queen licked his chapped lips, speaking finally in a baritone. "What's with you? You on drugs or something?"

Tony pointed his index finger at him. "If I ever come in here again and find you sitting on my bunk I'm going to kick your rotten teeth down your throat. Move your fuckin' ass."

The fag looked to the other prisoners for support, but found only averted eyes. "Well, all right," he said, shaking his shoulders. "You could have asked politely. I was here first, you know."

"Don't you talk to me unless I ask you a direct question."

Huffily, the queen scrambled from the bunk, pulling his blanket after him.

"Who's in charge of this cell?" Tony asked.

"Who is it that wants to know?" The man who spoke was a short, muscular black man about fifteen years Tony's junior. His thick features were surrounded by an uncut afro. His eyes were alert and cautious.

"I'm Tony Bartolini."

"What are you here for?"

"Forgery."

"Why do you want to know who's in charge?"

"I wanted to tell him that his maids forgot to wash the floor today."

"What if I like it this way?"

"Then we're going to have a very serious discussion."

"You're taking a chance."

"So are you."

"What makes you think so?"

Tony got on the bunk that now was empty for him, putting the folded blanket underneath his head. "I'm a reasonable man. You're a reasonable man, too. I'll give you twenty-four hours to find out whether the odds are in your favor or not."

I've got to keep very cool, Tony was reminding himself. *Everything I do will be observed. My chances all depend on keeping together.* Although with seven or eight hundred charges against him he wasn't particularly certain that anything would mean any less time to be served. But this was where class showed. The last three years had been only the preliminary rounds.

You bought the ticket. It's your ride. The cellmates talked in their corners, about women or about men. Tony felt that self-pity about his situation involved too much lying to himself to be acceptable. But the feeling of loss was terrific. That millionaire Tony Bartolini—who should at this very instant be flying to Aruba, where hotel reservations were already made and the champagne was now being iced—was slain today in a bar called Bill's by four believers in badly fitted suits. His body was laid to rest in the Federal Detention Center attended by guards with guns, filing clerks, pencil-pushers, and a knot of slavering fags that would just as soon work over the body of the dead.

Freshly pressed linen sheets were in his dreams that night. His body rose from the iron cot and basked in the golden sun of the South. Just once the bald man moved in his dreams, when Lacy the Fag unfolded his six and a half feet of erotic intensity and bent over his former bunk. No, old Lacy decided he did not want to get killed. He folded himself back down onto the hard floor, wondering how much further he had to sink. The bunk, after all, was the highest he had risen in twenty-eight years.

Tony's goal was to move to the section of the third floor where the "good people" lodged. The surroundings were similar to the rest of the third floor, the company being the main difference. The improved social rank was reached by both grace and financial mobility. It was the organization's turf, with a social order and stability exceptional in men's prisons; the Mafia discipline of the outside was just as effective inside the federal institution. Organization prisoners were encouraged to gather together. The authorities wanted these criminal professionals isolated from the rest of the convict population, since they had a propensity to "whack out" fags, goofs, jerks, riff-raff, informers, and other low-lifers, adding to prison violence statistics. And these frequently violent men tended to keep in order each other's homicidal impulses. And because it was financially profitable for guards and other prison officials to assign them cells together, since payoffs were a regular part of the jail economic system, and it was easier to supply the affluent prisoners special foods and alcohols *en masse* than to wander about the jail with a tunic filled with clanking or bulky booty. Thus, the jail's residents were divided like a layer cake. On the second floor, in segregation, dwelt the informers, the fags, the despised, and the ruined. The informers were kept here so that the ratted-upon wouldn't silence their songs with handy homemade shivs. The second floor was also where such substantial citizens as Sonny Franzese, the bank-robbery mastermind, dwelt elbow to elbow with such distinguished citizens as George Gillette, an ancient bootlegger of the 1930s, and Mad Dog Klinger. On the third floor were, from the criminal point of view, the outcasts, from the official point of view the *crème de la crème* of legal transgression: weird types such as draft evaders, tax offenders, white-collar executive criminals, and the ratted-upon. This was, from Tony's point of view, Federal Detention Center headquarters.

Throughout the prison, it took money to get a better standard of living; reputation and fame went only so far. So Tony's lawyer brought not only advice and strategies but also stacks of $5 and $10 bills. And sometimes, bad news.

"Tony. The word from a very good source is that the commissioner has asked the magistrate not to let you out on the street, which could make bail very, very high indeed. Which would end up being generally twenty-five thousand more than they think you are prepared to pay."

"Then why should I go through it? Besides, if I posted bond, I could lose one hell of a lot of money." Tony was thinking about the temptations of flight. He laughed. "If I sit here and don't cause them any trouble, maybe I'll get a break."

"There are a lot of charges against you."

"Maybe they'll get tired of prosecuting me."

"Never," the lawyer told him. "If you ask for separate trials in all the states with warrants against you, the government will be so pissed off about the money it'll have to spend that you'll be retirement age before you ever see freedom again."

"Maybe I should post the bond."

"Look, I have an idea. If you take Federal Rule 20, you can bring all the outstanding charges into one court. Plead guilty, to save the prosecution any work, and you'll get off. Maybe five years instead of twenty. It's the smartest thing to do."

"Then do it."

"It won't be easy."

"That means expensive, doesn't it? I don't care. It's my money, and my time, and I'd rather have a few years of my own someday. Speaking of money, I suppose that you've got something for me."

Nodding, the lawyer opened his briefcase, and under the

prison visitor's table he slipped Tony $500, which the convict slipped inside his underpants. The transaction did not go unnoticed by the guard, who would exact his own toll later on, patting down the prisoner for contraband every place but where he knew it was hidden. The money bought Tony's way to the emotional comforts of the second floor. Additional disbursements sent in his direction a cushy job in the jail kitchen, and five dollars here and there enabled him to join the underground postal service which brought mail in and out without attracting the attention of the authorities. Living off the welfare of the state in jail cost, in fact, about $500 a month, normal legal fees excluded. But a man who has developed a taste for Chivas has a hard time swallowing the prison rotgut brewed in buckets and balloons in every jail in the world.

Tony's six years in the Army had prepared him for discipline and confinement. Both the soldier and the gangster accept discipline and regimentation without protest in the absence of a realistic alternative. Tony had his friends and his status and enough money to exist in reasonable comfort. What he didn't have was peace of mind.

His dreams were disturbed by the smell of acetylene torches wielded daily by workmen who labored cutting away from the floors the iron tables in the recreation area in preparation for an increasing stream of new prisoners. As the Nixon administration solidified its power in Washington, a stern law-and-order attorney general had issued what the convicts referred to as the "get everybody" order without special regard for the subtle nuances of due process. Consequently, in the four-man cells first eight, then ten, and finally twelve prisoners were packed in together. Tony's perception was that a great part of New York City was being poured into the House of Detention like sugar from a bag, filling and finally overflowing the grim building. Some of the men claimed to be political prisoners. Tony's personal conservatism remained firmly convinced that all prisoners were almost certainly guilty of something. He *was* concerned however that real crooks like himself were being compromised by association with political dissenters. How could he hold up his head if his sophisticated undermining of the financial structure was equated by a vengeful bureaucrat with the noisy protests of a draft-card burner, some physical coward afraid to fight for his country in a time of war?

Despite his best efforts to stay cheerful, he was growing depressed. The stench, the crowding, the cockroaches, most of all the human failure and desperation, wore down his will.

His moral sensibilities were offended by the stealing that went on in the lockup, for not only was the smallest personal property—a comb, a package of cigarettes—a magnet to the greed of the other prisoners, but the authorities *themselves* stole. Those who kept the criminals were criminals; even the food on the prisoners' plates disappeared.

At work in the kitchen, Tony saw the boxes of meat delivered, clearly labeled as 120 pounds of pork loin. Yet the scales showed that the boxes contained no more than 60 pounds of meat, half having been snitched by the supplier, or the delivery man, or the civilian directors of the jail cafeteria. The shaved-down chops were as small as doilies and as thin as bacon, charred and curled up at the edges. The breakfast porridge was thin. The potatoes were watered. So Tony pilfered food from the kitchens to redress a wrong; he gave food to men he knew slept hungry.

One of the men he especially cared for was Mad Dog Klinger, an old man broken now from a lifetime in prison.

Despite his nickname, Mad Dog was a bent, gentle, elderly man coughing from the diseases he had caught working in the prison jute mill, toothless, with a ruined stomach that knotted and convulsed from contact with greasy food, spices, and nearly everything else. His helplessness reminded Tony of his mother's infirmities, and he began especially preparing for him poached eggs on lightly browned toast or thoroughly broiled chopped steaks with no seasoning.

The obstacle course lay between the kitchen and Klinger's cell, three sections of guards where prisoners were examined and shaken down on their travels through the jail. Tony was carrying to Klinger two steak sandwiches heavily wrapped in waxed paper taped to his groin when a guard at the third checkpoint decided he wasn't going to give any prisoner an easy pass. Jerking open Tony's belt and pulling down his pants, an experience as humiliating as being slapped in the face, the guard tore the sandwiches from his privates and threw them onto the floor as though they were his genitals.

The man who interrogated him had his sights set on getting the recipient but Tony claimed he planned to eat the sandwiches himself. For the next fifteen days his meals consisted of bread, water, potatoes, an occasional carrot or hunk of celery, eaten in a small solitary cell.

The cell was so barren, so devoid of any comfort, so systematically and deliberately brutal, that between rages Tony howled with laughter, imagining the luxurious Ibiza villa which languished so many miles and life styles away. The cell contained a metal cot without a mattress, a can to void in, and bare ceilings and walls. Confinement in solitary for reaching out to help a sick old man confused the spirit of penance he had brought to the lockup. How much of him, he wondered, should be taken away?

Calculating his earnings during the three years he spent breaking the law, Tony realized that he had grossed a few thousand more than $3 million, divided about equally between payments for moving bonds and securities to bankers overseas and direct earnings from forging. The magnitude of that wealth escaped comprehension. He hooked a finger in the large hole in the side of his undershorts, trying to hang on to sanity. They had taken from him a business worth a million dollars a year. They had taken away the apartments and the limousines and the villa and the women. Karin's body perched in an orange tree. They had even taken away the steak sandwiches from his loins. Giggling, Tony fell to his knees and beat the sides of his fists against the floor.

The week before the trial Karin appeared, her pink cheeks glowing above the collar of the honey-brown fur coat, his diamonds and gold ornamenting her ears and throat and fingers and wrists. The Tony she knew, so languorous and humorous and elegant, was strikingly changed. He was thirty pounds thinner, stooped at the shoulders with an old man's weariness, strains of worry corrugating the forehead and mouth, the color drained from his eyes until they had turned flat.

"Now don't make it hard for me by crying," Tony said.

Karin pressed his fingers curled on the table and then let them go. "When you come back to Ibiza . . ."

"I'll never get back there." The wry, self-deprecating smile of the gambler whose fortune has been lost on a single card at the gambling table.

"There must be something I can do."

"The rent's low here. The lawyer's paid. It won't be forever. You shouldn't have come here, Karin. The feds will follow you now. They'll haul you in to find out what you know. They don't know anything about my trips overseas and they can't find out or I'll never be a free man again. They have me on some other things here. Run, before they grab you. There's too much risk."

Karin wiped her nose, smiling. "When will I see you again?"

He learned from friends outside that Karin returned to Europe that evening, leaving no address behind.

One leg at a time he pulled on the trousers of the black mohair suit, wrinkled from storage, baggy on those thin prison shanks. The suit had been cut for another man than the one who would stand in the dock and swear that this particular truth was the entirety of all the truths a person could choose this January 12, 1969, but it was his suit, made to his specifications by a master craftsman. The cufflinks, the watch, poured their elegance into his wizened spirit. His eyes browned, golden motes swimming in the iris, a little color bloomed in his cheeks.

The handcuffs were removed in the courtroom. The judge was a dark bird with drooping suit and gold-framed eyeglasses. Tony welcomed the courtroom: wooden seats, harsh, echoing voices, yes, but no bars.

The clerk droned the charges from the mimeographed pages of formal record and Tony, finally permitted to speak, had only one sentence left.

"Guilty, your honor."

His mind crowded forward with excuses, justifications, rationalizations. But nobody heard the silent chorus. In fact, the judge had a slight hearing problem.

"What was that?"

219

Saying guilty again was like being married for a second time to a woman a man isn't all that certain about, but the clerk decided to help out, bellowing "Guilty" with the voice of an auctioneer selling the federal penitentiary to the highest bidder.

The learned defense counsel stressed the defendant's cooperation, Army record, and willingness to reform. His sentencing hung in the balance. The judge seemed not particularly horrified by Tony's crimes nor especially concerned in any way about the piece of gristly meat whose disposition was being argued over. The judge, the prosecutor, and Tony's own maneuvering lawyer were all three earning their living, as were the guards, bailiffs, court stenographer, and the man monitoring the boilers in the basement, by taking their various cuts of his guilt. *That's the way things are,* he thought. *Me, I've got a cigarette cough, a cold and no handkerchief.* He ran a finger under his runny nose and wiped it dry as unobtrusively as possible. A sign against his side.

But the prosecutor appeared to feel that things were not going all that well. Strutting like a bantam rooster and carried away with the conviction of his calling, the prosecutor brayed like a donkey kicked squarely in the nuts: *"The defendant is more dangerous with a pen in his hand than a man with a machine gun."*

The judge's eyes widened. The stenographer stopped typing for a moment, and the clerk turned to look at Tony, who lowered his eyes and as sweetly as a young girl furiously blushed, unwillingly seduced. At that instant he would have run to his own execution with those words emblazoned on banners behind.

Ignoring it all, the judge pronounced an initial thirty-day observation sentence so the psychiatrists could probe why an honest and successful man until thirty-five would have chosen thenceforth such a flamboyant life of crime.

Ungratefully, Tony concluded that it wasn't the right sentence at all. Thirty days of psychoanalysis could only determine the obvious, that his self-imposed restraints to obey the law as a *pro forma* exercise in free will had snapped at thirty-five. Tony thought of himself as a sinner, but the judge thought that he might be sick. Leave my head alone, he thought. It's all I've got left anymore.

The handcuffs went back on. The lawyer was congratulating himself for having brought his boy through it without losing the next two or three decades of his life.

"Sure, you did good," Tony said, nodding his head since he couldn't shake his hand in appreciation. "One hell of a job."

The lawyers for the next defendant were already pressing up against the bar. Maybe I *am* a nut case, Tony thought. Who the hell else would want to be "prince of thieves"?

Since his head contained the identities of several hundred people, three or four dozen professions, most of the geography of the United States and Europe, the Balearic Islands, Emil the Art Forger, and his universes which not only existed in space but historically in time also, what the psychiatrists wanted to get at had to be larger than a sentence or two. He visualized whatever it was they were looking for to be an object about the size of a watermelon, perhaps green-skinned, warm to the touch and pulsating lightly. He wasn't about to give up something as obviously important to his sanity as *that*.

The caseworker had scaly skin. He looked at Tony over his eyeglasses and at the records of the case, finding neither one of them especially appealing. He might not have been nuts about Dagos as a class.

"Tell me, Mr. Milano, why did you decide after all those years on the right side of the law to become a common criminal?"

"Well, sir," Tony said, "why don't you go fuck yourself?"

The man wrote "hostile to authority" on the examination sheet and dropped it into the manila file.

The psychiatrist didn't dawdle. "Tell me." A wash of sincerity nearly pushed Tony off his seat. "You can confide in me. Tell me about your sex life."

"My *sex* life?"

"Let's start with autoerotic development and adolescent homosexual experimentation. Did you ever do anything with boys?"

"What kind of a thing is that to ask somebody?"

"Did you?"

The patient was indignant. "Go fuck yourself."

"Confused sexual identity," the psychiatrist wrote, satisfied with his diagnosis.

The IQ tests were easy. The dexterity tests were fun.

"I never saw anybody who had finger dexterity like that," the technician told him.

The only test they didn't put him through was the catechism. Which he regretted.

"Holy Mary Mother of God, Jesus Christ," he prayed, standing in the cell block with his eyes opened, "now I'm making a promise. I'm going to go straight, because that's the right thing to do. Also, since I got caught, it's obvious that this string has come to an end. I'll serve my time. I won't turn informer on anyone, and I won't cause any trouble except to defend myself. Only please don't let those bastards screw around with my head."

"What are you doing standing there like that?" A guard stood looking at him between the bars.

"Isometric exercises."

The mental-health experts and social workers recommended that Tony serve five years in prison. The judge sentenced him to only two.

"Thank you, sir," Tony said. He was enormously grateful.

He arrived at the Federal Penitentiary at Lewisburg, Pennsylvania, on February 13, 1969. As he walked inside the prison gates, a bluebird flew away with a piece of dried grass in its beak. Just in time for Valentine's Day.

Chapter 10

Only this Valentine's Day was nothing to celebrate. He was going into a slaughterhouse. Of course it was his fault. He didn't give a damn.

The prisoners murdered each other, just like men did on the outside, for fun. Tony didn't know who the dead kid was. He was a nothing. A booster who had witnessed the murder of a guard in Leavenworth. An accident. He was in the wrong place at the wrong time.

But the kid knew who did it and the authorities knew that he knew. And the kid either told them who held the shivs or he didn't. Finally they transferred him to Lewisburg for his own protection. Only accidentally maybe, they also transferred another convict from Leavenworth, who spread the word that the kid was a rat. Rats die. A knot of prisoners like green flies moved, humming, in on the kid and the spoons, shined and sharpened, gleaming, stabbed. The flies buzzed away. Behind them, lying on the cold gray concrete, the kid spouted blood from two dozen holes. His time was finished.

It was as though the kid had been released from the grim fortress in order for Tony to take his place. That's nutsy thinking. He told himself throughout the seven day orientation and registration that the worst already happened. He was caught and sentenced. The psychiatrists wouldn't be digging into him. He was assigned to "G-2" block, Mafia row, where Al Capone once lived, where the connected princes held their court. He was one of them. Nothing to fear.

Only he wasn't sure who he was.

223

How could I forget something like that? I am the three-million-dollar man. It didn't connect.

"What job would you like while you're here, Tony?"

The assistant warden had his file open on the desk.

"How about a job in the clerk's office?"

"Christ! You'd sign your own release papers."

Right. And then walk out a free man. Get a new passport. A new identity. The next plane to Ibiza.

"You were in Army electronics, weren't you? How about working in communications?"

"What's that?"

"Plugging music, radio shows, stuff like that, into the prison headphone system."

"Sure, sure. Swell."

Lewisburg was one hell of a lot better than West Street. Good food. Cell blocks like college dormitories, individual cubicles. Tony Convict. There's a name. He could get used to that.

Victor Ciferelli was in "H" dormitory right across the way. Victor who ratted him out in Connecticut. Victor who caused the Philadelphia debacle. Victor whose flapping lips caused the FBI to take him from Bill's Lounge. The same rat bastard who brought him into this lousy fucking penitentiary sat in his cell reading *Time*.

Tony stepped into the cell. Victor knew who it was without looking up. Victor had been waiting for a month, since Tony set foot in the pen. There was no place to go.

"Get up, you rat cocksucker."

Victor sounded as though he was choking on a fishbone, deep in his throat. *Let me finish the goddam magazine,* Victor thought.

"I didn't mean to. I didn't mean to."

He held the magazine over his chest like a shield. He wouldn't look up. Tony's first blow clubbed the top of his head, a hammer banging down through the carefully combed black hair. The following blow landed someplace on the back of Victor's neck. He squirmed. He kicked. He wouldn't fight. Hitting. Hitting. You don't have to want to kill. You just let the rage flow. It comes so easily.

Victor didn't move when Tony walked panting out of the cell. His nose was broken. His cheeks and eyes were lacerated. Bruises welled darkly under the battered skin. He wasn't dead. But scared to death, almost literally. The heart attack two days later nearly carried him off. From the prison hospital, Victor was transferred for safety to the Lewisburg farm. Easy time, for a rat. The stool pigeons went to the farm or to the penitentiary's other "suburb," Alanwood. Nobody questioned Tony about the raw openings on his knuckles. Nobody cared. Victor was a second-class rat. Not like first-class rat, fat Vincent Teresa who eventually brought down two dozen men. Eating steak in cell-block "G-1" with the fags knowing that anybody there would get life if they had the courage to whack him out. So sure of his power to destroy.

"How's it going, Tony my man?"

"Fine, Vinnie."

"They only got you on the checks, they tell me. What about all the other stuff? What was it you were into? Didn't you do something for Raymond about bonds?"

"Bail bonds? What?"

"You know what I mean."

"I don't know what the hell you're talking about."

The obese greaseball made Tony gag. Vinnie who swaggered on fat legs into cocktail lounges boasting he was in "The Mob," for chrissake. Vinnie Teresa who bought a bag of diamonds from Jack Mace and handed them out like jelly beans to airplane stewardesses in order to get laid. Sitting here now, a black widow spider, drawing webs to catch other men, in order to get out. No looks. No life. No class. Who ought to be dead.

He was out before he was killed, given a new identity and set up free for his good services to society. It's nuts. Tony never talked. How could he? He wasn't even that certain about his name.

Don't let on that you feel screwed up. Take prison the easy way. One day at a time. Breakfast. Lunch. Dinner. Movies twice a week. Be reasonable. Keep your counsel. Do favors. Neither a borrower nor a lender be. Follow the golden rule. Pretend you are in Sunday school.

The only thing the prison library was good for was legal research. The bound volumes were well worn. Tony tried night after night to find a way to get out of the charges still pending against him in Connecticut. State detainers reached out for his future after his federal time had been served. No Section 20 nonsense for those creeps. The answer must be some place in the books.

Months of research, reading the law. Quiet and quietude fell upon him as an unexpected gift. With no women, even most of his dreams of lips and breasts and bodies fled. He slept quietly. He wanted to know the law. Other prisoners noticed and asked for help. He wrote briefs and appeals for convicts with legitimate beefs. He couldn't resist the impulse for action. The law gave him something to do. Tony, the jailhouse lawyer. Somebody instead of just an ordinary con.

He felt deep satisfaction when one of his convicts got sprung. He accepted fourteen clients, winning the appeals for thirteen of them. Justice might be cruel, but the law itself wasn't very hard.

"Most of the men in prison are guilty," he observed to a friend, "but they were put in against the law. Their constitutional rights were violated, most of the time, which is wrong. If a man is guilty, he still ought to be convicted according to the law. He should not be sent to prison for the wrong crime. He should not be sentenced illegally. The system has to be honest if you want the criminal to understand his guilt."

He was especially offended that most of the convicts he helped had been represented initially in court by public defenders.

"I'm not saying court-appointed attorneys don't know their jobs or that they're ripping anyone off," he continued. "But these people are so overloaded they don't have the time to check legal precedents and read previous court decisions that would help their clients. They have no time for anything. Some public defenders handle six, seven, even ten cases a day. They don't have the time to do the job right.

"General guilt or innocence isn't the issue. To jail a man for the wrong crime is a crime, but it's not always against the law."

Incongruous that he should be concerned about the niceties of the law. Hell, Tony What's-his-name might be the only prisoner in Lewisburg certain that he was guilty in both fact and substance. Nailed, as it were. Worse yet, he couldn't find any out for the charges still pending in Connecticut, a state he hated and whose jails he feared. The one client he couldn't help was himself.

The final answer to the charges in Connecticut came in executing the old extralegal maneuver, the fix. It took some doing, since Tony was not exactly in a position to sit down at dinner with Raymond Patriarca and lay out his request. But the letter got through, the jailhouse Pony Express once again riding through the bars.

Dear Raymond,

Connecticut has detainers out against me on sixty-eight different check charges, about two hundred sixty counts, which they will not drop. I thought you might be able to speak to somebody about this matter. I'd appreciate anything you could do.

Sincerely,

Tony Bartolini

Tony wasn't sure that the signature looked like his own. But since he had kept his mouth shut, Raymond owed Tony a lifetime of favors. Collectable now. The old man's chief fixer, he had confided to Tony, was a US senator, a staunch Republican pillar of law and order. *Fix it, Raymond,* Tony requested in a telepathic burst. *We've done too much business together for you to forget.*

Raymond remembered. He pulled strings in the right places. The retainers outstanding against Tony were suddenly dropped. One year served of his present sentence, and the future free and open again. With good time, only five or six more months to go. Freedom wasn't that far away any more.

"How did you beat the Connecticut rap?" Jimmy Hoffa asked the bald forger as the two men together turned over the mattress they tied in the penitentiary shop. "Who do you know?"

Tony liked Hoffa. The burly Teamster boss was a good-natured guy who shared his revulsion for drugs, fags, informers, and fools. And he also liked working with his hands. The mattress shop was more interesting than prison communications, where you sat on your ass and counted time.

"Just luck, I guess." Tony was positive that Hoffa had his own senators to intercede for him. Presidents too.

"You're a lucky guy." Hoffa scratched the hair on his chest. "It's hard to make a state forget about two hundred sixty counts."

Tony nodded.

But damn, he felt there was something wrong about such a powerful fix. He couldn't hold together in his mind how guilt and innocence, the law, justice, and the political system went together. He was starting to realize that they didn't.

Innocence was a theological state. Guilt was a legal definition. Justice was a moral concept. Politics was a power system that overrode everything but the final decision of God himself. Politics and money, the same thing, ruled all. Apparently he hadn't stolen enough money to escape the boundaries of the law. If he had stolen more he might not have gone to jail at all.

Mulling that over, sitting with his hands pressed together, smelling spring outside, Tony considered being free. In a few weeks, by June, 1970, because of accrued "good" time, the penitentiary doors would open for him. He had to figure out what to do then. Known forgers are always registered and watched by the police. He was no longer anonymous. Tony Milano was known to the authorities.

He left Lewisburg on June 2. Waiting for the Greyhound bus to carry him to Boston with messages for the family of a prison friend, he promised himself that the adventure was finished forever. He would stay straight. What the hell, he could always sell.

But by September he had learned that he couldn't always sell. Not with a felony record. The unvarnished truth wasn't much of a wanted item these days.

"Good morning. Mr. Milano, is it? You're applying for the job we advertised, selling Wild Rose Homes?"

Leaning confidently forward. "Have you had any previous sales experience?"

"Sure. Lots. I've sold everything from encyclopedias to home appliances. My last job was sales manager for the Wren Appliance chain in New York City."

"Why did you leave that job?"

"I was dissatisfied with the owner."

"I see. How long ago was that?"

"That was, ah, just about five years ago."

"Five years ago? And what have you been doing since?"

"Well you see, I was a professional forger for a while. And then I served fifteen months in Lewisburg Federal Penitentiary."

"You have a prison record as a professional forger?"

"Yes, sir. But I've served my time. I'm straight."

"I have your number. We'll call you."

"Give me a chance to show you what I can do. Just a chance. It can't hurt you."

"We'll think about it, certainly. Thank you for stopping in. You'll hear from us."

The reality was that an ex-con wasn't trusted anyplace near money. Nobody wanted a professional forger as a salesman. Tony, who could turn signatures into cash under the widest possible variety of false names and identities, whose very presence could inspire unquestioning trust, was worthless currency with the truth. Nobody wanted the honest penitent, searching for a straight living in the real world.

By September, after traveling around the country begging for executive sales jobs under his own name, he had virtually exhausted the possibilities. Factory jobs were plentiful and Tony was good with his hands, but he couldn't bring himself to come so far down. He wasn't some dirty-fingernailed stiff slaving away for four dollars an hour on an assembly line. For God's sake, he was a millionaire.

But it was damn hard to live like a millionaire with no money to back up the life style. No job and no chances. So if the problem was his identity, he knew how to change it. Getting desperate, he created a new personality named Curt Dean. Using friends and mail drops to back up nonexistent references, he found a job as a salesman for a large Miami automobile dealer.

He just sold like hell. He flirted boldly with the women,

joked with the men, talked mechanics with performance addicts, and laid down a line of bullshit and charm that had the folks' tongues hanging out to sign on the dotted line. Number-one salesman within two weeks. In line for sales manager within another couple of months. Tony thought he was being given the promotion when the owner called him into his offices.

"Good morning, Curt. Take a seat, will you? You've been with us ten weeks now, isn't that right?"

"Yes, it is."

"And I don't mind telling you, you've done one hell of a job."

"Thank you, sir."

"But there's a serious problem that's come up, Curt."

Tony's bowels churned. *I'm going to be fired,* he thought.

"The bonding company tells me there's no Curt Dean. The credit investigators find no record of any Curt Dean anyplace. I thought they were mistaken and asked them to recheck it all. They're positive. That means you're somebody else."

"Look. I've sold a hell of a lot of cars for you. You know that's true. You said it yourself. Does it make any difference who I am?"

"You lied to me, Curt."

"Because I needed a job. Do you want the truth now?"

"I'd like to know."

"My real name is Peter Milano. I'm an ex-con."

"I see. What did you do, Mr. Milano? Or should I call you Curt?"

"I was a forger."

"*My God.* I mean, I'll have to let you go."

"But I've made money for you. I'm straight. You *know* that."

From the way the man looked at him it was plain that he knew nothing of the kind. After Tony left the office, the owner ordered emergency auditing of all agency books, checks, and records. The owner was certain he narrowly had missed being wiped out by a clever criminal.

Half a dozen new jobs, identities, lives, began to assume a workable illusion of reality, then crumbled away. The truth was unacceptable. The imaginary creations were unstable. Tony slid. There were more and more days spent looking at blank walls or sitting on a bench under Miami's sunburned palm trees. Guys he knew from New York, guys he spent time with in West Street and Lewisburg, appeared now and then, well dressed, pockets filled with spending money, on the move.

"Good to see you, Tony. What are you into, man?"

"Nothing. I'm clean. I'm straight."

"If you don't mind my telling you, Tony, you look a bit down."

"It hasn't been easy."

"Look. I know this guy. He's got a lot of real fresh traveler's checks. A good price. I'll loan you a grand or two, get you back into business."

"I appreciate it, but I'm going to keep my nose clean."

"It's up to you. But you've got one hell of a good rep, Tony. It would be too bad to waste it."

"Tell that to the people who hand out jobs."

"Ah, what the hell. The square world sucks. Want to have a drink?"

Swallowing his pride. "Sure. Just one. I've got to meet this fella."

The luxury of the Palm Beach cocktail lounge seeped into Tony's parched senses. Conversation dragged. They were, after all, on different sides of the law.

"Good to see you again, Tony. Here's a number where you can reach me, if you're interested in anything."

A handshake. Three $100 bills. Charity. But a man has to eat, dammit. Christ.

The bald man with bowed shoulders and a hooked nose slumped in the chipped wooden chair of the Miami rooming house. Sweat ran down under his thin arms and his bony back. His large hands were red and puffy with eczema, an allergic reaction to the harsh detergents of the cheap Cuban diner where he washed dishes. His bare feet on the bare wooden floor.

The $10-a-week room came furnished with a worn mattress on sagging springs, a tottering nightstand and a small mirror whose peeled-away silver pock-marked the face that had the courage to look into it.

On the floor, a battered, once-expensive suitcase lay with its top open: inside only a few pairs of much-washed undershorts, undershirts, and a hand-scrubbed dress shirt slightly gray now with age. A neatly pressed navy-blue silk suit with the right arm coming unfixed at the shoulder hung on a nail on the door.

From downstairs came the loud sound of the evening news on the proprietor's television set. The newscaster's analysis of the Democratic National Convention opening that day in Miami mixed with the plaintive moan of a Cuban balladeer on a record played endlessly by the tenant next door.

Moths, mosquitoes, and other insects fluttered at the rusted windowscreen in their desire to join the bug party which danced at night around the bare bulb in the ceiling. In the dark far corner, cockroaches were coming out of the cracks for their evening foray. The roomer had long since stopped worrying about his insect companions.

The roomer's dark eyes reflected virtually no light at all. But if an observer stared deeply into the bald man's skull-like face and eyes, he would notice the flickering flame of what actually was a dinner party going on in the man's mind. Around a huge table, dozens of magnificent men and beautiful women were being served by the host, a tall, muscular, handsome man with eyes as golden as the Ibiza sun. Then there was the apparition of the interior of a Mercedes limousine where the same man, wearing a curly white wig, was lazily counting through American hundred-dollar bills that filled the attaché case on the seat.

"Hey, Tony. Tony." The voice from downstairs persisted. "You asleep up there? There's some guys here who want to talk to you."

The roomer straightened up, opened the door, and peered down the stairway.

"You callin' me, Salvatore?"

"You damn right I'm callin' you. There's two guys here to talk to you. You want 'em to come up?"

"Nah. Hold on. Who is it?"

"How in a hell am I supposed to know? Two guys all dressed up."

"Tell 'em to wait a minute."

Tony closed the door, considered a moment, then put on the dress shirt, tucking the tails into the pants. Nobody knew where he was living. They must be cops. Screw them. He was clean.

Two men who looked like undergraduates stood uncomfortably on the wooden porch outside, disdainfully looking at the crumbling block of old houses. A new four-door Chevrolet was parked at the curb.

"You Tony Bartolini?"

The bald man shook his head. "My name is Peter Milano."

"Yeah." The young man who spoke had very short hair and wore a dark ivy-league suit. "It's the same guy. You're the forger, aren't you?"

"You FBI? You've got no claim on me. I served my time."

The two men looked at each other. "Come on out here," the thin-faced one said, a surprisingly forceful note of command in his rather reedy voice.

"Hey," the man repeated, "I said come here."

"You having some trouble?" Salvatore called.

"Just some friends," Tony responded. He opened the door and joined the two men on the porch.

The man with the short hair said, "Look, let's be friends."

"Sure."

"We're not the kind of feds you're used to. I mean, we're not cops or FBI."

"Then what are you?"

"Who the hell are *you* to ask *us?* You're the criminal, for God's sake."

"I don't have to take this from anybody."

"The hell you don't. Don't fuck around with us, buddy. We'll cream you. I mean it."

"Nothing you can do to me but kill me," Tony said to him. "You might as well."

"We can send you back to jail forever." The thin-featured one showed his teeth in an ugly smile.

"I served my time."

"Not for the bonds, you didn't."

Tony's skin felt prickly.

"What do you mean?"

"Think nobody knows about that, Tony?" The sharp-chinned one took his arm. "Come on down to the car. We want to talk to you."

Reluctantly, Tony entered the car. The slight one got behind the wheel and drove them to the Fontainebleu Hotel.

"What do you want?" Tony asked. "What am I doing here?"

"We got a job for you to do for the government," said the one with short hair.

"How do I know you're government?"

In the elevator to the fourth floor, the skinny man showed him identification imprinted with the seal of the President of the United States. He held his fingers over his name.

"I missed the name."

"It's none of your fucking business."

The large hotel room contained no luggage or personal effects.

"You want something to drink?" The short-haired one was attempting to be friendly. Tony was certain they were feds of some kind, but he had no idea who carried identification with the Presidential seal on it.

"Yeah, I want something to drink. A whole bottle."

"Anything you want."

"Make it Chivas."

"Sure. Ice? Soda?"

"The whole shooting match. And cigarettes. Two packs of Marlboro."

"Sure thing. Want something to eat?"

In the light of the hotel room, the two young men didn't seem to have any authority at all. They seemed like fraternity boys. Creeps. Punks.

"I want a nice porterhouse steak. Mushrooms. Sliced tomatoes."

"Coming right up."

They called room service. Tony sat in the easy chair, the two government men standing in front of him. He stared at them, his eyes blazing.

"You better tell me what this is about."

"We know about everything."

"Maybe."

"Sixty-two trips overseas to London, Zurich, Paris, Copenhagen, Berlin, Beirut, Madrid, Lisbon. Want more?"

Tony shook his head "No."

"Villa on Ibiza. Girlfriend Karin Nilsson, the Swedish stripper. You were a courier for Jack Mace, Raymond Patriarca. Patriarca fixed your Connecticut case, didn't he?"

Tony was sweating again, despite the air conditioning. "I don't know what you're talking about."

"Tony, we've got enough on you to send you back to Lewisburg for a hundred years. You'll never get out. Understand?"

"I don't understand anything. If you're going to charge me, I want a lawyer, right now."

For the first time the short-haired one appeared a little worried. "You don't need a lawyer for this. I told you, we just want a favor from you."

"Some fucking favor," Tony said to him. "You're giving me heart failure, talking about a hundred years like that. I want my goddam lawyer."

"We're going to offer you an alternative." The thin one answered the knock at the door, then wheeled in the cart himself, careful not to let the waiter see inside the hotel room. The short-haired one opened the bottle and poured Tony Chivas over ice, adding a twist of lemon.

"How much soda?"

"I'll drink it straight."

"Here's the deal," said the thin one. "One thousand dollars if you write two signatures for me."

Tony drained the glass of scotch, coughing, cleared his throat and lighted a cigarette from one of the new packs. "Mind if I eat?" He indicated the steak. "I like 'em better hot than cold."

The government men shrugged. Tony ate the steak, cutting away the fat along the edges, chewing carefully. He hadn't eaten a porterhouse for nearly a year. When he was finished he put the plate aside, and poured himself another Chivas.

"I'll tell you something. If you think that I'm going to take the chance of going back to the penitentiary for a thousand bucks, you're nuts."

"It isn't that," said short-hair. "It's back to jail *or* make yourself a thousand."

"Now I know goddam well you're not FBI."

"You can't be sure."

"The hell I can't. The FBI doesn't make deals like that. That's one thing you learn."

"Let's stop fucking around." The thin-faced one seemed nervous. "We're from the central government. That means Washington. Understand?"

Tony didn't.

"The Administration. The executive branch."

Tony's face was full of wonder. "You mean the President?"

"Right." The short-haired man's voice was harsh. "Come on, Tony, we're not kidding about your choice."

"Maybe you're not." Tony's hands were sweating, his fingers were trembling. "I don't know if I could do any signatures. I put the pen away when I came out of jail."

"You're born with that kind of touch." The thin-faced man was opening up a flat white envelope, extracting ten sheets of paper. "What do you need?"

"Right now I need a clean towel to wipe off my hands. Then I need pens. Do you want ink or ball point?"

"Ink." The short-haired one brought a clean towel from the bathroom. "You want to work at the desk?"

"Yeah." Tony drew up the chair. Short-hair placed two fountain pens on the desk next to him. "Let me see the signatures. I'll need to practice them first."

"Here." Hatchet-face placed the bottoms of two letters in front of Tony.

Tony looked at the signatures and pushed away from the desk, glowering. "Fuck you. Send me away forever. I won't do it. You're crazy."

The signatures were "George McGovern" and "Hubert H. Humphrey."

"You *gotta* do it!" Short-hair pushed him back down into the chair. "We'll give you more money."

"No."

He opened a long, thin wallet, counting out $2,000.

"No."

He counted out $3,000 more. "I won't go any higher."

Tony looked at the money—$5,000 or 100 years in the penitentiary. He wanted the money. Goddammit, he needed the money. "How many signatures each?"

They looked at each other, smiling. "Two."

"Another thousand."

"You're holding us up."

Tony was in command now. "Then fuck it."

Short-hair handed over another grand. "How long will it take?"

"Depends if I can still do it."

He picked up the thinner pen for McGovern's signature, writing it several dozen times over and over on hotel stationery. Using the pen with the broader nib, he repeated the process with Humphrey's, and poured himself some more scotch.

"OK. I'm ready. What do you want them on?"

From the same white envelope, thin-face lifted two sheets of each man's official stationery. "At the bottom, where they would normally sign."

"These letters are blank."

"We *know* they're blank."

"How in hell do I know what's going to go on them?"

"That's none of your business."

"For chrissake." Tony looked up. "It could be *anything*."

Short-hair was exasperated.

Tony wavered. "I want to know. I'm doing this directly for the President?"

"This comes from right on the top," said thin-face. "Just sign them and get it over with."

Tony wrote two George McGoverns, and two Hubert H. Humphreys, looking at the signatures while the ink dried. "You know, this gives me a funny feeling, doing something like this."

Short-hair placed the stationery into his envelope. "Don't know why it should bother a crook."

Tony stood up, straightening his shoulders, holding the glass of scotch; his eyes were raging. "You punks got your terms wrong. I'm a criminal. *You're* crooks."

"Christ, listen to *him*," said short-hair. The pair went to the door. "Nice meeting you, Tony. Maybe we'll do business sometime again."

Tony lifted his glass. "I hope you pricks get run over by a truck," he called after them.

With $6,000 in the pocket of his baggy khakis and the nearly empty fifth of Chivas Regal in a brown bag under his arm, the bald man sat on the sands of Miami Beach, watching the waves build and break. He was watching the leisurely progress of a two-masted yacht on the far horizon.

"Why are you sitting there like that in your clothes?" asked a little girl in a red bathing suit with two blue stars on the chest, looking at him curiously.

The little girl's mother hurried down the beach, pulling her forcefully away. "Come away from that man, Melinda. Can't you see he doesn't want to be bothered?"

Nodding his head gravely, Tony tried to find the yacht whose progress he had been following, but it had disappeared. All the scotch had also disappeared.

Only the yellow sun hadn't disappeared. The sun and the waves. Somehow, it gave him a feeling of great hope. He got up and returned to the rooming house, where he bathed, shaved, and fell asleep. He had the most extraordinary dreams.

In the summer of 1973, when the Watergate hearings occupied the attention of most Americans, a successful San Francisco real estate salesman who had once been called Peter Milano looked intently at every new witness: he was looking for somebody, a repugnant young man with a boyish face who had made him commit the one crime he had wanted no part of.

Finally one day that very man sat before Senator Sam Ervin nervously admitting some of his crimes. His juvenile, bland features appeared twisted and sinister in the eyes of the salesman, who followed the testimony with a thin smile on his mouth. He had hurried home that evening after work, as he had since these Watergate hearings began, arriving at the small frame house in which he lived with his new wife, Susan, and her two daughters, in plenty of time to watch the evening news.

"I never knew you were so interested in politics," his wife commented from the kitchen.

The plain, plump woman came out of the kitchen to peer over his shoulder at the face of the unimpressive young man trying to explain some of his sins. She had never seen her husband look so fierce.

"What are you so excited about?" she said soothingly. "They're all crooks in politics. Why is that man special?"

"Because he's a blackmailer," the man exclaimed.

"How do you know that?"

"I heard about him when I lived in Miami."

"Did you know him?"

"Of course not. A person like that is scum, worse than a common criminal. But now they're getting the bastard! I hope they give him life!"

He stood suddenly and switched off the television.

"Well, I don't know," she said uncertainly. "I guess I don't understand very well what it's all about."

After dinner was finished, the salesman lit a cigarette and sat down beside his wife on the sofa, putting an arm over her shoulder. The fierceness had left his countenance.

"I'm lucky to have you," he said. "You've been good for me. The house. The kids. Everything could be so much different."

"Why, yes, of course dear." Susan smiled, a little surprised.

"You make me happy, too," she said. "But sometimes I do wish we were richer."

Just before going to bed he stepped outside, and looked upwards. It was a brilliant, clear, starlit night. He imagined writing name after name in stars, and the sensation held him transfixed. In his mind, a shower of money seemed to pour out of the sky above him, a flood of riches.

"Tony, are you coming to bed?"

The spell was broken. He raised his hand, flexed his fingers, then dropped his hand to his side without regret. He knew where to find the pen if he ever needed to write with it again.